William MacGillivray

Creatures of Air, Land and Sea

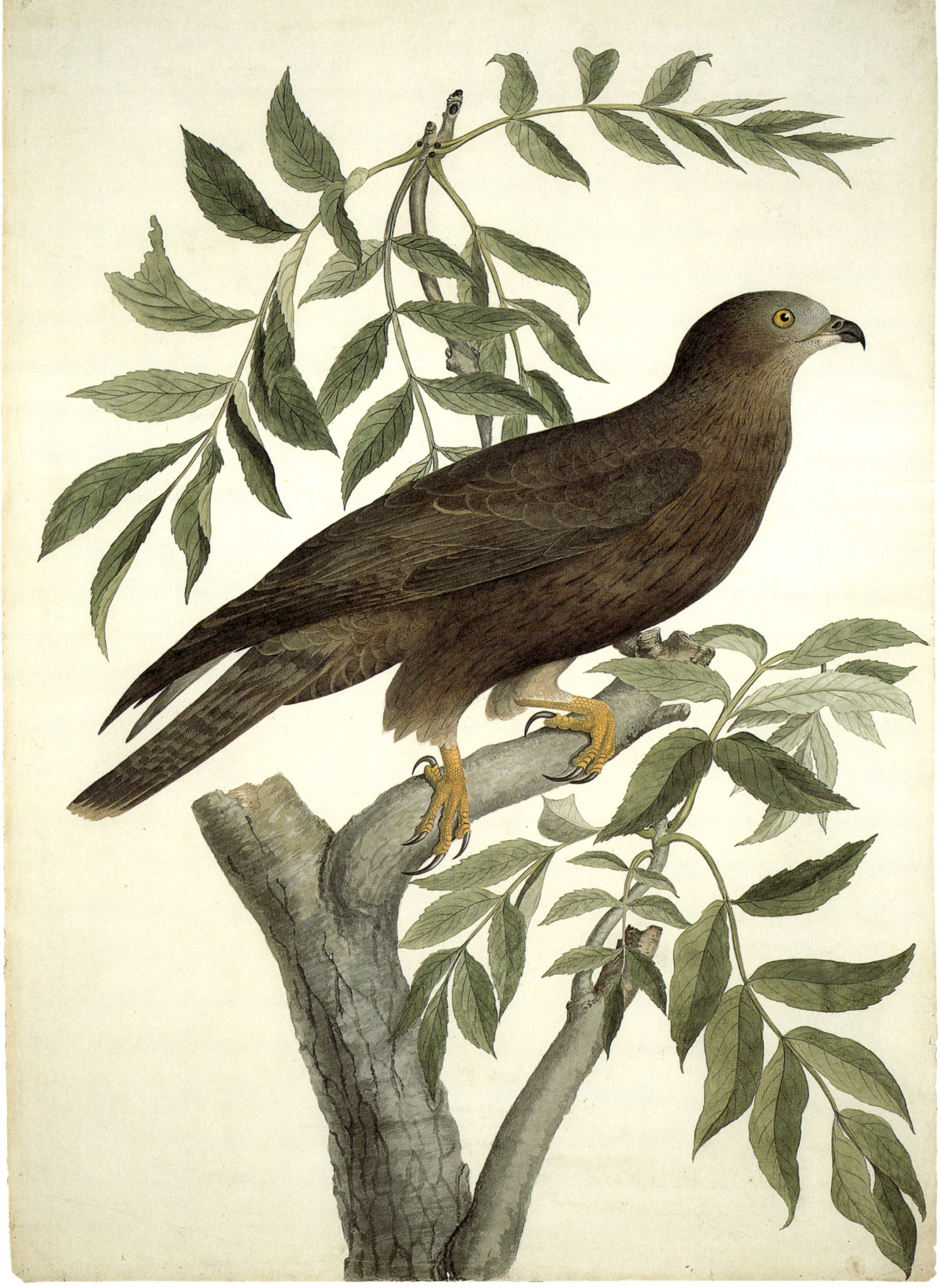

William MacGillivray

Creatures of Air, Land and Sea

ROBERT RALPH

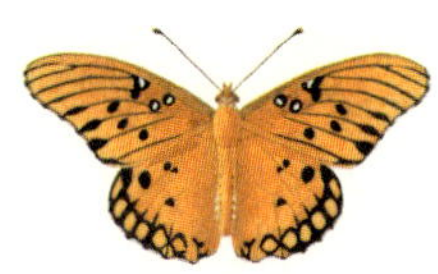

MERRELL HOLBERTON
PUBLISHERS LONDON
and
THE NATURAL HISTORY MUSEUM, LONDON

Unless otherwise stated, all photographs are taken from the books and portrait collections of The Natural History Museum, London.

The Natural History Museum would like to thank Ewen C.S. Macpherson for generously supporting the publication of this title.

First published in 1999 by
Merrell Holberton Publishers Ltd
42 Southwark Street, London SE1 1UN
and
The Natural History Museum, London

Distributed in the USA and Canada by Rizzoli International Publications, Inc.
through St. Martin's Press, 175 Fifth Avenue, New York, New York 10010

British Library Cataloguing in Publication Data
Ralph, Robert
William MacGillivray : creatures of air, land and sea
1.MacGillivray, William, 1796–1852 2.Wildlife painting – Great Britain 3.Painting, Modern – 19th century – Great Britain
I.Title II.British Museum (Natural History)
759.2

ISBN 1 85894 088 5 hardback
ISBN 1 85894 100 8 paperback

Designed by Roger Davies

Produced by Merrell Holberton Publishers
Printed and bound in Italy

Front jacket/cover: William MacGillivray, Grey heron *Ardea cinerea, ca.* 1835

Back jacket/cover: William MacGillivray, Bass *Dicentrarchus labrax* [*Labrax lupus.*]
(see also plate 34)

Frontispiece: William MacGillivray, Honey buzzard *Pernis apivorus*, 1839

Contents

Acknowledgements

I should like to thank Jane Hogg of The Natural History Museum Publishing Division for helping to bring this book into being, and Trudy Brannan and Lynn Millhouse for their help along the way. Most of the colour illustrations and some of the black-and-white photographs in this book were produced by Pat Hart of the Photographic Unit of the museum and I am grateful to her for her help. I am also grateful to Rex Banks, who first introduced me to the collection of MacGillivray's paintings in the Museum Library.

I owe a great deal to three of MacGillivray's descendants living in Australia, Carol Tebbutt, Marion Truman and Paul Truman, who sent transparencies of paintings and objects in their possession.

The Record Office for Leicestershire, Leicester and Rutland holds the unpublished letters of James Harley, a close friend and correspondent of MacGillivray, and I am grateful for permission to quote extracts from the letters (Record Office accession number 13D56). I am also happy to acknowledge the help given by the staff of the Aberdeen University Library Special Collections and Archives Department and their permission to quote extracts from MacGillivray's notebooks held by them. Mike Craig, the Head of the University Library Reprographic Unit, was particularly helpful in preparing several of the illustrations.

Robert Ralph

The Natural History Museum would like to thank Ewen C.S. Macpherson for generously supporting the publication of this title.

The museum holds 214 watercolours by William MacGillivray, presented by his second son, Paul Howard MacGillivray, in 1892.

Introduction

William MacGillivray was the Regius Professor of Natural History at Aberdeen University from 1841 until his death in 1852. One of his lasting legacies to the university was to establish a natural history museum, which still exists today in the Department of Zoology. In the museum there is a small collection of very old bird specimens, a dozen of them, all from North America, labelled with their Latin names and dates between 1831 and 1838, written in MacGillivray's handwriting. I came across them in 1988 when I was a senior lecturer in the department and curator of the museum. I was intrigued by the words on the backs of the labels, "presented by Mr Audubon". The only Audubon I had heard of was John James Audubon, the famous American naturalist and bird artist; why had he given some specimens to MacGillivray? From a brief biography of MacGillivray written by an unrelated namesake, William MacGillivray, at the turn of the century, from his journals in the Aberdeen University Library, and from his published books and papers, I realized that the bird specimens in the museum were a tangible reminder of a close friendship between the two men – a friendship that had a remarkable influence on the development of ornithology in Britain and the United States. I also learned more about the life of a remarkable man, an extraordinary field naturalist who also painted birds – paintings thought by Audubon to be every bit as good as his own and which are now in The Natural History Museum Library.

In 1989 I met Rex Banks, then the Head of Library Services at The Natural History Museum, who showed me the collection of watercolours of birds, mammals and fishes painted by MacGillivray. They were intended to accompany MacGillivray's written work, especially the five-volume *A History of British Birds*, but he was never able to afford the expense of producing them; because of this they have never received the attention and acknowledgement that they deserve. Indeed, MacGillivray himself, as a naturalist and ornithologist, has never received adequate recognition, either in his native land, or in the United States for his work with his friend Audubon. I hope this book will make his name more widely known.

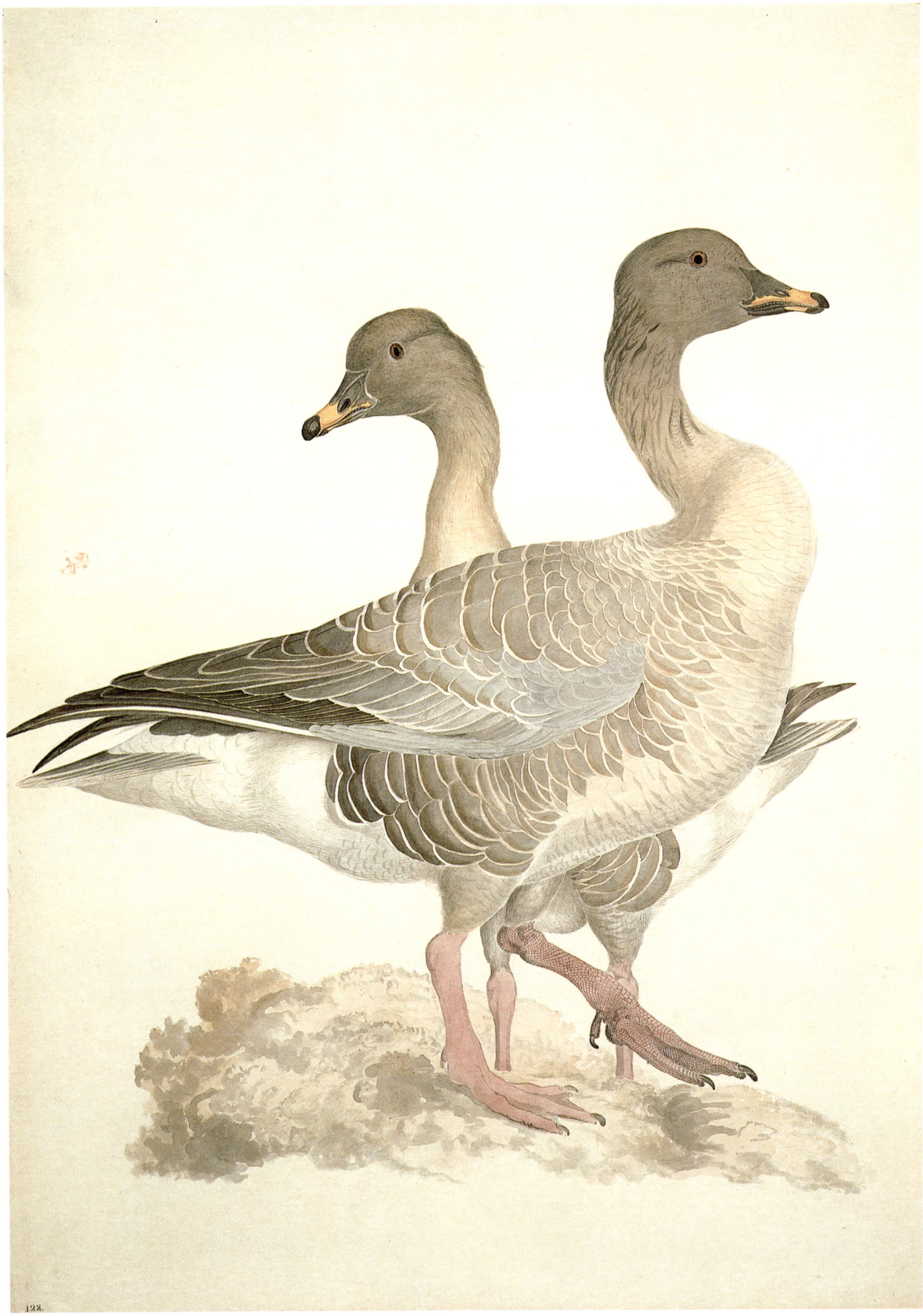

Edinburgh

A Hotbed of Genius

MACGILLIVRAY PAINTINGS

All the plates illustrated here are from the collections in The Natural History Museum, London. The captions open with the current common and scientific names. If MacGillivray's annotations differ from this, his common and scientific names follow in square brackets. Any other of MacGillivray's annotations are given in italics. Although MacGillivray didn't use the modern convention of italics for scientific names, it is used here.

PLATE 1 Greylag geese *Anser anser*

Sometime in October 1830, somewhere in Edinburgh, two men met for the first time, a meeting that developed into a life-long friendship between them. Today, one of them, John James Audubon, is known around the world as the artist who produced the famous paintings in *The Birds of America*,[1] paintings that have become the most expensive bird paintings ever sold, and the man whose name has become synonymous with birds and the conservation movement. The other man was William MacGillivray, a dour, taciturn Scot from Aberdeen, a man whose name and work as an ornithologist have been almost completely forgotten, but a man who produced paintings of birds, the best of which were comparable with Audubon's, and a man who, through his contributions to the subject, deserves to be remembered as one of Britain's finest ornithologists. Between them the two men produced ornithological works that were to lay the foundations of the subject in their respective countries. For Audubon this was his *Ornithological Biography*,[2] the letterpress that accompanied *The Birds of America*, five volumes and a synopsis that described the taxonomy, behaviour, and distribution of each species of bird illustrated by him. The work was published from Edinburgh in the 1830s and although Audubon's name is the only one that appears on the title pages, he could not have produced it without MacGillivray's help. MacGillivray's major contribution to British ornithology was through his own life's work, the five-volume *A History of British Birds*.[3] The first three volumes were published between 1837 and 1840 but were greeted with critical hostility and failed commercially so that it was another twelve years before the final two volumes were published, just weeks before MacGillivray's death. Today, 150 years or so after their publication, both sets of books have been largely forgotten but at the time of their publication and for many years afterwards they were the most detailed, most reliable accounts of the ornithology of Britain and North America.

When Audubon and MacGillivray met in 1830, Edinburgh had been MacGillivray's home, off and on, for nearly ten years. Audubon had been there just once before, in 1826–27, when the first plates of *The Birds of America* were produced, but the two men had not met then.

TURDUS MERULA. THE BLACK THRUSH, OR BLACKBIRD.

OUZEL. GARDEN OUZEL. MERLE. LON DUBH.

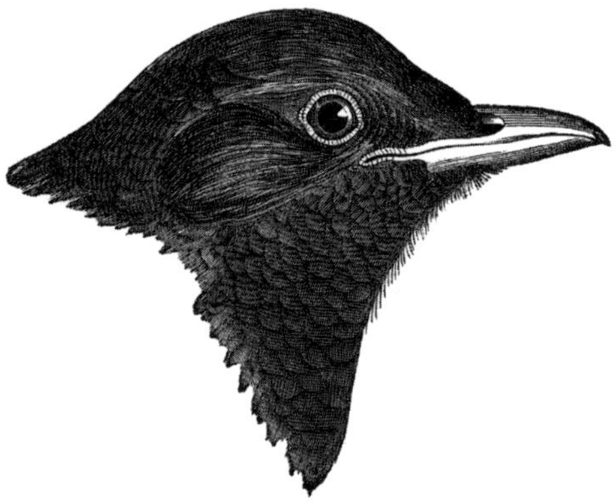

1 Blackbird *Turdus merula* from *A History of British Birds*, vol.2 (1839), p. 81

TURDUS VISCIVORUS. THE MISSEL THRUSH, OR SHRITE.

MISSEL THRUSH. MISTLE THRUSH. GREY THRUSH. STORM COCK. HOLM THRUSH. SCREECH THRUSH.

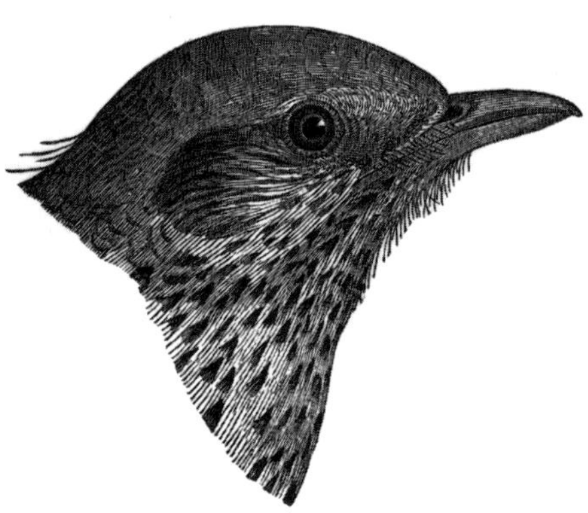

2 Mistle thrush *Turdus viscivorus*; 'missel thrush' from *A History of British Birds*, vol.2 (1839), p. 114

Edinburgh in the 1820s and 1830s was a remarkable city, after nearly a century of 'The Scottish Enlightenment' – the extraordinary outburst of intellectual activity that took place in the eighteenth century – and the printer and biographer William Smellie, who played a major role in writing and printing the first edition of the *Encyclopaedia Britannica*, was able to write, in 1800:

"Mr. Amyat, King's Chymist, a most sensible and agreeable English gentleman, resided in Edinburgh for a year or two. He one day surprised me with a curious remark. There is not a city in Europe, said he, that enjoys such a singular and noble privilege. I asked, What is that privilege? He replied, Here I stand at what is called the Cross of Edinburgh, and can, in a few minutes, take fifty men of genius and learning by the hand."[4]

These men 'of genius and learning' were individuals such as David Hume, one of the greatest philosophers of the western world; Adam Smith, the founder of economics; Adam Ferguson, the philosopher now regarded as the founder of sociology; and the historian William Robertson. Science was represented by men such as James Hutton, the founder of modern geology, Joseph Black, the chemist who discovered carbon dioxide, and the professors and doctors at the University's medical school who had made it internationally famous. In other fields, there were the architects Robert and James Adam and the portrait painter Sir Henry Raeburn. The intellectual calibre of these men, and many more like them, made Edinburgh "a hotbed of genius".[5]

By 1750 the population of the Old Town of Edinburgh was around 36,000 and the city had a reputation for squalor and violence that sat uncomfortably with a growing polite social life. The Act of Union in 1707 had seen the loss of the Scottish Parliament but, in spite of this, the minor nobility and substantial gentry of what was now referred to as 'North Britain' focused their lives on

PLATE 2 Greylag goose *Anser anser*
[Grey Goose. *Anser palustris.*] *From an adult Male, bought in Edinburgh, 1834. Edinburgh, December 1834. WMcG.*

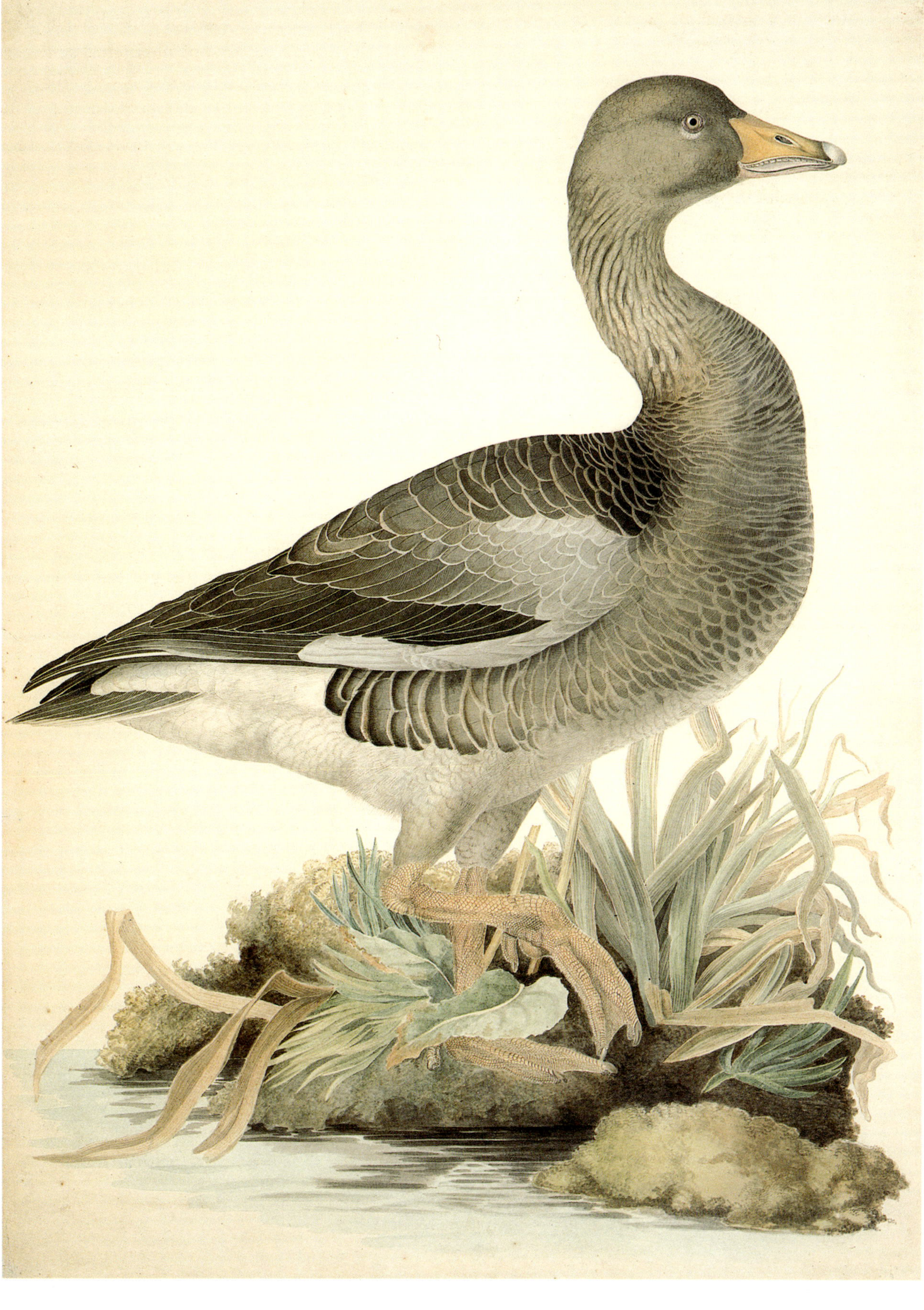

Edinburgh; London was too far away and too expensive. The life of the city was dominated by landowners, by the legal establishment, by the university and by a small number of families linked by professional interests. Clubs and societies, new journals, new lending libraries were established; a mood of improvement was in the air, an improvement of man's understanding of himself and of society, of the natural world around him, and of the environment in which he lived and worked. The mood was picked up by the City Council in an ambitious project to improve and develop the city. The last three decades of the eighteenth century were marked by the building of the New Town, a development of neo-classical buildings and splendid Georgian houses, a physical expression of the drive for improvement that led to the growth of a middle class that had the time and the affluence to be interested in the arts, in literature, in the natural world and in science.

Edinburgh University had been established in 1583, the fourth Scottish university after St Andrew's, Glasgow and Aberdeen, but in England in the eighteenth century there were still only Oxford and Cambridge, neither of them with scientific societies of any significance. For almost a hundred years Edinburgh was the only place in Britain with a university and a thriving intellectual community, which met regularly in various clubs and societies. The city's own Royal Society was established in 1783 and before the end of the century there were the Academy of Physics, the Royal Medical and Royal Physical Societies, the Chirurgo-Physical Society, the Natural History Society of Edinburgh, the Edinburgh University Chemical Society and the Agricultural Society of Edinburgh.

By the time that Audubon and MacGillivray met in Edinburgh at least two more societies had been formed. In 1808 the Wernerian Society of Edinburgh, a Scottish counterpart of the Linnean Society, was established by Robert Jameson, Professor of Natural History at the University, and in 1823 the Plinian Society of Edinburgh, a general scientific society, came into being. Many of these societies published their own journals, so that Edinburgh was home to a large number of periodicals, among them the *Memoirs of the Wernerian Natural History Society, Edinburgh Philosophical Journal* and *New Philosophical Journal, The Quarterly Journal of Agriculture, The Transactions of the Plinian Society* and the *Edinburgh Journal of Natural and Geographical Science*, journals that between them reflected an almost insatiable desire for information about the natural world.

The Scottish Enlightenment was an extraordinary phase in Scottish history; there is no simple explanation for it, perhaps it was no more than a chance coming together of minds and circumstances, but when MacGillivray and Audubon met in Edinburgh in 1830, it was in a city at the height of an intellectual golden age, perhaps unmatched by any other city in the world.

NOTES

1 Audubon (1827–38).

2 Audubon (1831–39).

3 MacGillivray (1837–52).

4 William Smellie *Literary and Characteristic Lives of Gregory, Kames, Hume, and Smith* (Edinburgh 1800), pp. 161-62.

5 The expression "Edinburgh – a hotbed of genius" was used by the character Dr Lewis in the novel *Humphrey Clinker* by Tobias Smollett (Edinburgh 1771).

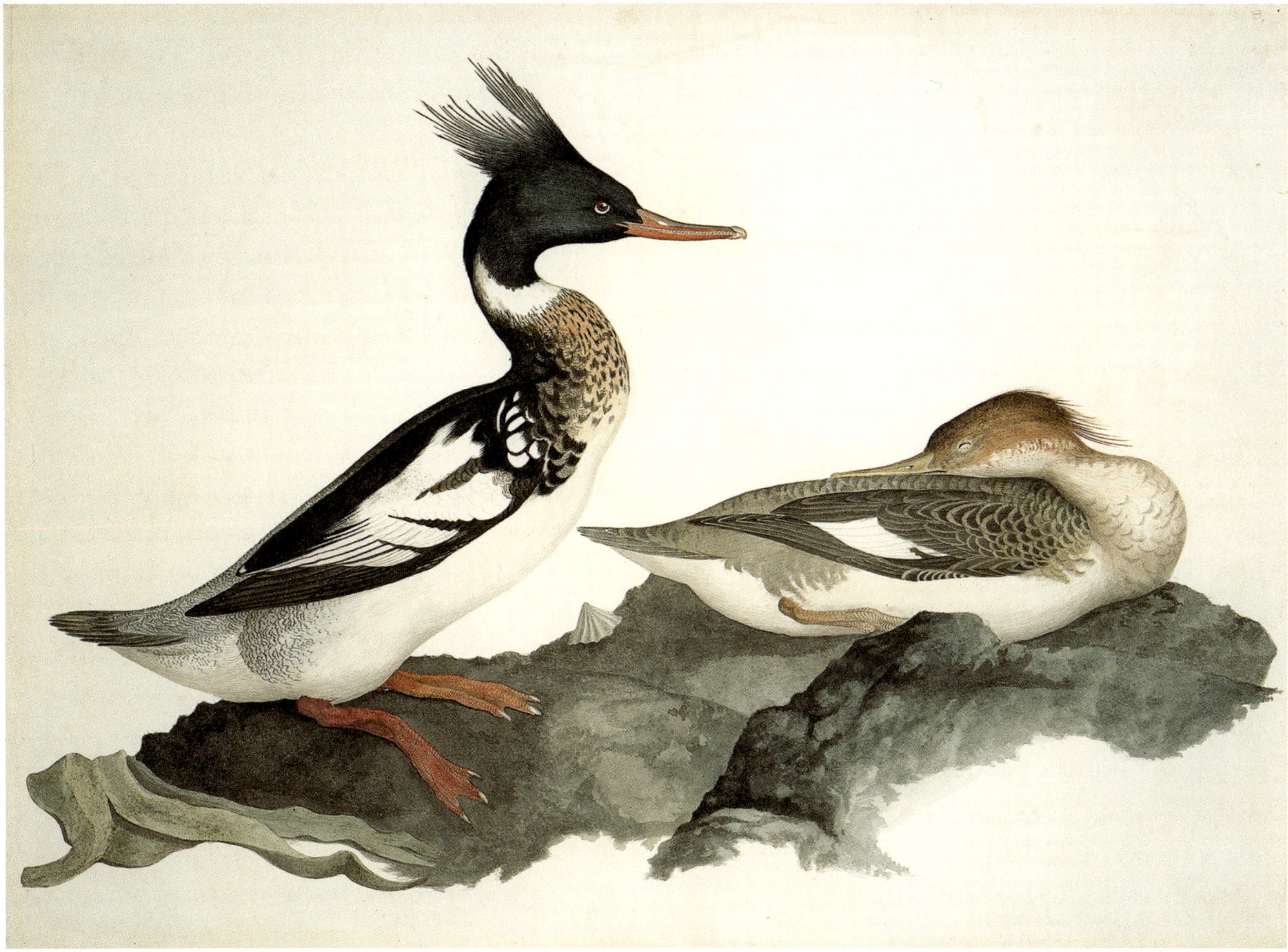

PLATE 3 Red-breasted merganser *Mergus serrator*

[Red-breasted Merganser. *Mergus Serrator.*] *The Male from a specimen obtained in the Edinburgh market, in April, 1837. The Female from a purchased skin. Edinburgh, 28th April, 1837. W.Mc.G.*

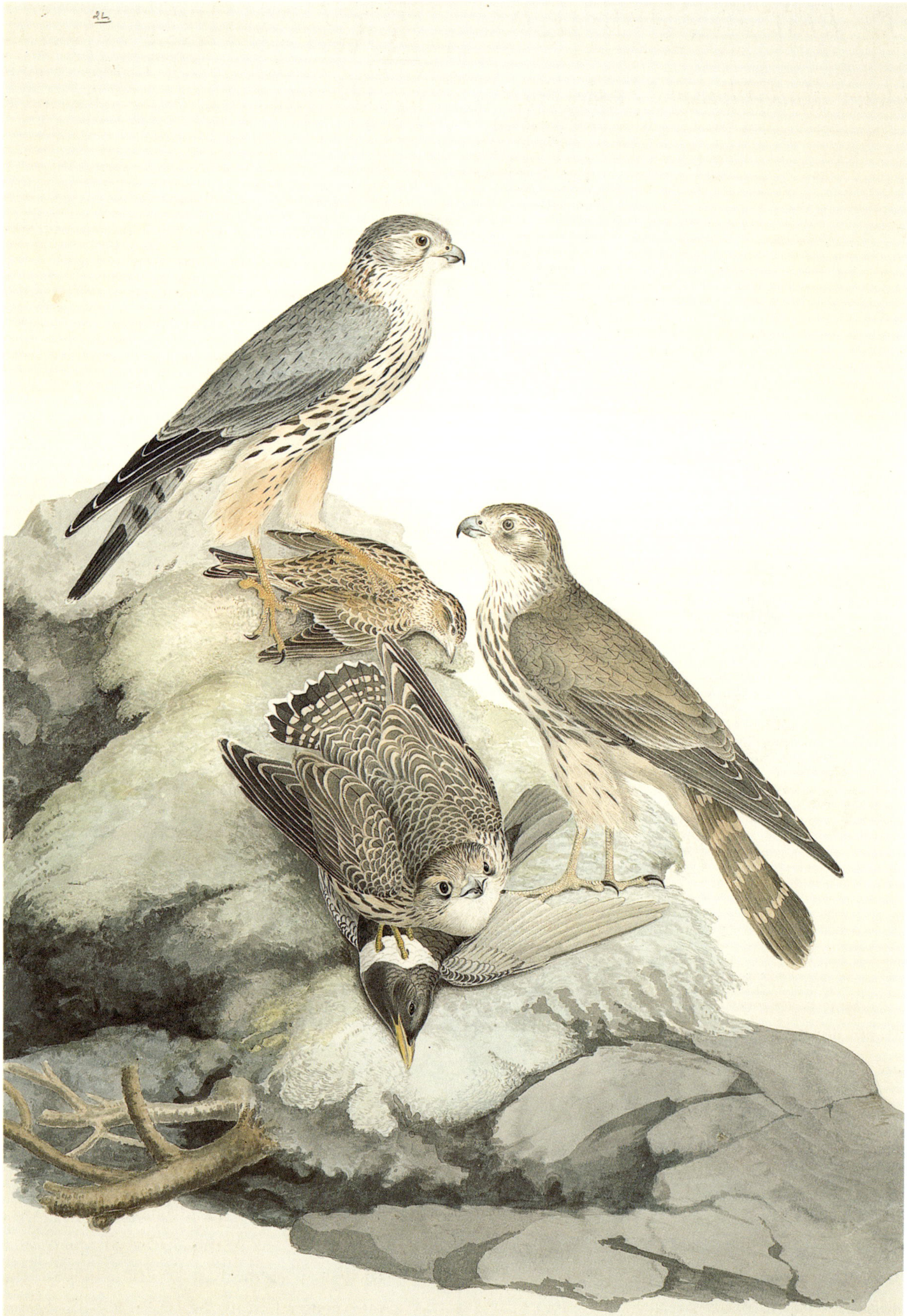

The Path to Edinburgh

William MacGillivray's Early Years

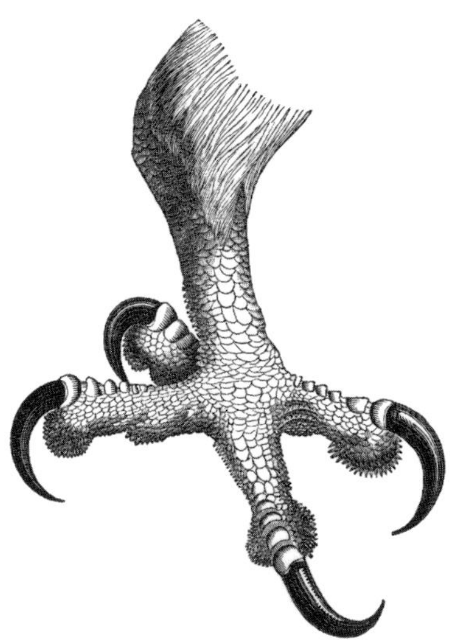

3 Osprey claw *Pandion haliaetus* from *A History of British Birds*, vol. 3 (1840), p. 251

PLATE 4 Merlin *Falco columbarius*
[Merlin. *Falco Aesalon.*] *Male, Female and Young with a Lark and a Ring ouzel. From specimens obtained near Edinburgh. Edinburgh, September 1835.*

William MacGillivray was born in Old Aberdeen in north-east Scotland on 25 January 1796. The record of his birth is in the Old Machar parish register, not in the expected place among the entries for January, but several pages back, tucked away at the bottom of a page with the records for the previous month, December 1795, put there perhaps by an economical minister determined not to waste an inch of space at the bottom of a page.

MacGillivray's start in life was not a particularly auspicious one. His father, also William, was a student at the local King's College in Old Aberdeen; all that is known of his mother is her name, Anne Wishart; they were not married, so that like Audubon, MacGillivray was illegitimate and knew little of his natural mother. The student records at King's College show that William MacGillivray senior came from Inverness-shire but did not complete his degree. Shortly after the birth of his son, he left Aberdeen to join the Cameron Highlanders and went on to serve with them in the Peninsular Wars. Various accounts of MacGillivray's life suggest that his father became a surgeon in the regiment and was killed at the Battle of Corunna in 1809, but in the records of the regiment there is no record of his name in the casualty lists after that battle. The Cameron Highlanders were involved in many actions in northern Spain at about this time but the name of William MacGillivray appears just once in the regimental casualty records – a private William MacGillivray was killed in a later battle, the siege of Burgos, in 1812.

Nothing is known of the earliest years of the young William's life, but when he was just three years old he was taken from Aberdeen to Harris in the Outer Hebrides. His father had married Euphemia (Effie) MacNeil, a daughter of William MacNeil of Pabbay, but MacGillivray was brought up by his uncle, Roderick MacGillivray, and his family on their farm at North-town on the south-west tip of the island. The ruined walls of the house are still there today, used as a sheep fank, a fold, by the crofters in the nearby village of Northton. North-town is at the base of the 1000-foot-high Ben Capval, sheltered from the westerly Atlantic gales and overlooking the machair and the spectacularly beautiful

AQUILA CHRYSAËTUS. THE GOLDEN EAGLE.

BLACK EAGLE. RING-TAILED EAGLE. BROWN EAGLE. IOLAIR DHUBH.

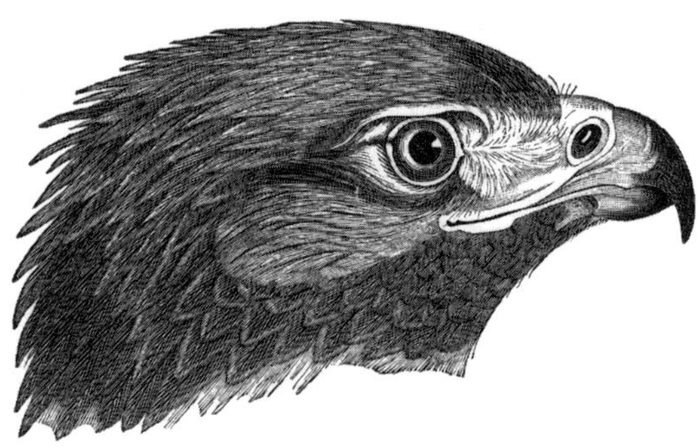

Fig. 215.

4 Golden eagle *Aquila chrysaetos* from *A History of British Birds*, vol. 3 (1840), p. 204

Luskentyre sands. The young William went to the village school at Obbe a few miles from Northton. Considering the time and the place, the beginning of the 19th century on an island little known to the rest of Britain, he received what seems a remarkable education, learning among other things Latin and Greek. An idea of his opinion of Latin, at least, comes in his description of the rock dove in the first volume of *A History of British Birds* (1837) where he recalled that, as a boy, he kept a tame one: "Whenever I escaped from the detested pages of Virgil and Horace, the pigeon was sure to fly to me, and sometimes alighted on my head or shoulder, directing its bill towards my mouth, and flapping its wings".[1]

There are occasional references to his childhood in some of his later works, as in his account of the Golden eagle in *Descriptions of the Rapacious Birds of Great Britain* (1836) where he wrote about learning to use a gun:

"My first aquaintance with the Golden Eagle happened in the following manner. On the farm of North-town in Harris, at that time held by my uncle, great havoc had been made among the lambs by the eagles, which resorted to that peninsula from all parts of the mainland, and from the neighbouring island of Shellay. I had just commenced the use of the gun, under the guidance of my uncle, and had only as yet fired five shots; with the first of which I had riddled a table, with the second demolished a rock-pigeon, killed two with the third, and with the rest had done nothing to my credit as a marksman. The sixth was destined for a higher deed. Not finding any flesh or fish, recent or putrid about the place, I laid hold of a white hen, to the legs of which I fastened a bit of twine and a wooden peg, filled one of my jacket-pockets with barley-grain, the other with old newspapers; and, taking the hen under my arm, and my gun on my shoulder, proceeded to the farther brow of the hill. There I fastened the bird to the turf by means of the peg, left her the barley, put up a double charge of buckshot into the gun, and shut myself up into the pit. [Pits were dug into various parts of the hillside as hides from which to shoot eagles attracted to carrion bait.] Before I had been there an hour, the rain had made its way through the roof, the newspapers had ceased to amuse, and I had fallen into a sort of slumber, from which I was awakened by a shrill scream. My first motion was to peep through the hole, when I beheld an eagle perched on the back of the hen, which crouched close to the ground in terror; my second was to raise to my shoulder the butt of the gun, of which the muzzle lay in the aperture of the hut; and at the moment when the eagle was in the act of raising his head, as if to inflict a blow on his unresisting victim, I fired, and received a serious contusion on the cheek, the gun having been overcharged. Impatient to know the result, I raised the roof on my back, forced myself through it, and running up to the

PLATE 5 Honey buzzard *Pernis apivorus*

From a specimen shot near Stirling in the beginning of June, 1838. Lent by Mr. MacDuff Carfrae on the 9th June when its outline was taken. Finished, Edinburgh, 12th July 1839. W.Mc.G.

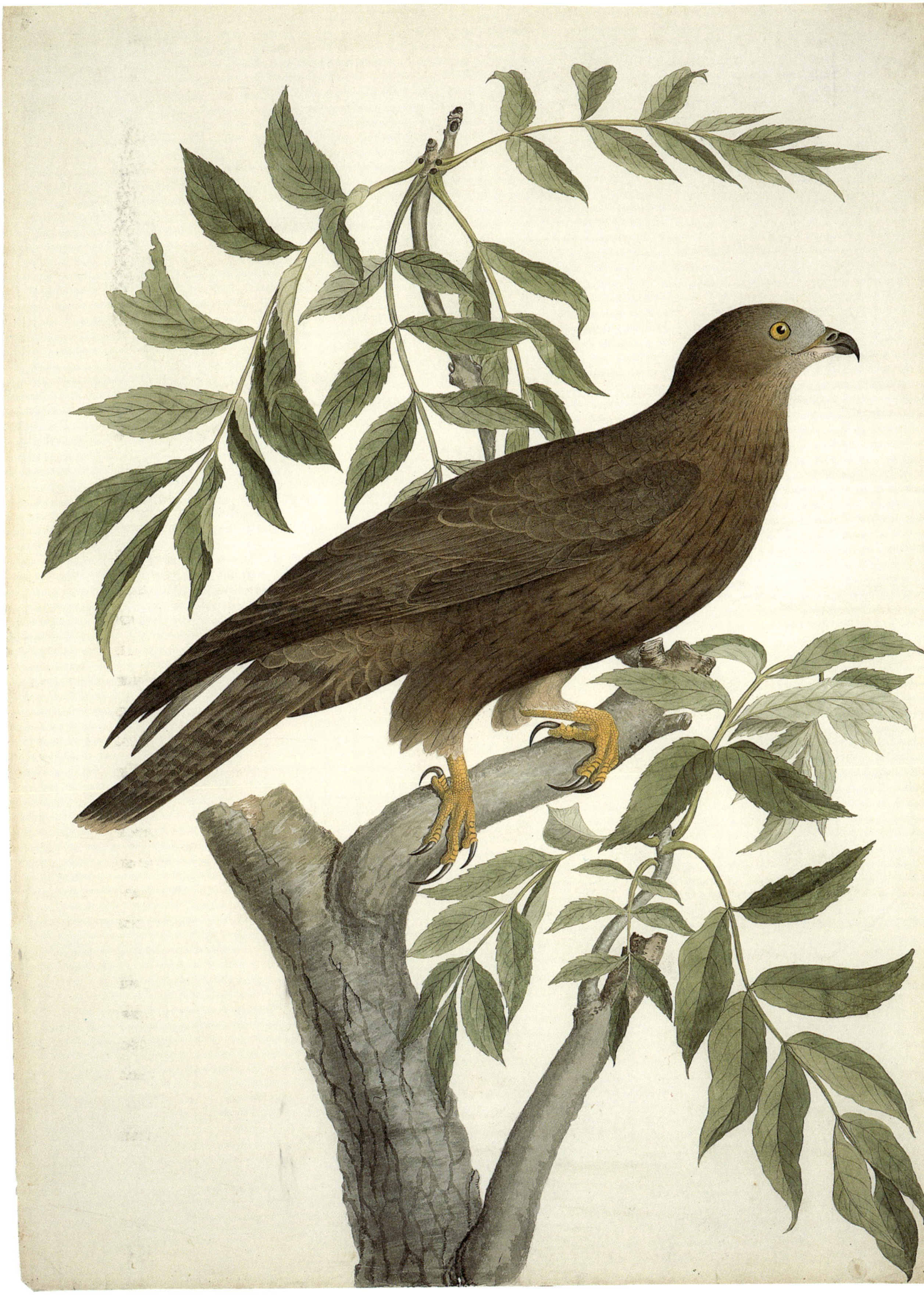

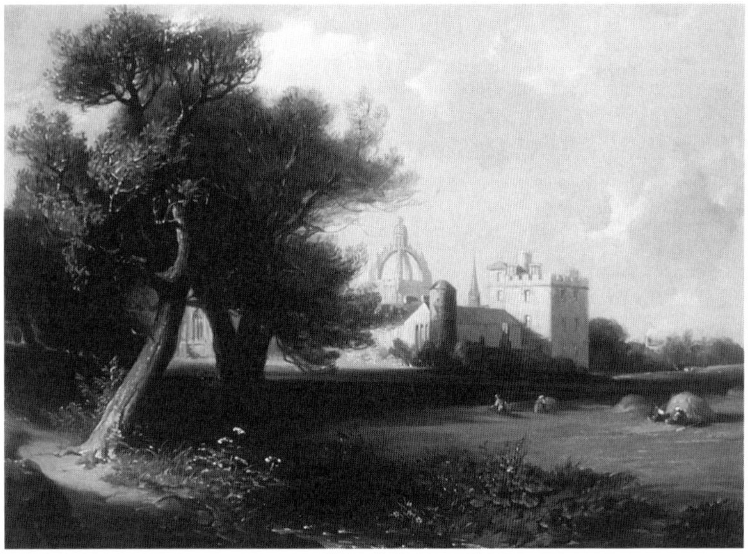

5 King's College in 1848 by James Cassie, much as it would have been twenty years earlier when MacGillivray was a student there.

place, found the eagle quite dead, the whole shot having entered its side. So, this is all, I thought, an eagle is nothing wonderful after all. I remember feeling precisely in the same manner after shooting my first deer. I threw the eagle upon my back, brought a leg on each side of my neck, tied the feet before, put the hen, which had been but slightly injured by the grasp of the tyrant, under one arm, the gun under another, and thus accoutred soon made my appearance on the brow of the hill. As I descended the people came out to see what I had got, some thinking it a bunch of heather put up with the view of deceiving them, others alleging that *Uilleam beg* [his Gaelic name] had actually shot an eagle. My uncle was as proud as myself, for I had proved a hopeful scholar and had saved him half a score of lambkins. As I was not then a naturalist, the bird was allowed to rot on the dungheap, without having its quills counted or its bill measured. As to the hen which had been in such peril, first from the talons of an eagle, and then from the shot of a raw recruit, it still continued useful in its way, reared a brood of chickens, and was finally eaten."[2]

MacGillivray's academic potential must have been noticed by someone in his local community, the schoolmaster, his uncle, or the local minister perhaps, because at the age of eleven he returned to Aberdeen, went to a local school for a year, and then entered King's College to take a general MA degree. At this time, the beginning of the nineteenth century, it was not uncommon for students in Scotland to attend university at such a young age. Students at Aberdeen came from all over the north of Scotland, from the Shetland Islands in the north to the Outer Hebrides in the west. It would have been commonplace for these students to walk from their homes to Aberdeen and back again; for MacGillivray this would have been a journey of around 180 miles, including a boat crossing of the Minch.

PLATE 6 Honey buzzard *Pernis apivorus*
[*Honey Buzzard.* Pernis apivora.] *Adult male. Drawn by Mr. MacGillivray Aug 13th 1835*
From a stuffed specimen lent by John Bushnan Esq. Surgeon, Dumfries. (appears on front of picture)
Young male. From an individual shot at Dramlanrig, Dumfrieshire. Lent by John Bushman Esq. Edinburgh, July, 1835. W.Mc.G. (appears on back of picture).

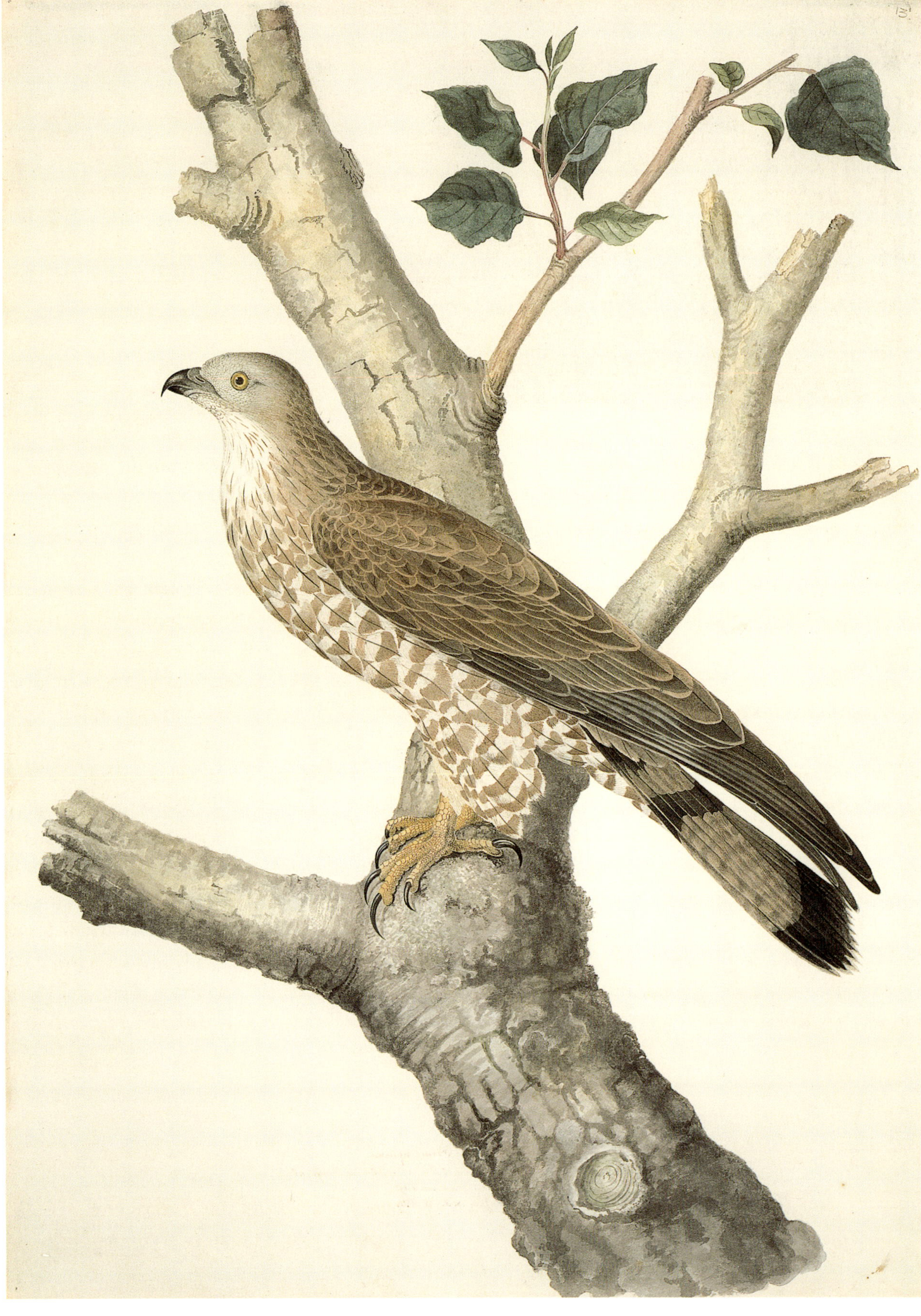

In 1814 MacGillivray began studying medicine, still at King's College, but he was increasingly drawn to natural history, and after a few years gave up medicine to become a naturalist. In the Preface to his *Descriptions of the Rapacious Birds of Great Britain*, MacGillivray presents "a few particulars of my history", the closest he ever came to any kind of autobiography.

"I commenced the study of Zoology in 1817, while qualifying myself for the medical profession at Aberdeen, a city not less famed for learned professors than for dried haddocks. My only guides were Linnaeus and Pennant, for at that period I knew no living wight who had any knowledge of the subject, excepting a fellow student, Mr. William Craigie, now in Upper Canada, who accompanied me on my rambles, and most zealously strove to add to our common store of knowledge, both in Zoology and Botany. How many pleasant and successful excursions, in quest of plants and animals, we made together on the romantic braes of the Don, the pebbly shores of the Dee, the rocks of the Cove, the sands of the seashore, and the bleak moors of the interior, I cannot now tell. The fascinations of these pursuits were such that, after studying medicine for nearly five years, during part of which time I officiated as dissector to the lecturer on Anatomy at Marischal College, I resolved to relinquish it, and devote my attention exclusively to Natural History."[3]

The decision to give up medicine left MacGillivray with no settled plans for the future or for a career and in August 1817, aged twenty-one, he left Aberdeen to go back home to North-town on the first stage of a trip intended to take him through the highlands and islands, through Skye, Ross-shire, Caithness, Inverness-shire and Cromarty, the intention being to widen his experience of natural history, especially in botany. The journal that he kept during the trip has survived, and is now in the Aberdeen University Library. The first entry, Old Aberdeen, Sunday 3 August 1817, begins:

"I am again determined for a tour through part of the Highlands and Isles. In regard to my motives – the principal one is connected with the article pecunia but it would be doing injustice to my favourite study, not to say that Natural History also put in its vote for the expedition. Mr James Shand [a student friend], actuated by a desire of extending his knowledge in Topography and Zoology, intends to accompany me. He has already made his departure, but will meet me tomorrow at Kemnay. My baggage will be heavy: but I submit with cheerfulness to any temporary inconvenience, when it becomes the mean of procuring permanent benefit. I may here with propriety enough give an account in detail of my accoutrements: In the first place. My clothes differ in nothing from those commonly worn. I take some changes of femoralia and pectoralia [breeches and shirts], linnen, stockings, and two pair of shoes. My hat is just like those of my neighbours, without the vast umbelliform brim, which characterises the physical or Linnoan cut! [After Linnaeus, the Swedish taxonomist.] For my studies and amusement by the way, I take the first part of the First and the Third Volume of the Systema Natura: Smith's Compendium Flora Britannica; Campbells' Pleasures of Hope; drawing paper, pencils, paint & crayons; paper, ink and pens; one pound of gunpowder, six pounds of shot, flints and bullets, powder horn & fowling-piece, hair-line and hooks and a quarter of a pound of snuff. The other articles which can scarcely be reduced to any distinct class are the following: pocket compass, knife, soap, razors, silk-thread, wax, buttons, sharping stone, needles, lancets, opium, a flute & some small boxes. All, excepting my gun, packed into two small bundles, clapped upon my

PLATE 7 Kestrel *Falco tinnunculus*
[Kestrel. *Falco Tinnunculus.*] *Adult Male and Three Young Birds. From specimens lent by Mr. MacDuff Carfrae, May 1835. Edinburgh, May 1835. WMc.G.*

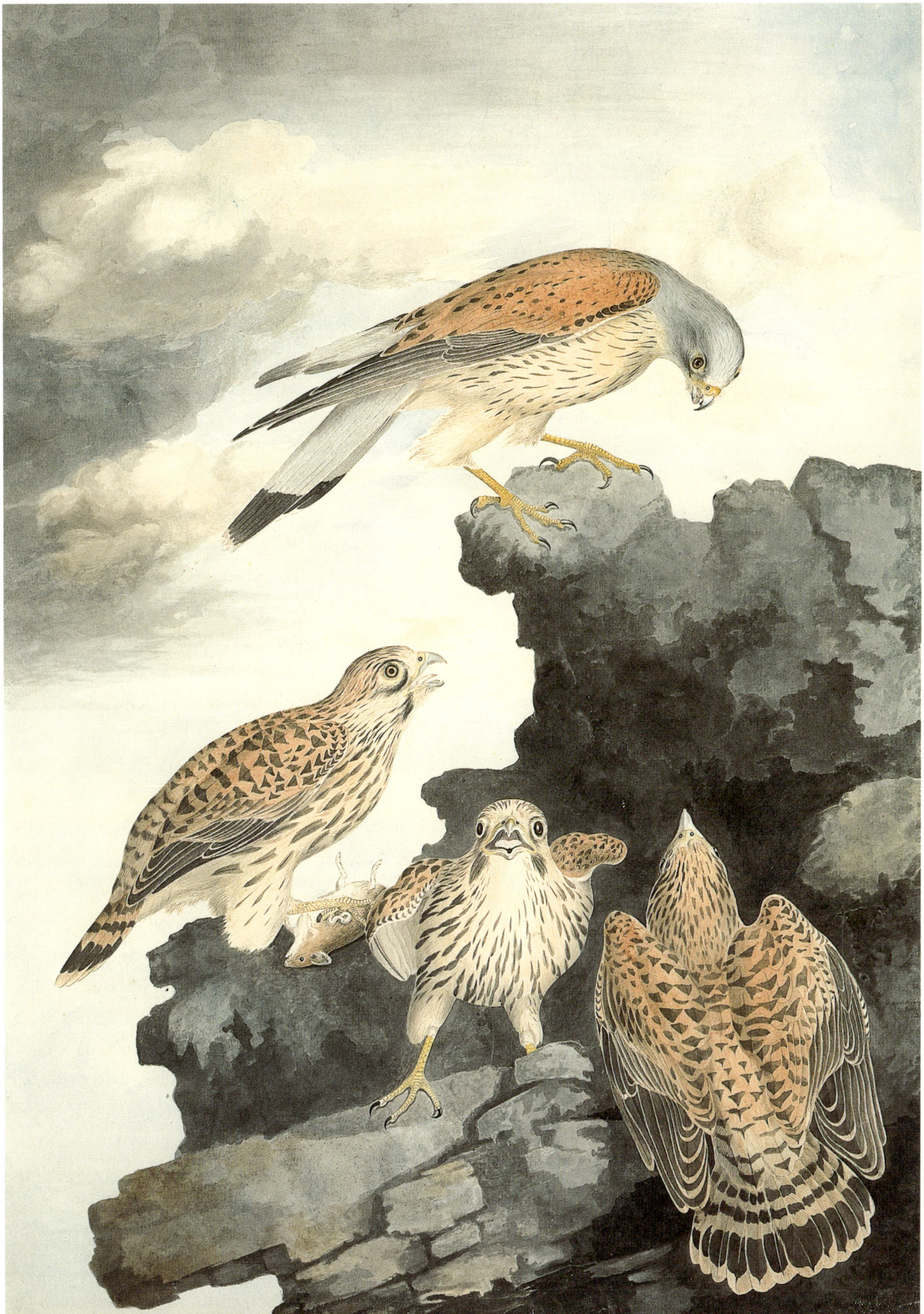

shoulders, after the manner of a knapsack. The objects in view are money to be obtained from some of my friends to enable me to prosecute my studies, my improvement in Natural History, particularly in Ornithology, Ichthyology and Mineralogy: Botany too – inurement to hardship, the habit of early rising, dexterity in the use of the gun, proficiency in physiognomy [judging character and disposition from a person's external features]. Knowledge of men and manners, romantic ideas, practical imagery, sketches of landscape drawings in Zoology or Botany. If I catch rightly at opportunities, I have a fair chance of accomplishing all these ends."[4]

There is no suggestion in the journal that he had any success with the article "pecunia" as he put it, or that he obtained any money from his friends or relatives, and, as events turned out, he spent almost a year at home in North-town. It is clear from the materials that he took with him that he intended to draw and paint, but there are no sketches or drawings in the journal and nothing else that he might have done at that time has survived. The journal is full of comments on people that he met on his travels, visits to relatives and friends on Harris and Lewis, and descriptions of medical treatments administered to various patients, but the main threads running through it are the descriptions of the natural history of Harris, the plants and animals, and especially the birds. It also reveals much of MacGillivray's character. As his moods changed he could be humorous or grave, spirited or despondent, lapsing into bouts of melancholy and self-doubt, or roused to fierce indignation by, for example, the treatment of crofters by their lairds. However, he was always simple and direct in his opinions, a characteristic that was to make him enemies in later life. When he arrived at North-town he met his foster-mother's younger sister, Miss Marion McCaskill; he was twenty-one, she just fourteen. The entry in his journal for Tuesday 26 August 1817 records his impression of her:

"I took a walk with the ladies – and in the evening went with Marion to the fold. Marion is a very fine girl, tall and genteel in her figure, but rather simple and unsuspecting. Sweet flower of the rural shade! full easily might you be by love's simplicity betray'd, and guileless trust, but blasted be the heart that could harbour a thought inimical to your virtue."[5]

The journal does not record any intimate feelings MacGillivray may have had about young Marion's virtue, inimical or otherwise, but romance quickly blossomed between them, as he wrote in his journal a few weeks later:

"On regaining the house, I got supper, drank some warm milk, shifted my pedicles [changed my socks], warmed me by the kitchen fire, succeeded in obtaining about a dozen kisses of all dimensions from Miss Marion, and retired to bed."[6]

The rest of the year at North-town was spent walking and riding over much of Harris, observing and collecting birds, plants and rocks. On one excursion he made the first recorded ascent of Clisham, at 2,600 feet the highest mountain in the Outer Hebrides:

"The hail came in great showers, the wind was exceedingly keen, and the summits of the hills were covered with snow. ... and I proceeded towards Clisheim. In despite of hail and snow, and frost and whirlwinds I clambered to the summit, and well was my labour repaid, for from this I enjoyed a very sublime spectacle. I was on the highest pinnacle of that range of islands denominated the Long Island, throned upon a precipitous ridge of rocks. The islands of Uist, Harris and Lewis lay under my feet. Towards the east and south in the extreme distance appeared the mountains of Ross and Inverness shires, with the hills and capes and plains of Skye. Toward the west a long series of pointed summits, commencing at Clisheim, forming a

PLATE 8 Black grouse *Tetrao tetrix*
[Black grouse. *Tetrao Tetrix.*] *Adult male. From an individual procured by Mr. Carfrae. Edinburgh, April, 1836. W.Mc.G.*

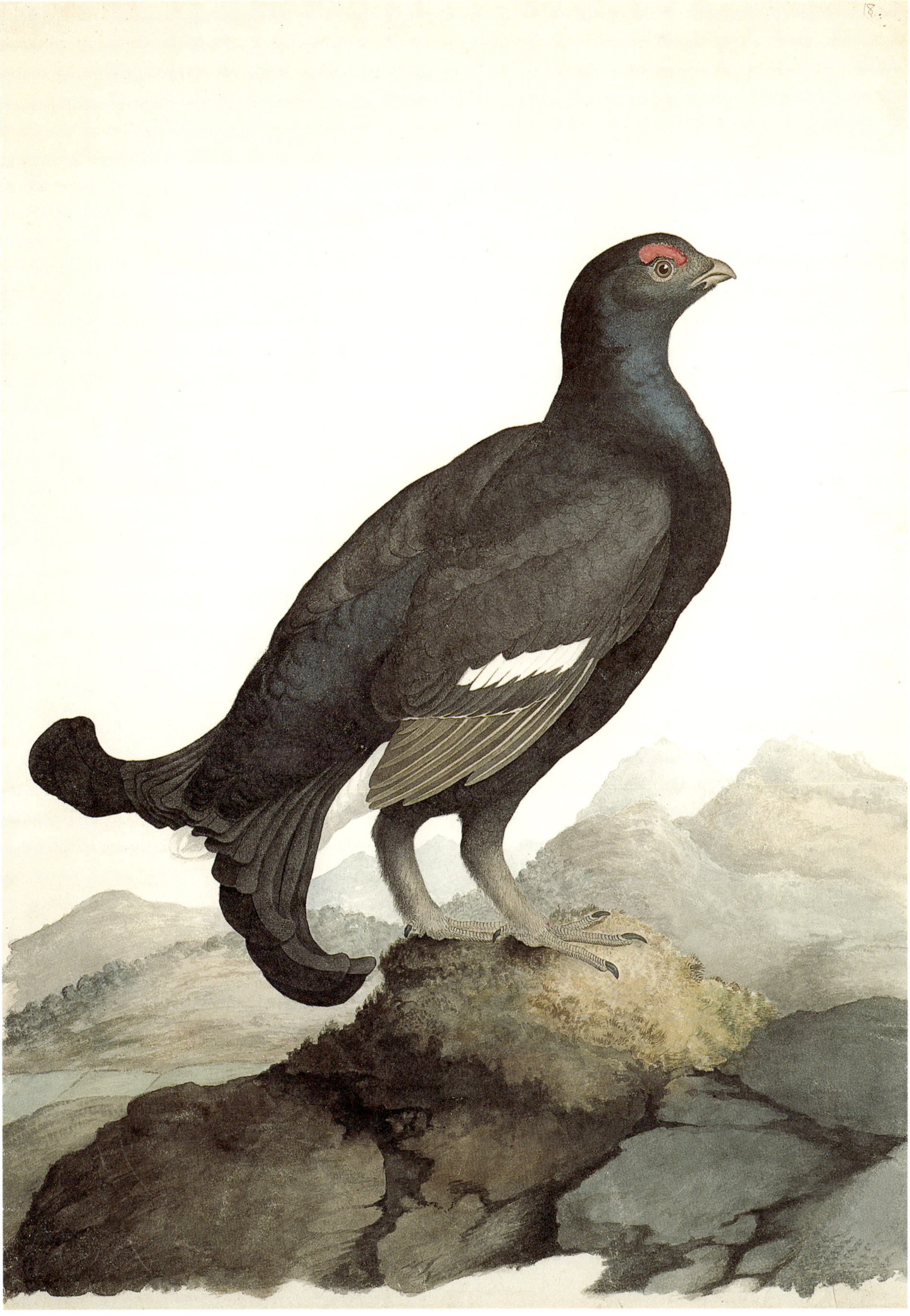

broad ridge, extended for several miles. The snow came on so thickly, that I was apprehensive of being smothered in it. I felt too, for the first time perhaps the disagreeable effects of cold – my feet and fingers were almost senseless, and I began to feel sickish and faint. I got warm however by walking briskly, and after passing the deep glen of Langadal sat me down upon the western side of it to take a pinch of snuff, and soon discovered tokens of cultivation at the distance of three or four miles."[7]

He spent his time on his studies of birds, plants and rocks, teaching at his old school at Obbe and putting into practice some of his medical training. On one occasion he records receiving a letter and two plates of material from a friend in Aberdeen, material with which he inoculated the local children against smallpox. He seems also to have shown great perception in his diagnoses:

"I met the Gaelic schoolmaster of Strond, who told me he was much troubled with headache, and requested my advice. I found that his complaint was hypochondriasis, and advised him to use a purgative occasionally."[8]

The journal is a detailed account of daily life in the Outer Hebrides in the early part of the nineteenth century. MacGillivray recorded the smallest details of what he ate, what he drank, the clothes that he wore and the games that his family played in the evening. The journal also contains the only references he ever made to his father and to the woman his father married, Euphemia MacNeil. She is referred to several times as Mrs MacGillivray, without explanation as to who she was, and there are just two passing mentions of his father. He refers to "some papers relative to the distribution of my father's effects" and to "the farm promised to Mr. MacNiel of Kyles, for his sister Euphemia, my father's widow".

It was, however, in the pursuit of natural history that MacGillivray spent most of his time. He regularly shot birds to examine, dissect and identify them, comparing their descriptions with those given by Linnaeus, the only zoological work available to him. He made careful descriptions of each species that he collected, together with notes on their distribution, migration and behaviour, and even when his ideas on taxonomy differed from those of Linnaeus, he had confidence enough to record them.

Everything was of interest to him. In December 1817, a walrus was shot as it rested on a rock near North-town and MacGillivray measured it and dissected it. He sent a notice about it to the *Inverness Journal* newspaper[9] and a few years later wrote a more formal account in the *Edinburgh Philosophical Journal,* his first scientific paper.[10] Later, in 1838, MacGillivray wrote the volume on 'British Quadrupeds' in Sir William Jardine's *The Naturalist's Library,* where he added another piece of information about the North-town walrus:

"The occurrence of so rare an animal caused great astonishment at the time, and the courage of the person who ventured to shoot it was highly extolled. It formed the subject of many a conversation over the whole district; and its ghost appeared to a young woman in a dream, stating that it had visited their inhospitable coast in search of a lost brother."[11]

MacGillivray took every chance to add to his knowledge and experience of comparative anatomy, dissecting everything that came his way. There were the stranded seals and dolphins to be expected in the Outer Hebrides, but more unusually there was the chance to dissect a bear that a local laird had kept in a cage in his garden. When it was eventually decided that the bear should be shot, MacGillivray agreed to carry out the task and then stuff it:

PLATE 9 Lesser black-backed gull *Larus fuscus*
[Smaller Black-backed Gull. *Larus fuscus.*] *From an individual shot by W. MacGillivray, at Preston Pans, on 6th May, 1836. Edinburgh 7th May 1836. WMcG.*

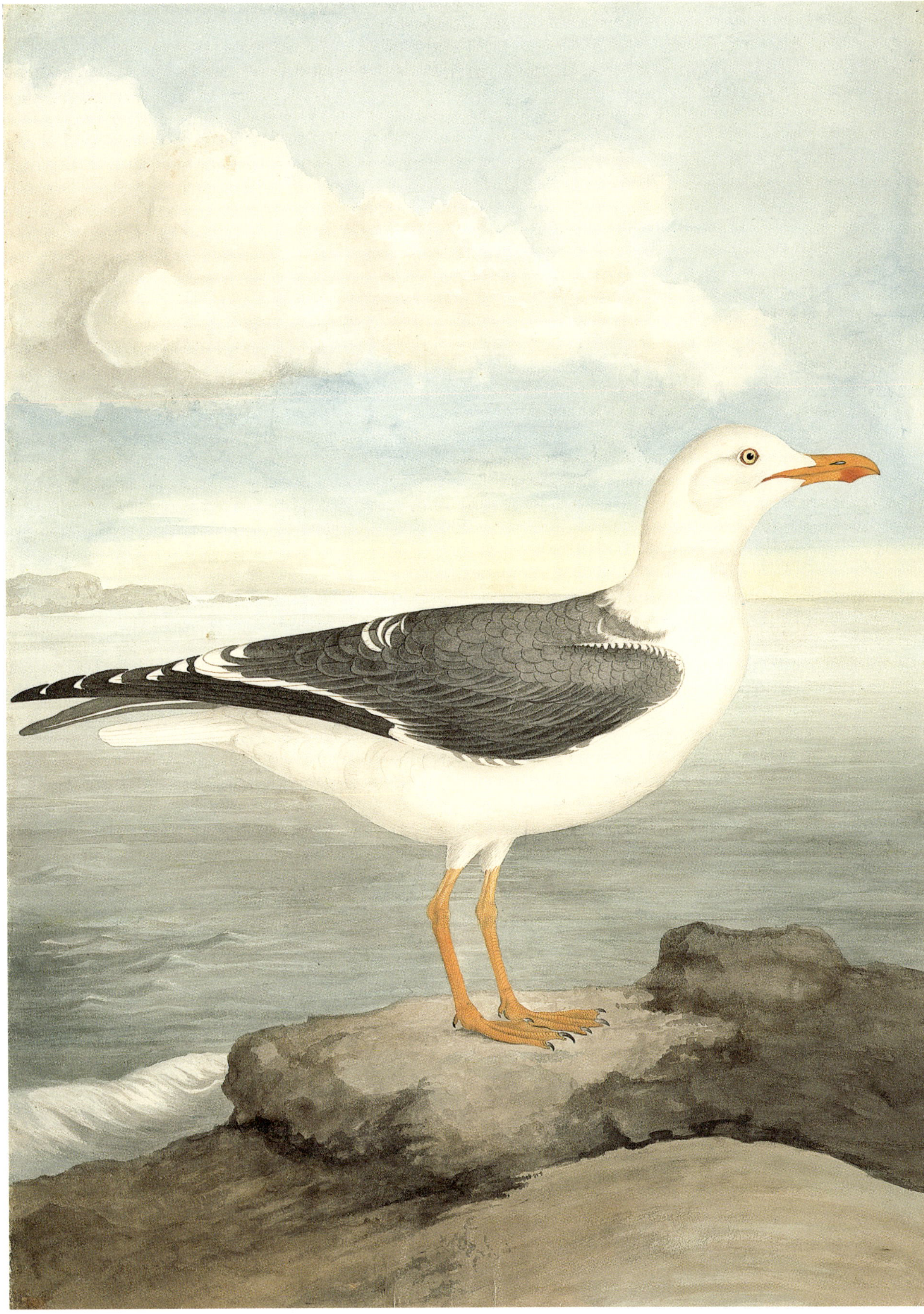

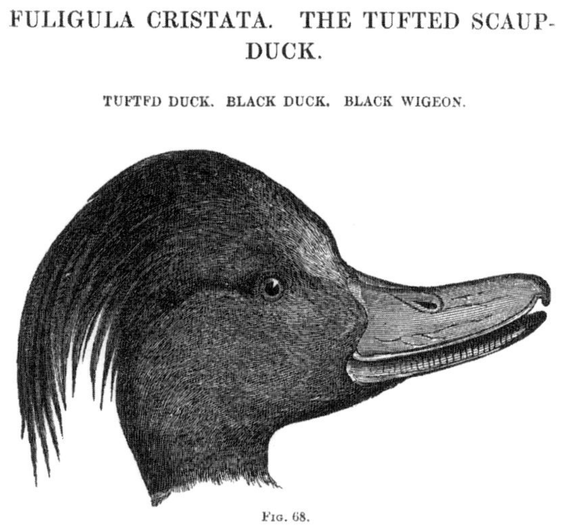

6 Tufted duck *Aythya fuligula*; 'tufted scaup-duck', *Fuligula cristata* from *A History of British Birds*, vol. 5 (1852), p. 121

"I found a musket and charged it with powder in due quantity and a lump of lead. So poor Bruin was shot through the head. After breakfast I skinned him. The plan which I took up was this. First I got a frame made to support the stuffing; it consists of a stick for the back, two cross ones to which were affixed those substitutes for the bones of the legs, and a neck piece. Upon these straw and hay were moulded into the natural form of the animal, and the whole secured by ropes. I then sewed up the skin, and slit it from the tail to the head along the back – and thus the skin was easily drawn upon the legs, and from thence pulled over the whole body – The head was supported by a rope. In the evening I put him out, and was amused with the apprehension with which the dogs and some little boys regarded him."[12]

Towards the end of his time at North-town, MacGillivray went through a period of introspection and self-analysis. He was twenty-two, in love, had no money and not too much in the way of prospects. What was he to do with his life? In his journal for Monday, 27 April 1818 he wrote:

"From reading with considerable attention De Luc's Treatise on Geology I find that I need not be under the apprehension of ever exhausting those parts of the study of Nature which best suit my peculiar constitution. New subjects, I am persuaded will daily present themselves for investigation. The observation of geological indices will henceforth occupy much of my time. On my way to Aberdeen I might acquire considerable mineralogical knowledge, if I possessed the necessary books and instruments – but in the deficiency of these I may even do something. I shall at least become acquainted with a few species. I have not yet seen an account of the Birds of Britain with which I am entirely pleased; and I have of late been thinking upon the subject. Perhaps it might not be a mad scheme to attempt the ornithology of Scotland. I certainly would not engage for more. But whether this alone would be acceptable I cannot yet determine. However I shall begin to note every particular regarding it, which I can observe, or collect from creditable authority.

My acquirements may be numerated in few words, of most of the physical sciences, I have got a smattering. In Zoology I have made considerable progress, particularly in Ornithology. I have just begun the study of Mineralogy, but Botany with which I began the study of Nature, and which I have cultivated for two years has been peculiarly captivating. Yet though I may be well acquainted with the principles and terms of the art I have not examined above 500 species.

On the fine arts, I may say I have bestowed considerable attention. Poetry is my favourite, and I am told that my performance is not quite despicable, and that I ought to pursue the study with unremitting attention. I am at times inclined to think so, but at others the fear of never attaining any considerable degree of merit in this department prevents me from occupying much of my time with it. For painting I have a natural genius, and in as far as I have tried this art I have succeeded well. Flower drawing however is the only branch of it in which I have made considerable progress. As to Music, I can just read an air with difficulty, with the violin and German flute, of its theory I know little or nothing.

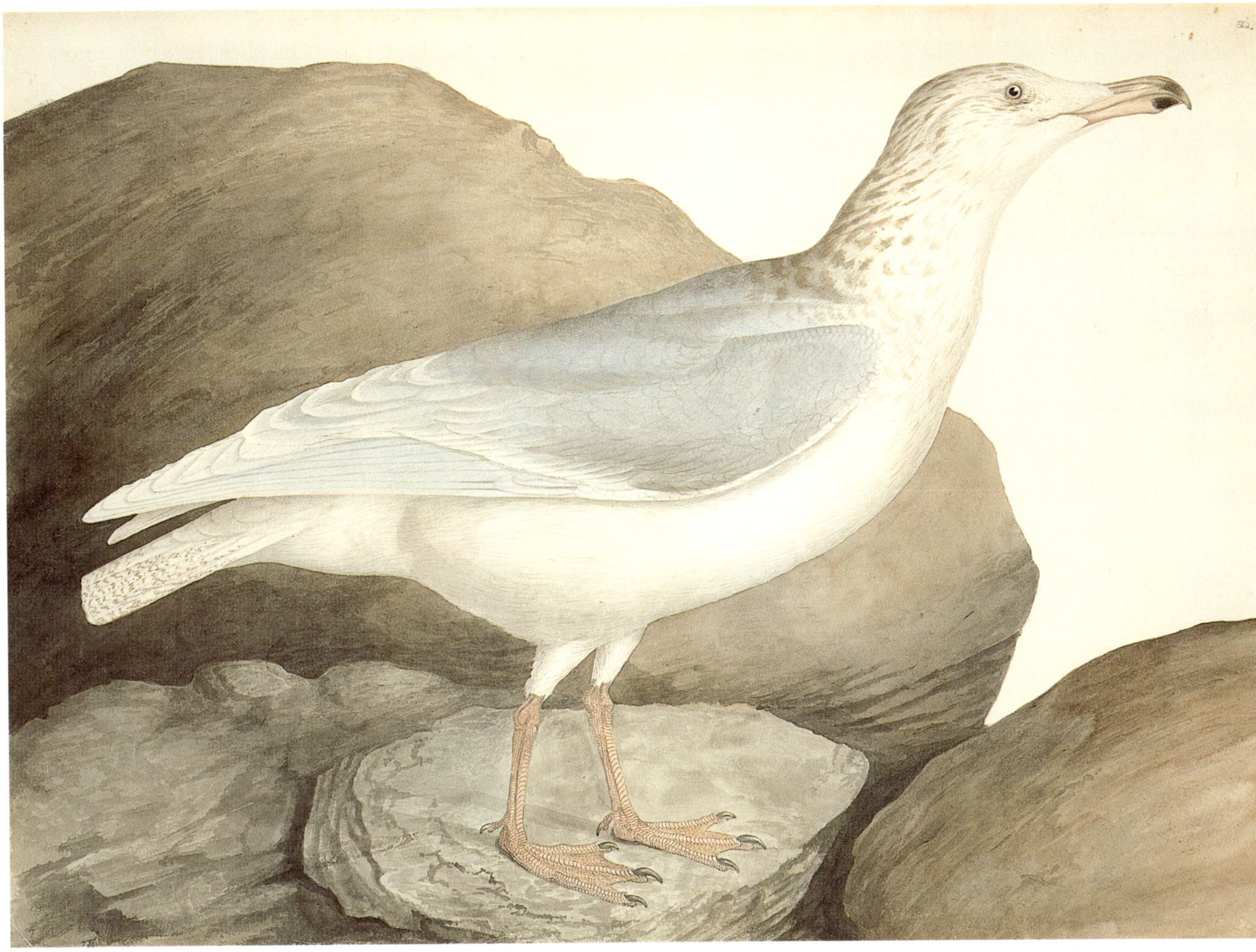

PLATE 10 Glaucous gull *Larus hyperboreus*

[Glaucous Gull or Burgomaster. *Larus glaucus.*] *From a specimen shot at Musselburgh in February 1837. Lent by Mr. MacDuff Carfrae. Edinburgh, 16th March 1837. W.Mc.G.*

These are the departments of Science to which I am most inclined by nature – consequently those in which I ought to excel. There are many others which I have tried – some indeed in which I have made considerable progress.

Of Medicine, including Anatomy, Physiology Medicine proper, Surgery and Pharmacy, I know a little, and just a little Chemistry as applicable to medicine engaged my attention. I have heard lectures on it, and studied it with some attention.

The other sciences of which I have just a smattering and nothing more are Mathematics, Philosophy Natural and Moral, and Agriculture. Of Civil History I know very little.

Thus I cannot boast of having acquired a thorough knowledge of any one science. Yet I must confess I am in a fair way – and if I can but acquire habits of industry and assiduity, may before the end of four or five years be eminent in something. I have certainly laid a good foundation – and the knowledge which I possess of so many sciences, little as it is, will enable me with greater ease and certainty to excel in any one of them, or in any other."[13]

The visitor to Northton today, standing among the ruins of the house that MacGillivray was brought up in, ruins that are used as a sheep fold by local crofters, will see much the same scene that MacGillivray looked on 180 years ago. It is easy to appreciate the influence that his surroundings had on him, and how they shaped the child and the man.

A walk along the Luskentyre and Scarista sands will turn up the same species of shell that MacGillivray collected, and the same flowers grow on the sand dunes, the machair and the sides of Ben Capval. The sands attract spectacular numbers of migrating sea birds, starlings nest in the holes in the ruined walls of the house, as they must have nested in the roof heather thatch, and golden eagles are seen occasionally, although it must have been a long time since three flew together along the brow of Ben Capval, as he once recorded.

On leaving Harris, MacGillivray probably went back to Aberdeen and made some money by teaching classes in botany and working as an assistant dissector in the anatomy class. He had planned to make a tour to the other parts of the Highlands but whether he did is not known. If he did he would surely have kept a journal, but a family story maintains that some of his journals were destroyed in a major library fire in Australia, so that the record covering the next few years of his life is full of gaps. Whatever he did in the year after he left Harris, his interest in ornithology developed and in the late summer of 1819 he made a decision that was to set the course of his life: he decided to visit the British Museum in London to see the major bird collections there.

NOTES

1 MacGillivray (1837).
2 MacGillivray (1836).
3 *Ibid.*, p. 2.
4 MacGillivray's original journal is in the Aberdeen University Library, MS1033. An edited version of it has been published by Ralph (1996).
5 Ralph (1996), p. 30.
6 *Ibid.*, p. 35.
7 *Ibid.*, p. 49.
8 *Ibid.*, p. 45.
9 *Inverness Journal*, 18 September 1818.
10 MacGillivray (1820).
11 MacGillivray (1838).
12 Ralph (1996), p. 108.
13 *Ibid.*, p. 126.

PLATE 11 Great auk *Pinguinis impennis*

[Great Auk. *Alca impennis.*] *From a preserved specimen belonging to J.J. Audubon Esq. the same as that figured by him in his 341st plate. Edinburgh 6th, July 1839. W.Mc.G.*

When MacGillivray painted this bird, the species was just five years away from extinction; the last living specimens were seen in Iceland in 1844. MacGillivray never saw a live example, he saw just two preserved specimens; one was in the British Museum, the other belonged to Audubon who had obtained it in London.

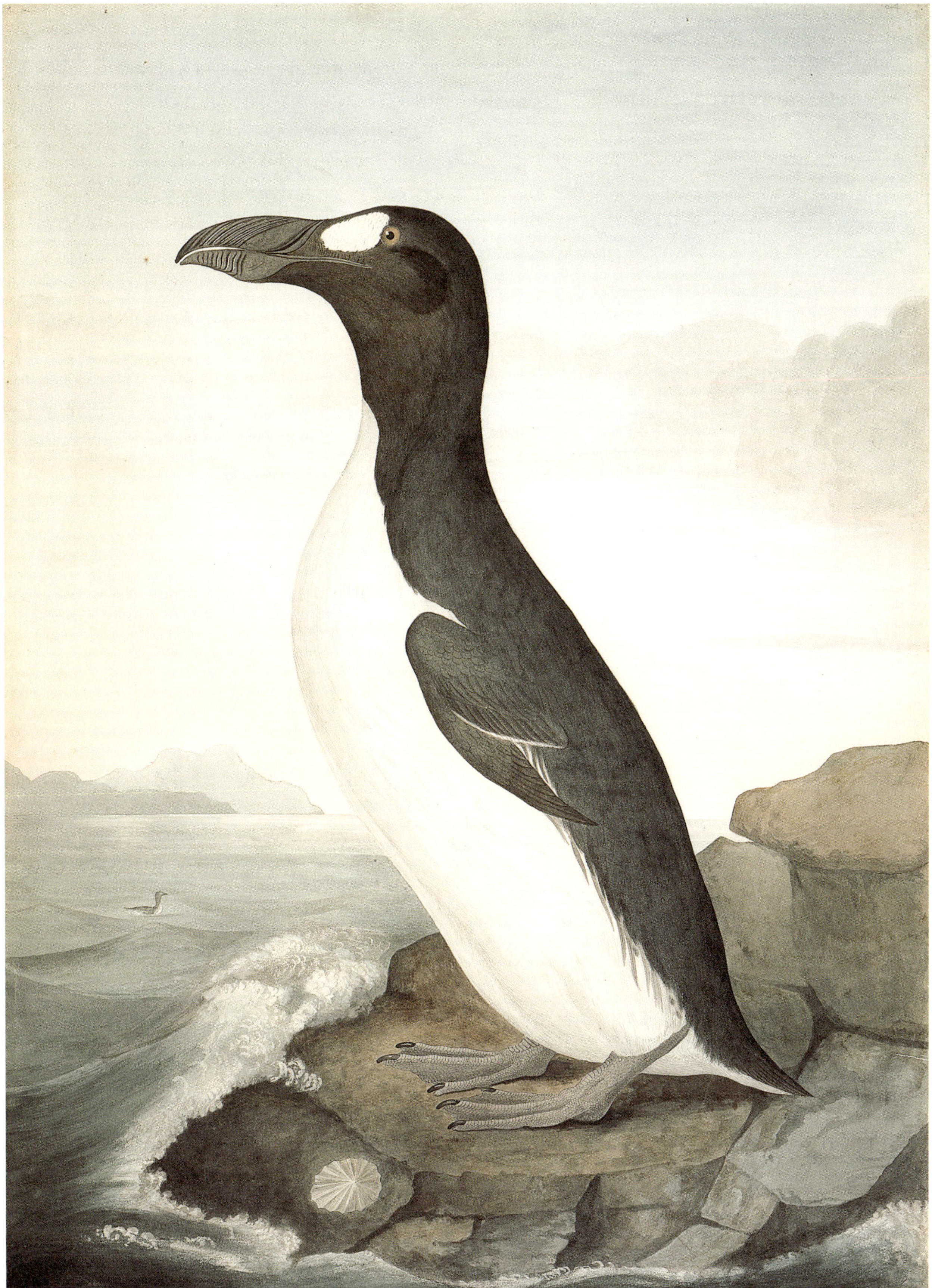

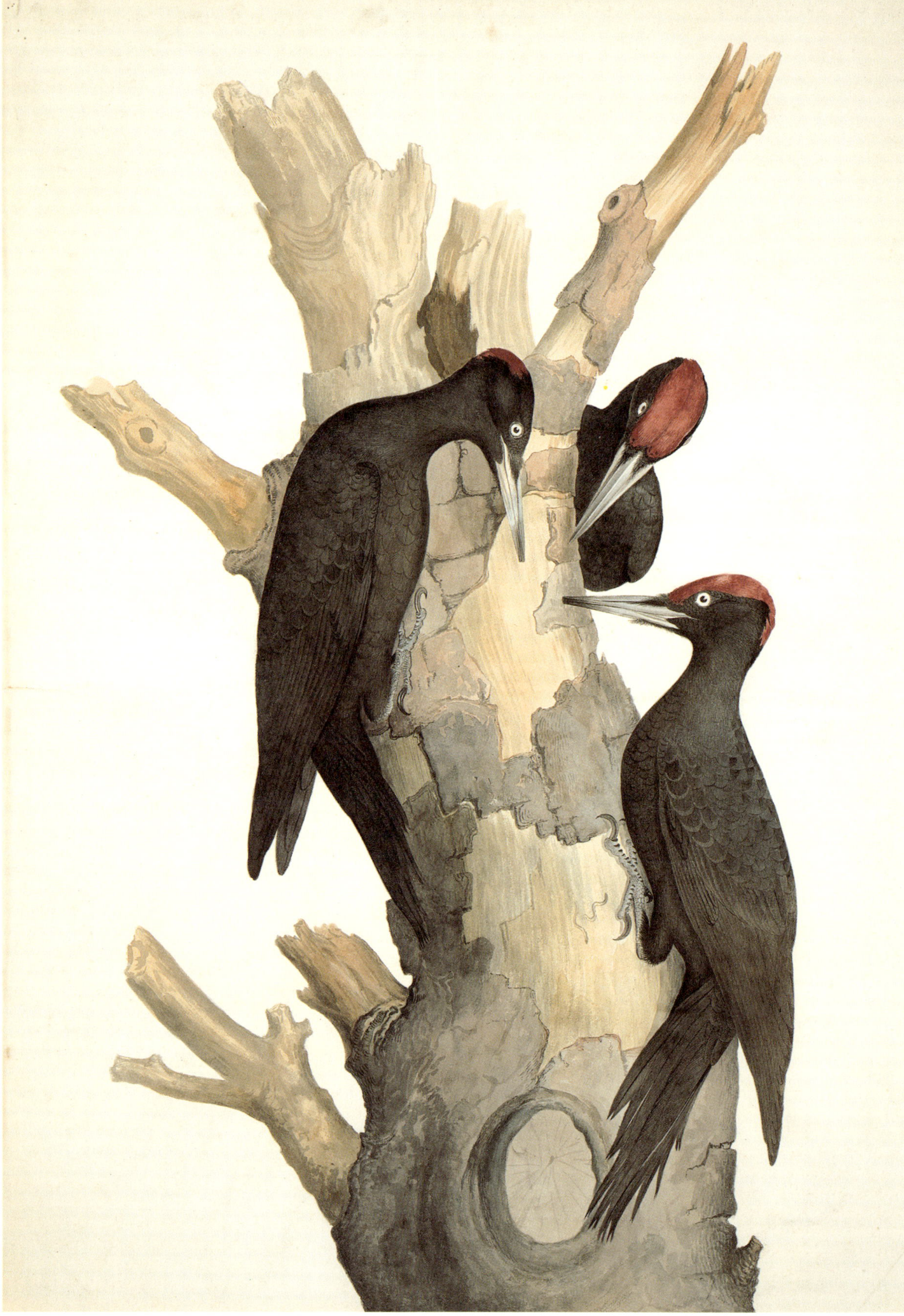

A Walk to London

PLATE 12 Black woodpecker *Dryocopus martius*
[Great Black Woodpecker. *Picus martius.*]
Edinburgh 16th July 1839. W.Mc.G.
This bird is not on the British Ornithologists' Union check-list of British birds. In *A History of British Birds* MacGillivray writes that he had two specimens in his collection, "purchased from a Dr. Madden, to whom they had been sent by their owner, as having been shot near Nottingham. That gentleman afterwards obtained for me a certification of the fact by the person who had procured them." It seems unlikely that two specimens should have come from the Continent to be shot near Nottingham in the 1830s, and almost certainly MacGillivray was the unwitting victim of fraud or mistake.

In 1819 MacGillivray was just twenty-three; he had already walked many hundreds of miles through the Scottish Highlands and islands and had slept out in the heather or in a mountain cave many times, so it is no surprise that he planned to walk to London. By the most direct route it is about 500 miles from Aberdeen but MacGillivray planned to see parts of Scotland that he had not visited before and he covered 501 miles before he crossed the border into England, at Carlisle.

During the trip MacGillivray kept a detailed journal, which has survived and which is in the Aberdeen University library, some 200 closely written quarto pages of around 60,000 words, written with quill pen and portable inkwell, by candlelight in lodging houses and inns, in the shelter of barns during a break in the day and under hedgerows with frost-chilled fingers. He describes the events of each day, the places that he saw and the people that he met, but pays special attention to the botany of the areas that he passed through and finishes each entry with lists of the plants that he had seen. At the beginning of the journal he provides a detailed account of the equipment he was taking with him:

"I refrain from laying down any general or particular plan either for my journey or journal. Only I shall drink a mouthful from the source of the Dee, and give three cheers to myself on the top of Ben Nevis; and till that time keep a regular list of all the plants and birds which may occur. On my back I carry a knapsack eighteen inches by fourteen, and three and a half in depth, made of very thick oiled cloth, and fastening with two leather straps. This machine which cost me six shillings and sixpence contains the following articles; a large portfolio containing a quire of large fine paper folded and marked at the margin for my journal, and seventeen pieces of drawing paper of the same size with the former. Two travelling maps, one of Scotland, the other of England, a small portfolio with a parcel of paper for drying plants, a few sheets of clean paper, stitched, Compendium Flora Britannica, a bottle of ink, four quills, China ink, paints, two black lead pencils, eight camel hair pencils with stalks, Indian rubber, a shirt, a false neck [cravat], two pairs of short stockings, a soap box, two razors, a piece of soap, a toothbrush, a sharping stone, a lancet, a pair of scissors, some thread, needles. My clothes are, an oldish hat, a flannel undervest, linen shirt of course, a blue long coat, gray trowsers, and black vest, the three last old materials, a pair of short stockings, a pair of stout shoes and a coloured neck cloth, a greatcoat, and a pair of old gloves. Of money I had just Ten Pounds Sterling when I left Aberdeen; nine pounds in bank notes put into a small pocket in the inner side of my flannel undervest, one in silver, secured in a purse of chamois leather, kept in a pocket of my trowsers. Other articles will be mentioned tomorrow, after I have set out."[1]

The other articles, carried in his knapsack and his pockets included a penknife, a small ink piece with pens, a small itinerary of Scotland, a glass for drinking by the way and a towel. So he woke up at half past four on 8 September 1819, breakfasted about five and set off. The natural direction to take from Aberdeen to London is south but MacGillivray set his course westwards along what is now known as Royal Deeside, towards Braemar. The first entry in his journal was written in the Aboyne Arms Inn at Charlestown of Aboyne, about 30 miles from Aberdeen. There are three closely written pages detailing the walk, the places, the people, the scenery and then long lists of the plants and animals that he had seen, all given their Latin names. The plants are recorded in great detail, with the 30 miles from Aberdeen divided into four sections; the plants in each section are listed separately and recorded as being in or out of flower. There are nearly 300 plant names in the list, although of course they are not all separate species, as some species were found in more than one of his arbitrary divisions of the distance. He wrote until eleven at night when his candle burned down and then began again next morning to finish the lists.

Much later, in 1831, MacGillivray used some of these records in a paper in which he described the distribution of plants along the whole length of the River Dee, from its source high in the alpine conditions of the Cairngorm mountains to where it meets the sea at Aberdeen.[2] This paper has been described as the first ecological paper to be published in Britain, several decades before the word ecology had been invented.

The next day MacGillivray moved on to Braemar and again spent the evening writing up his journal, although as on the previous evening he did not complete it. The next morning, after washing and shaving in a nearby stream ....

"I returned to the Inn, and now let me finish my narrative of yesterday's journey which I was obliged, partly by lassitude and partly by cold to leave off last night. It is certainly hard work to travel all day, and sit in wet clothes four or five hours into the evening composing and writing an account of the achievements of the day."[3]

Hard work it may have been but he was an enthusiast for it. He even decided to stay an extra day at Braemar to climb a mountain he had seen that morning:

"As I was returning from the river in which I washed this morning I observed the rocky summits of a mountain in the north towering above the intermediate hills. This, thought I, is in all likelihood the highest mountain here, I shall go to its top. It was at least twelve o'clock before I set out."[4]

It turned out to be a long day. It was half past nine at night before he made his way back to the inn, having walked for two hours in darkness, and when he got there he found his bed taken by someone else! Even so he sat up writing his journal until his candle gave out at one

PLATE 13 Great spotted woodpecker *Dendrocopos major*
[Greater Spotted Woodpecker. *Picus major.*] *Male and Female. The former from a stuffed specimen, the latter from a recent individual shot at Invermoriston and lent by Mr Carfrae. Edinburgh January, 1834.*

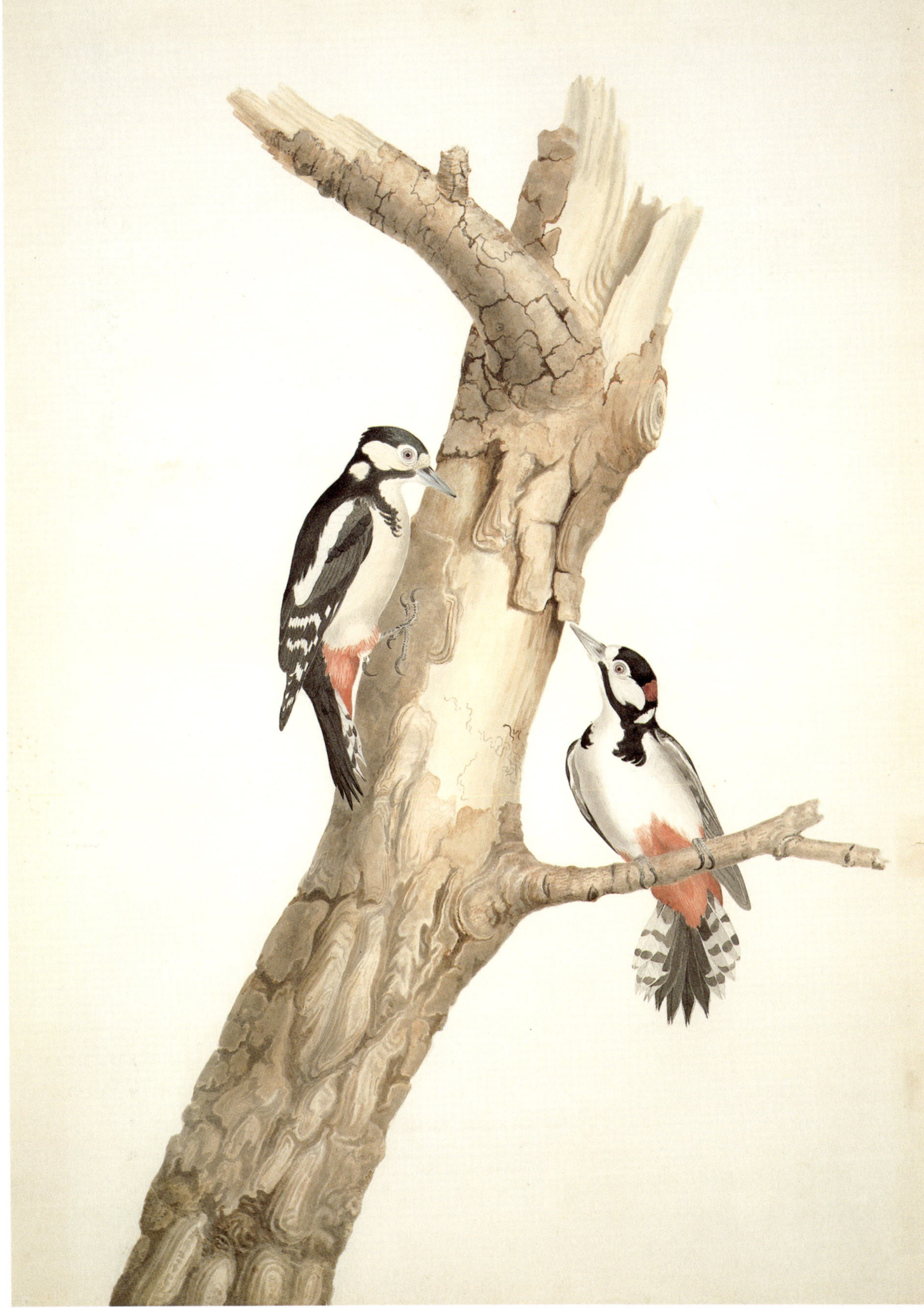

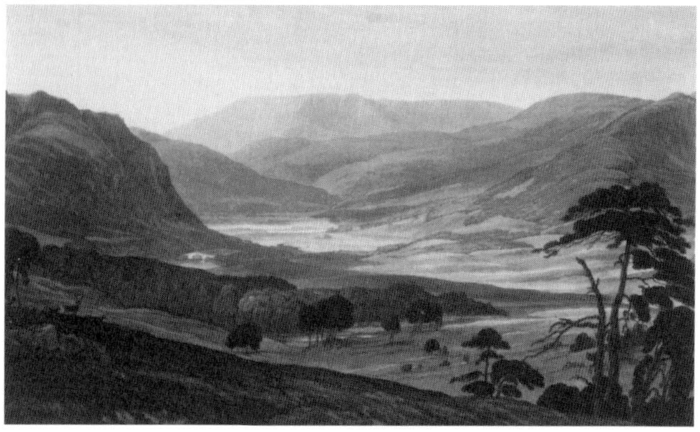

7 'Ben-Y-Bourd', from *Scenery of the Grampian Mountains* (1819) by George Fennel Robson, gives an impression of Upper Deeside at the time that MacGillivray passed through it on his walk to London. In the far distance is Beinn a' Bhuird, the mountain that MacGillivray climbed from Braemar.

o'clock. It was not until the next day that MacGillivray discovered the name of the mountain he had climbed, Beinn a' Bhuird, 3,924 feet high, and nine miles from Braemar.

At this point in his journal he gives an insight into what he felt was the proper way to study the natural world, by getting out into the field and examining it there:

"This, say I, is the proper way of studying botany – let who will say otherwise, the Fellow at Oxford or Edinburgh makes what he deems a glorious morning excursion among parterres [a formal ornamental flower garden] of blooming beauty – flowers I mean – with book in hand and perhaps 'spectacles on nose' – Shakesp. – or at least quizzing glass to eye, is just like a parrot chattering over the jargon of scientific nomenclature, without knowing anything more of the matter. Everybody is too conceited to think others can do better than himself."[5]

MacGillivray was always contemptuous of what he referred to as cabinet naturalists, men who bought specimens or paid others to collect for them, and then spent their time endlessly arguing over varieties and different classification systems. All through his life he was insistent that simply to give a species a name meant nothing: a species had to be observed in its natural habitat to know something meaningful about it. Being able to mock the cabinet naturalists with a quote from *As You Like It* is a measure of the breadth of his interests and education.

After spending a day resting at Braemar he was on his way again, through the mountains, across the summit of Cairngorm, to Kingussie on Speyside, a distance of thirty-six miles with a night spent in the open. On his many walks from Harris to Aberdeen and back he must have spent many nights in the open air, sleeping in the heather or in a cave, but on this occasion the experience is vividly described:

"It was by this time completely dark and I determined to rest myself. Unfortunately I had proceeded so far up the glen which terminated high among the mountains that I had left behind me the region of heath, so that I could not procure enough to make a bed. However I got a sheltered place, and feeling warm after my exertions, thought that I might sleep all night without a covering of heath, as it was by no means cold. I soon found however, that the night air, mild as it was, chilled me and so I rose and pulled some grass and moss and spread them beneath me in a snugger place than that which I had before chosen. Melancholy ideas had been rising in my mind for upwards of an hour before this, but I contrived to repress them almost instantly. I knew that they could only add to the want of comfort to which my situation exposed me. I was never before aware that I could exert any control over these ideas, but now found to my satisfaction that I could completely suppress them. I endeavoured to compose myself to rest after eating some of my provision which consisted of a quarter of a barley cake and a few crumbs of cheese, and not feeling the most distant idea of danger, succeeded so far as to produce a sort of slumber between sleeping and waking. About midnight I looked up and saw the moon with some stars. They were at times obscured by masses of vapour which rolled along the summits of the mountains. I had now a better view of my

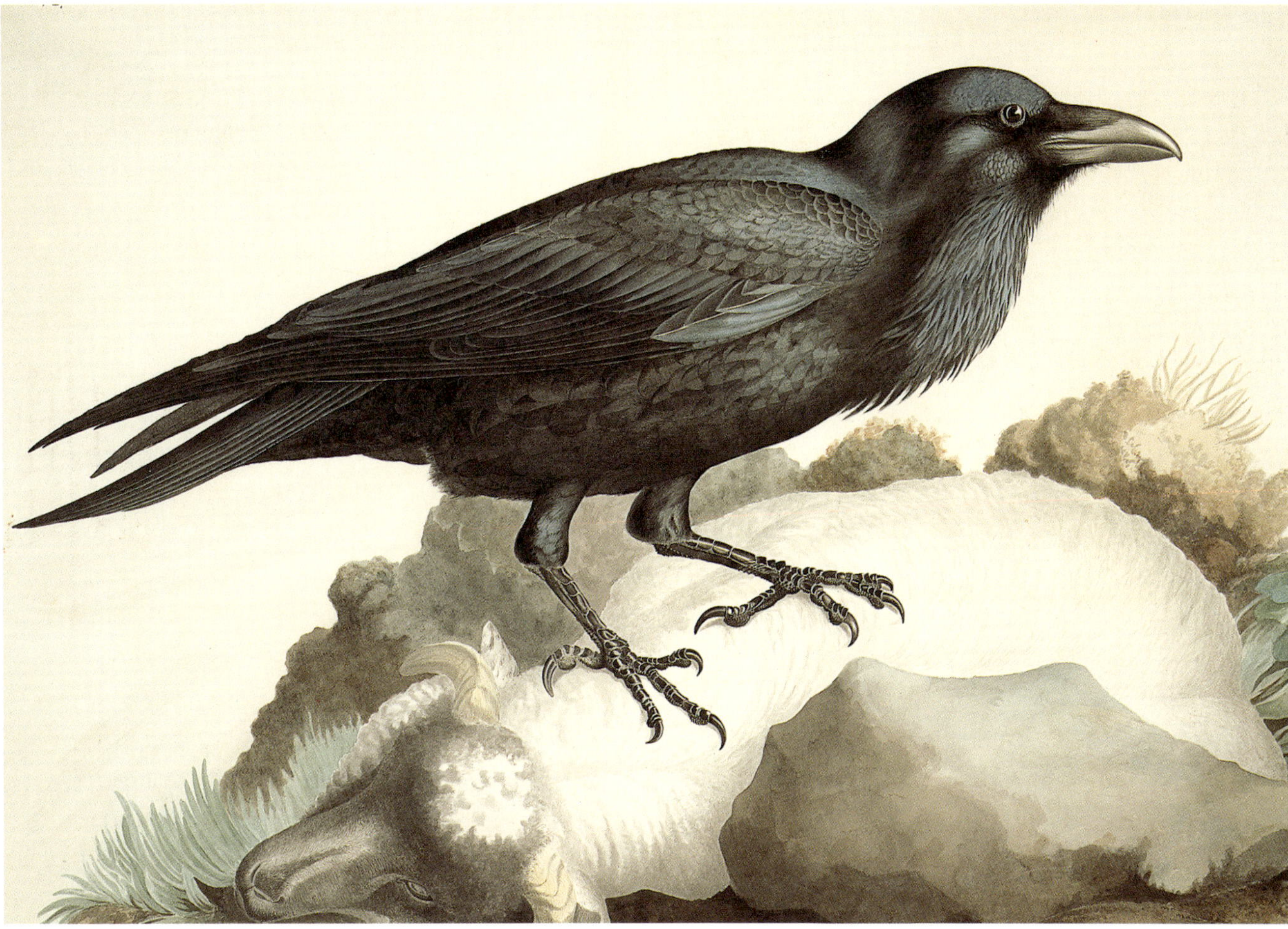

PLATE 14 Raven *Corvus corax*

[Raven. *Corvus corax.*] *From a fine adult Male shot near Edinburgh, and presented by Mr. MacDuff Carfrae. Edinburgh, June 1832. W.Mc.G.*

situation. I was near the upper end of a high valley completely surrounded by masses of rock. Behind me in the west and at the upper end of the valley was a high mountain involved in clouds, on the right hand was another in the form of a pyramidous rock and contiguous with it a peak of less elevation, on the left hand a ridge running from the mountain in the west and terminating at the mouth of the valley in a dark conical mass, and straight before one in the east at the distance of nearly a mile, another vast mountain. The summits of all were at times enveloped in clouds. The wind which blew from the west was not keen, and the night was such as would be termed a warm one. Yet on wakening from my slumber I felt chilly, and soon after began to shiver. I then rose and gathered a few large stones, and a good deal of grass and short heath which I picked from among the stones. With these I formed a somewhat snug sort of bed or couch, and unloosed my pack and took a night-cap and a pair of stockings from it which I applied to their proper uses for my feet had been wetted and my hat alone did not keep my head warm. Then after eating some more of my scanty store and drinking two or three glasses of water from a rill which trickled near me I lay down, put heather and my knapsack over my feet, and placed myself in an easy posture, and fell asleep. I awoke fresh but weak this morning about sunrise, and put myself in trim to continue my journey."[6]

This description of his route is so detailed that a modern-day walker through the Cairngorms can follow his route directly. He carried on down the Great Glen to Fort William where he took the time to climb Ben Nevis, Britain's highest mountain at 4,409 feet. Then it was on by Loch Leven, through Tyndrum, Inverary and Dumbarton to Glasgow. In Glasgow he saw gas-lit streets, wrote his journal in a gas-lit room, saw steamboats on the Clyde and visited the botanical gardens, but he was not impressed by the city or by its inhabitants, who came under his physiognomic scrutiny:

"Countenances were seen every now and then with the horrid marks of urban vulgarity or rather of blackguardism, I know no word as applicable as this, urban vulgarity I say in opposition to rustic, though the term urban is commonly used in a very different sense, for they are widely different. The ignorance of the peasant may excite a smile and the uncouthness of his manners may afford subject of ridicule, but the diabolic depravity of the city blackguard however blended with awkward vulgarity, must excite pure horror and detestation. To the former one even feels kindness, and wish to overlook his little innocent blunders – but with the latter we have no sympathy. The very women in this district had a masculine air – rather their countenances expressed extreme coarseness of sentiment, and habitual impudence, or at least want of delicacy. And as to beauty, there was none of it. I have not seen a beautiful girl since I left Aberdeen, though I walked today over a great part of this city. I saw one handsome, but not beautiful young lady indeed yesterday, near Luss. The peculiar features of the highlanders have no connection with those expressions of depravity in the lowlanders. The former may sometimes appear savage, but the latter are diabolic. Of the different sorts of faces which attracted my attention here the most ridiculous were those of some dragoons which I met, whiskered and mystachioed from the chin to the ears. One of them in particular had very long red mystachioes which near the mouth assumed a whitish tinge, they looked of all things like the whiskers of an old red cat which had been licking cream. These blockheads think to render themselves formidable by leaving their beards uncut. I am much mistaken if an honest soberly decent man is not in a good cause worth two of such scarecrows. The British soldiery have always been noted for their plainness, and for their bravery, and I am apprehensive that when foppery is introduced among them, weakness and irresolution will accompany it. Perhaps I am mistaken, and perhaps when a fellow is 'bearded like the pard'

PLATE 15 Hooded crow *Corvus corone cornix*

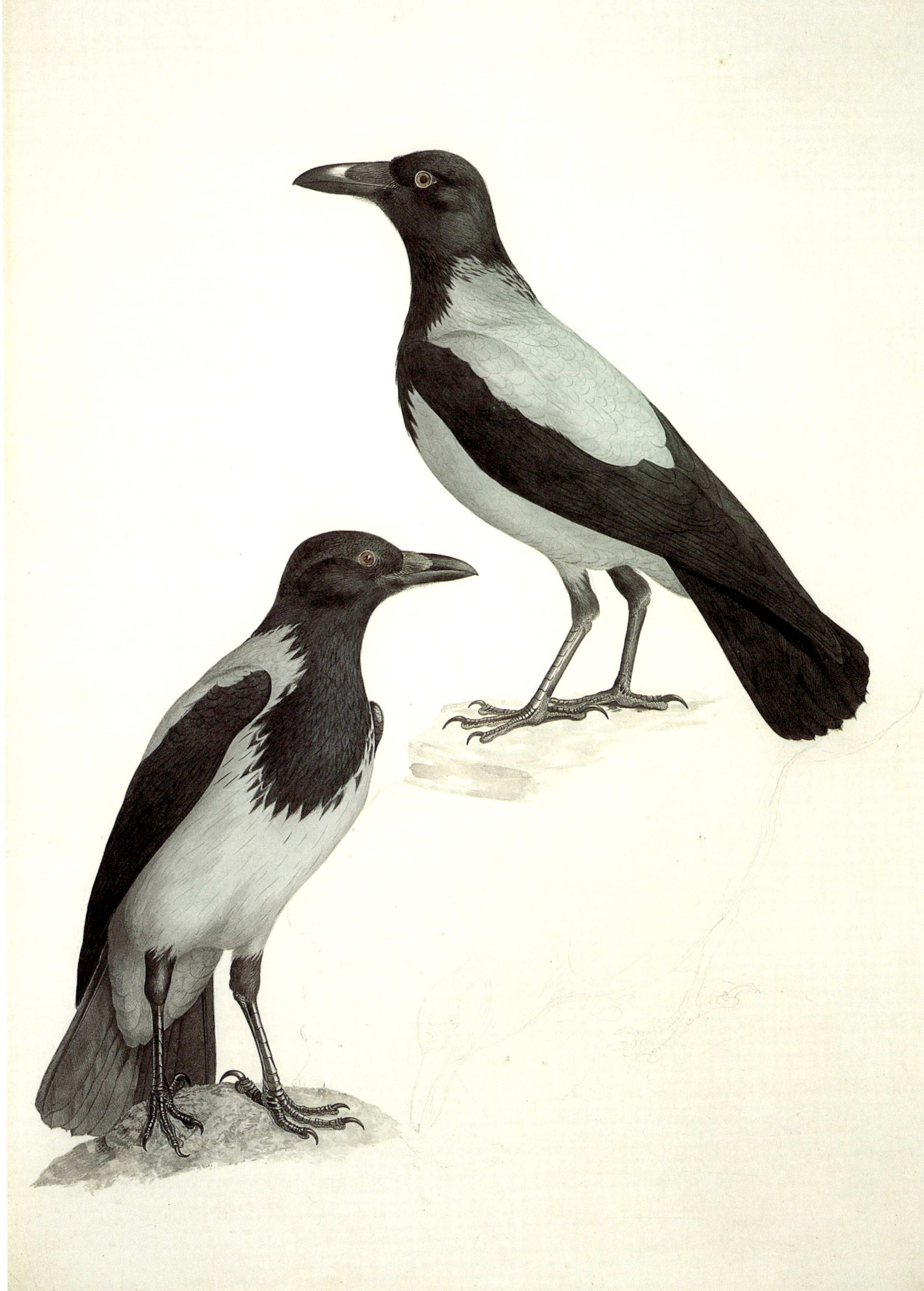
33.

[pard = leopard from *As You Like It* again] he assumes as a necessary consequence the ferocity of that animal."[7]

MacGillivray seems to have been indifferent to being tired, cold, wet or hungry, his biggest problems coming from a source unfamiliar to the modern-day traveller, from the bites of bed bugs. As he walked on from Glasgow towards Ayr he was in great distress:

"Both my wrists and one cheek are swelled enormously from the bites of bugs which I got in Glasgow. I had thought the animals were to be dreaded only in old houses, but even in the Inn at Luss on Lochlomond, I got a bite on the temple. The bite of a bug, though to some people very trifling, is to me a serious disaster, for my skin is so irritable that the least cut or scratch always festers. The tumour on my cheek was last night as large as a hen's egg, and today it has a scab upon it from serous effusion. Those upon my wrist and two upon my right arm were nearly as large, and have small blisters on the top. A bite which I got on the wrist three years ago, suppurated and was a month in healing, and its mark remains to this hour."[8]

He journeyed on, taking the long road around the coast, through Ayr, Girvan, Port-Patrick, Stranraer, Castle Douglas, Dumfries and Gretna where he crossed the border into England noting that the first object that attracted his attention on entering England was a pig. By this time he had spent five of his original ten pounds and in Carlisle he went to a bank and changed his money into English pounds, something he was to regret over the next few days. Unknown to him forged English notes had been circulating in Cumberland and when he tried to buy food or hire lodgings he found that no one would take his money. The difficulties that this caused and the problems it gave his conscience are vividly recorded:

"As I was determined to be economical I did not go to a large Inn, but searched among the smaller sort for lodging but could find none, nor could I get change for one of my notes. I proceeded and marched along the Keswick road till about seven o'clock. I then entered a public house, but was refused lodging. About half a mile further on I entered another. They had no beds. I ordered supper however, for by this time I was hungry having eaten nothing all day, but a two penny cake. Previously to the good woman's beginning to prepare it I informed her that unless she could give me change she needed not bear the trouble as I had no silver. She said she could give me change, but on my mentioning that my note was of the Bank of England a new difficulty arose, for none of them she said were taken in Cumberland on account of forgeries which had been made. It was in vain that I told them I had got my notes at the Bank. Her husband said that I indeed spoke like an honest man, but that had once been cheated and had resolved never to take again a Bank of England note. I told them I should not have cared upon another occasion, but then I was hungry and fatigued, and could scarcely proceed on my journey. No matter, it wouldn't do – and on I trudged. The road in this part was a narrow lane hemmed in with high hedges. The mire covered the whole of it, and I was wetted to the ankles. Cross-roads occurred frequently, and at length I thought I was going in a wrong direction judging by the position of the moon which sent a few dim rays through a cloudy atmosphere. I was on a wrong road – but at length I came to some houses and was put right. Soon after I got to an Inn, but here the beds were all occupied and they were unwilling to let me sleep in an outhouse, and wouldn't be at the trouble of preparing some supper for me. However I got directions in abundance and was told to go first to the left, and then to the right, and to hold straight up the common. As a cross-road, I went to a farm house to enquire. The door was shut. I found myself in a farmyard, and spying a cart shed went into it, and mounted a cart where I lay down. I had not been long there when I found a loft near me and got upon it. Here I found a bundle of wattlings, another of rushes, and a bit of mat and I had carried a bag with me from the cart. So I put off my knapsack, and laid

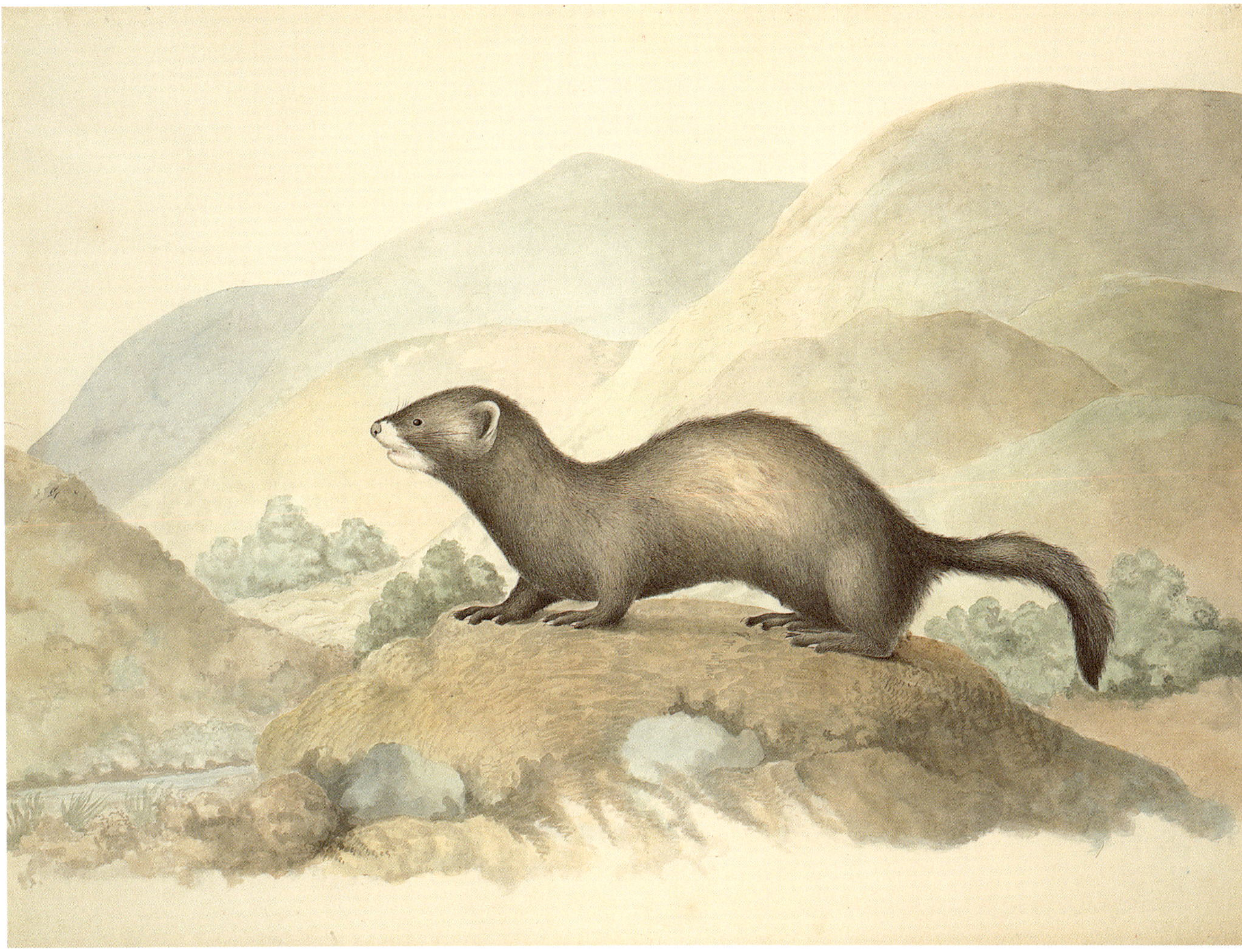

PLATE 16 Polecat *Mustela putorius*

[Fumart. *Mustela Putorius.*] *From a specimen obtained at Birkhill, top of Moffat Water. 4th September 1832. Edinburgh. September, 1832. WMc.G.*

the bag under my head on the wattle and rushes, and spread the ragged mat over my legs, and slept, but not soundly. About midnight my feet felt very cold for they were very wet. So I put off my shoes and wrapped my feet in the mat. Wet shoes are good conductors and bad containers of caloric [heat]. The mat answered better for one foot soon got warmish, and that was enough for a strong chap like me. So I fell asleep and when I awakened today the people were up feeding the horse and the poultry. I descended from my celestial mansion, to wade again among the mire. I felt very weak but did not experience the sensation of hunger. My hat was so crumpled that I could not get it put right, and my clothes were and are still covered with dirt of various kinds. When I had proceeded about two miles I found an Inn and entered it. Here I breakfasted upon tea, bread and butter, and eggs. But a dispute arose between the good man and the good woman about my note. They said they believed they were perfectly good, and if I had any other note, especially a Scotch one, they would readily give change, but none of the Bank of England were taken, and they chose rather to lose the shilling for my breakfast than to run the risk of taking a bad note. This was tormenting and I felt that I had done wrong in not telling them about it before I took my breakfast. The people were very kind and good-natured, and wished me not to be concerned about the matter, for said they, it is of no consequence and you are welcome to the breakfast. I am not sure but that my conduct verged upon dishonesty. However I shall not act so again. I write this in the open air sitting upon a tuft of grass near the road."[9]

Once in England, MacGillivray gave up the systematic noting of the plants that he saw but the journal is still full of candid impressions of the people and the land. His Scottish Presbyterian upbringing was especially offended by his first English Sabbath:

"I am now seated in an easy chair by a large fire in the parlour of an Inn in Kendal, the chief town of Westmorland. On the other side of the fire are two fellows smoking tobacco. I applied at several inns in town before I got lodging, and I was surprised to see the number of people tippling in them. It is not so in Scotland thought I. Far different is the occupation of the Scottish tradesman and peasant on Sunday. I like not to see the Sabbath violated by people who profess the Christian religion. Today for the first time I saw it violated, and I was shocked. In one place I saw boys flying a kite, in another I met a parcel of pedlars, the bread and fruit shops were open everywhere, and on a lake I saw people sailing for pleasure. I like to see the Sabbath kept even with puritanical strictness. This may be a Scotch prejudice, no, it is no prejudice, devotion of one day in seven to religious exercises is absolutely necessary to keep in mind the chief end of our existence. It serves to confirm religious habit and when the Scottish peasantry begin to think lightly of breaking the Sabbath they will become less virtuous. I would have expressed my ideas on this subject more clearly and more at length, had not two other fellows come in and raised such a clatter as to exclude the possibility of thinking unless I were deaf."[10]

His route to London now became more direct, through the Lake District, Lancaster, Preston and Manchester. The latter city had much the same impression on him as Glasgow had had, and he left it without regret:

"About ten o'clock yesterday I left Manchester, and such an abominable dunghill of a town I never before saw. Narrow, irregular, dirty streets, misshapen brick houses daubed over with paint and whitening. Hideous manufactories with their sooty smoke-disgorging chimneys towering amongst the pestilential clouds that rolled over the city – crowds of ill-looking

PLATE 17
An unfinished painting of a Golden eagle *Aquila chrysaetos.*

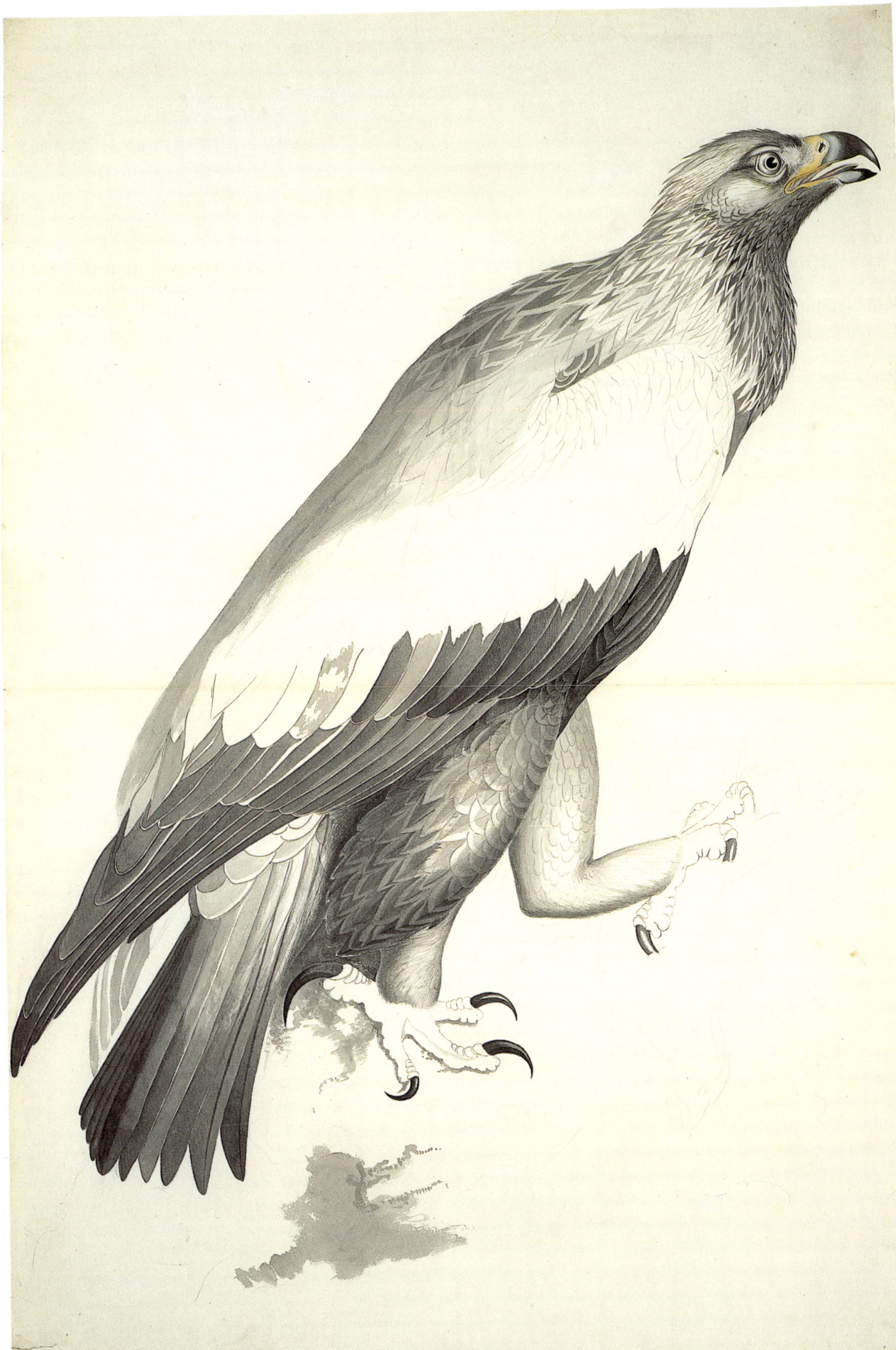

and deformed raggamuffins, waggons laden with coal and beer butts, the intolerable stench arising from tallow chandleries, tanneries, sewers, and butchers stalls, etc, etc. The skirts of the city are however not so bad. Here the streets are wide, and the houses large and regular. On getting onto the London road my spirits revived. The sight of a stone marked with 'To London 182 miles' inspired me with fresh vigour, and for sometime I trudged along as cheerily as if I had been within three hours march of the great city, the goal at which my wild goose chase is to terminate."[11]

Manchester was a source of temptation to MacGillivray; he had enough money to be able to buy a stage-coach ticket to London, but he had determined to walk to London and, putting the city behind him, he walked on, a powerful demonstration of his strength of character and his determination to achieve self-set goals. The next day, at Buxton, he noted that "London is still 150 miles. I propose to be there on Thursday at about 2 o'clock, that is at the rate of twenty-six miles a day". In fact he arrived there a day earlier. Just south of Leicester he had to sleep, or at least try to sleep, in the open:

"The sky became suddenly overcast and rain began to fall. A barnyard with some large stacks appeared irresistibly inviting and so I clambered over the fence and sat down by a stack where I amused me for some time with picking oats. I then rose and searched for a convenient dormitory, at length I found a heap of straw, and making a hole in it, entered and lay down with my knapsack under my head and a handkerchief about it. The night was very cold and the wind blew through the straw so that I could not sleep. About midnight I rose and gathered more straw about me, but it would not do. There is a degree of cold which effectually prevents sleep. The sky was clear and the keeness of the air indicated frost, so about two or three o'clock I got up and continued my journey. I met several people but nobody molested me. When the sun began to appear I found myself at the 80th milestone from London. I felt weak and my feet were sore, for the road was extremely hard. The grass was white with frost, and I was obliged to keep my hands in my pockets for I had lost my gloves about three weeks before. About eight o'clock I got some bread in a village and lay down by a haystack to eat it. Here I cut my thumb, I believe to the bone. The weather soon after grew warmer, but I grew more tired, so that it was two o'clock when I reached Northampton. Here I dined by a dyke on two pence worth of bread and two pence worth of cheese, and then entered an alehouse where I drank a cup and smoked a pipe and read a piece of a newspaper."[12]

When he wrote this he had walked fifty-one miles without proper sleep, and eating only bread and cheese. He was still nearly sixty miles from London, had a shilling and a penny-halfpenny left of his money, and was in a bad way, "my shoes and stockings were in tatters so that the gravel was getting in and tormenting me". The rest of the journey was completed in one stretch, fifty-eight miles more with nothing but bread and an apple, almost on his knees, and having to sit to rest his feet every two or three miles. The weather was unkind to him, for the last twelve hours he walked in torrential rain, soaked to the skin:

"At length I got to Highgate about twelve o'clock and soon after entered London. The rain poured down in torrents and I was wetted to the skin. A bundle which I had directed to be sent me from Aberdeen was addressed to a Mr Cowie, a bookseller, No 31 Poultry. So I managed though with great difficulty to crawl there. My parcel had arrived and in it I found a letter from the Isles from Mary MacCaskill. This however did not ease my feet which were intolerably sore and I was obliged to stand for several hours waiting for a servant of Mr Cowie's who was to procure lodging for me. Mr Cowie is a Scotchman from Banff. I was

PLATE 18 Golden eagle *Aquila chrysaetos*

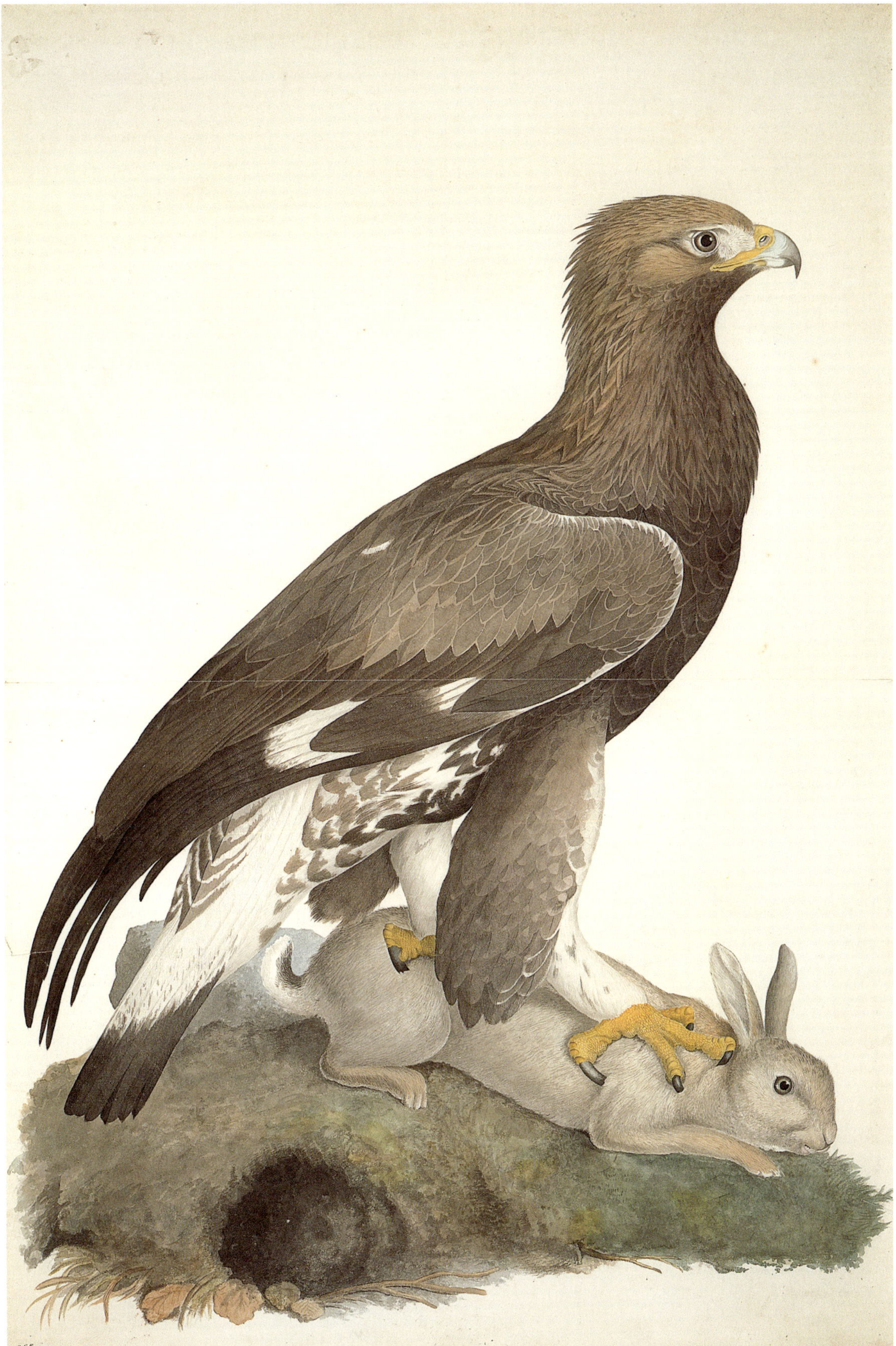
165.

BERNICLA LEUCOPSIS. THE WHITE-FACED BERNICLE-GOOSE.

CLAIKIS. CLAKIS. CLAIK-GOOSE. BARNACLE. WHITE-CHEEKED BARNACLE. LAND BARNACLE.

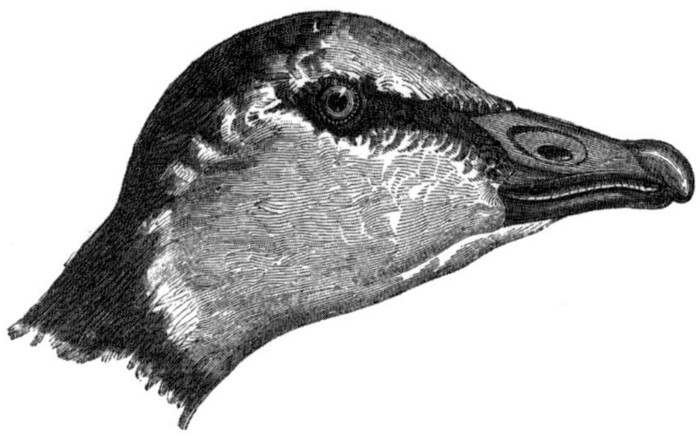

FIG. 58.

8 Barnacle goose *Branta leucopsis*; 'white-faced bernicle-goose', *Bernicla leucopsis* from *A History of British Birds*, vol. 4 (1852), p. 622

directed to him by Dr Barclay. he was very kind and affable and I dined with him. At length a room was got for me and I proceeded to it with my baggage. After washing my feet with warm water I got into a famous bed and had a glorious snoring bout until nine this morning, when I arose and breakfasted. I have now got into decent clothes, and I had need as may readily be believed after performing a journey of eight hundred miles on foot.

I have now finished my journey and I am satisfied with my conduct. It is not every young man who would readily undertake to walk eight hundred miles, and very few who would accomplish such an undertaking, under the provoking allurement of every now and then falling in with a stage coach that might carry them to the end of their journey in a very short time and with less expense than if they walked. Once indeed I was very nearly lost, that is my resolution was nearly overcome, and I had almost determined when at Manchester to take a seat. But I knew that I would have repented this for years and I persisted and I am glad of it. When at Buxton it may be remembered I determined to be at London on Thursday by twelve o'clock and to spend only ten shillings and sixpence, and this too I accomplished, for I got here a day before the time, and did not expend more money than the sum mentioned. This was not effected without some painful effort. It cost me the lack of sleep for two nights, and obliged me to travel at one stretch 51 and at another 58 miles, and to live a day upon bread and water. But I consider these as very trifling hardships compared with those which I might undergo on a serious journey, to the interior of Africa, for instance, or to China by Tartary, and I am now glad that I kept my resolution. With a sufficient motive, and an alluring object in view I would undertake to travel to the uttermost corner of the earth."[13]

MacGillivray never made what he referred to as "a serious journey" to the interior of Africa, or to China. In fact, he never travelled outside of the British Isles, but it is doubtful if there is anything in Britain in recent times to compare with his journey from Aberdeen to London. Incredibly, despite the exertions and hardships of the previous few days, MacGillivray was out sightseeing the next day "strolling through the city and peeping everywhere". He seemed to be in no rush to visit the British Museum, the object of his exploits, but spent the day climbing the Monument to the Great Fire of London, counting the 322 steps and admiring the view from the top, "although the smoke prevents one from seeing too far". On the Saturday, it was 2 October, it was very cold and a great deal of snow fell during the night, so that he did not get out until lunchtime and then spent the afternoon visiting some private museums. Sunday was spent sightseeing. He visited St Paul's, Westminster Abbey, Hyde Park and the Tower, and then, at last on the Monday, he went to the British Museum:

"Today I went to the British Museum. The rooms were open at eleven, and I was among the first there. I

PLATE 19 Eagle owl *Bubo bubo*

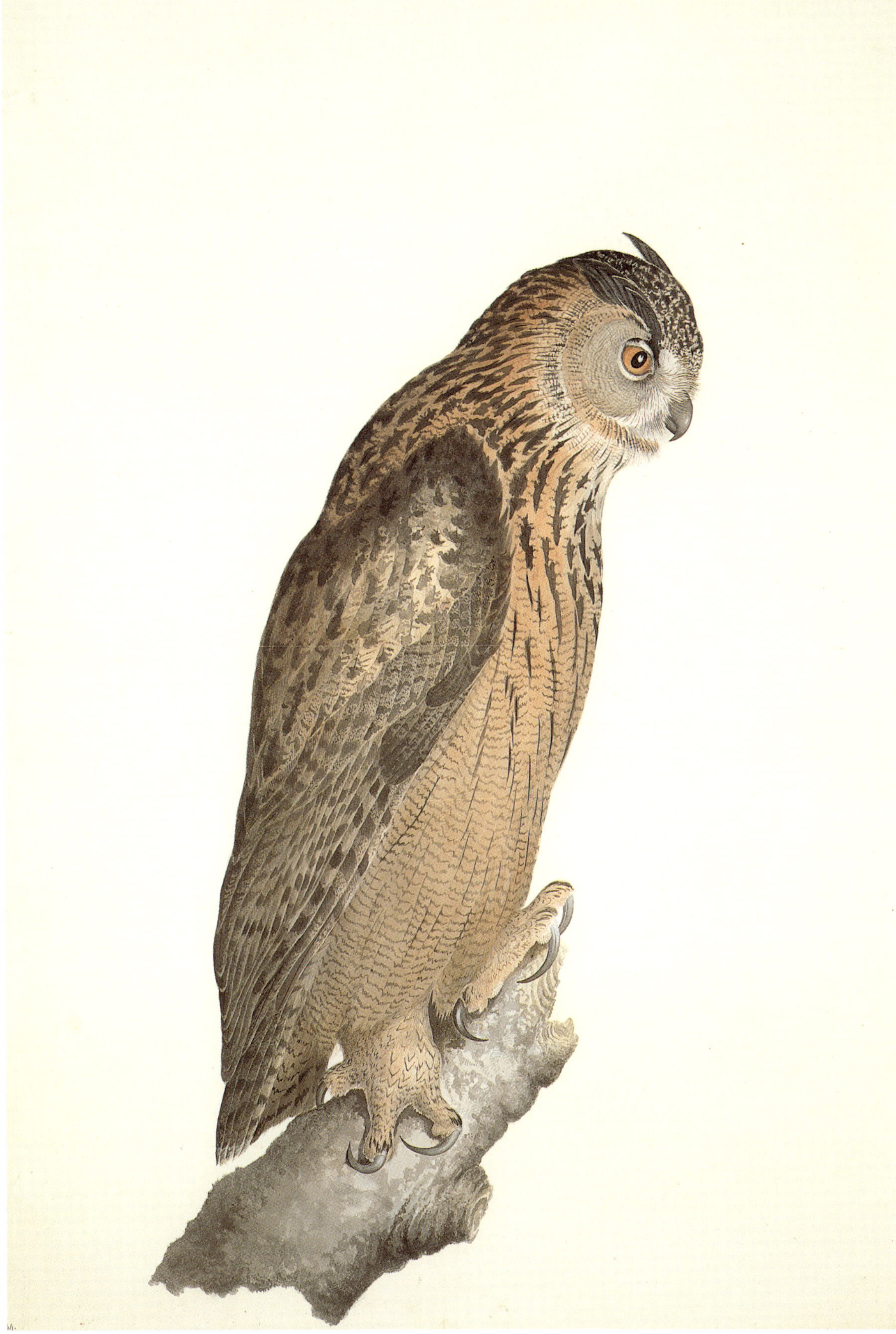

was not surprised. I had formed high ideas of the museum of the greatest nation in the world, nor was I disappointed. It is richest in minerals and shells, but I paid most attention to the birds, particularly to the collection of British Birds which occupies a separate apartment. The system of Linnaeus has been superseded by that of Cuvier, and justly in my estimation. I was glad to find that most of my opinions regarding the genera of birds were deemed correct, for the improvements upon the Linnaean system which had occurred to me on my journey through the Western Isles last year were here realized, and I felt proud that I had been able to think for myself on such a subject, and think correctly too. However I do not altogether agree with modern ornithologists, and possibly I may become some day the author of a new system, at least I have the assurance to think so. I had promised to go and see the rest of Mr Brooke's museum today, but I could not prevail upon myself to leave the British Museum, and so I wandered through the rooms till two o'clock, and latterly began to inspect the company which came in crowds. I was amused with one creature who was acting as demonstrator to some young ladies and who was positive that a species of fish in one of the apartments was a Salamander, as he called it. I was pleased, very much pleased, to find that my opinion regarding the snake of Harris was correct, namely that it is the *Anguis fragilis* of Linnaeus [the slow worm], and that it is not poisonous. I felt my love of Natural History very much increased by the inspection of the museum. At the same time I felt convinced that to study nature I must have recourse to nature alone, pure and free from human interference. The division of the genus *Anas* [a genus of ducks], which I had proposed is here adopted. *Pelecanus bassanus* of Linnaeus [the Gannet] is a distinct genus, as I had imagined it, and what struck me as very odd was that they had given it the very name which I had proposed to myself – *Sula*. I am afraid my vanity will be too much increased by this visit. At least I am now more determined to think for myself, as I have done for about two years. Ornithology is my favourite study and it will go hard with me if I do not one day merit the name of ornithologist."[14]

MacGillivray stayed in London for a few more days before returning to Aberdeen by sea, on the smack *Expert*. He spent two long days of misery in the forecastle before upgrading his ticket to a cabin berth. By the time he was home again he was clearly physically and mentally exhausted, having travelled 837 miles on foot to London and 450 miles back to Aberdeen by sea. The last entry in his journal is dated 12 November and contains the phrase "I can scarcely brandish a quill" and ends rather abruptly. After walking for eight weeks to get there, he made just one visit to the British Museum and spent just a few hours there; but the effect the visit had on him was a lasting one that had set the future course of his life, to "merit the name of ornithologist".

NOTES

1 MacGillivray's original journal is in the Aberdeen University Library, MS1032. An edited version of it has been published by Ralph (1998).
2 MacGillivray (1831).
3 Ralph (1998), p. 20.
4 *Ibid.*, p. 22.
5 *Ibid.*, p. 29.
6 *Ibid.*, p. 35.
7 *Ibid.*, p. 65.
8 *Ibid.*, p. 69.
9 *Ibid.*, pp. 101–103.
10 *Ibid.*, pp. 104–105.
11 *Ibid.*, p. 116.
12 *Ibid.*, p. 121.
13 *Ibid.*, pp. 123–24.
14 *Ibid.*, pp. 133–34.

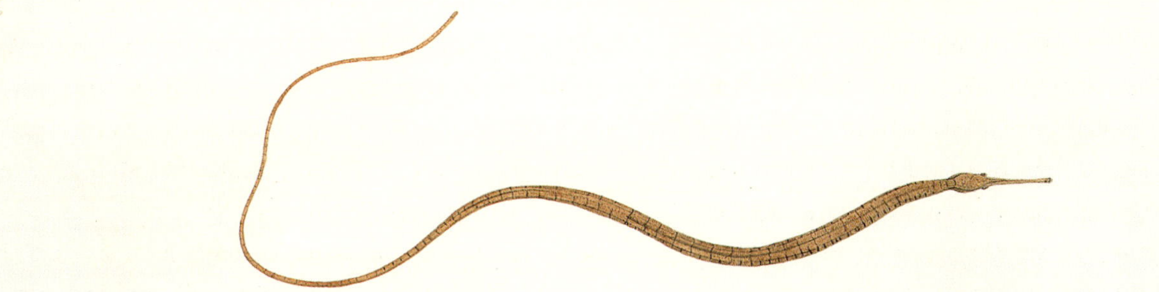

PLATE 20 Straight-nosed pipefish *Nerophis ophidion*
[*Sygnathus aegorbus.*]

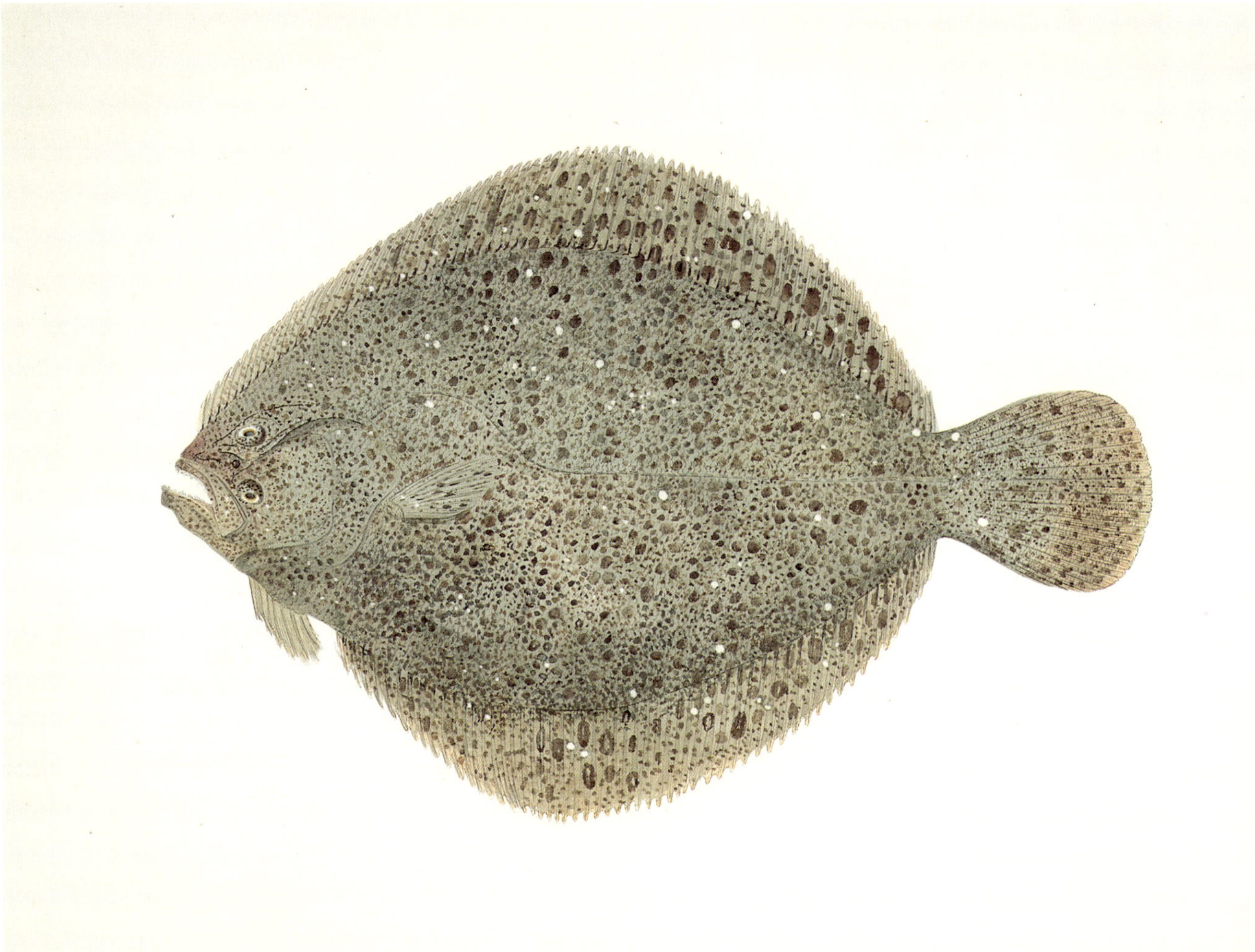

PLATE 21 Brill *Scophthalmus rhombus*
[*Pleuronectes rhombus.*]

The 1820s

Years of Uncertainty

The next ten years were among the most unsettled in MacGillivray's life, as he wandered between Aberdeen, Edinburgh and the Western Isles, looking for permanent employment and a regular source of income. This is also the period in his life about which the least is known; he probably kept a journal, as he did for most of the other periods in his life, but nothing has survived. There are some hints about what he was doing in the introduction to *Descriptions of the Rapacious Birds of Great Britain* where he presents "a few particulars of my history". Describing what he did after his walk to London he says:

"Having been advised by a friend to engage in a kind of mineralogical speculation, I afterwards went to Edinburgh, where I had the advantage of hearing Professor Jameson's lectures. I then betook myself to the Outer Hebrides, where I hammered at the gneiss rocks, gathered gulls' eggs, and shot plovers and pigeons, until finding the trade dull, I returned to the civilised part of the country. I now became assistant and secretary to the learned Professor of Natural History in the University of Edinburgh [Professor Jameson], under whom I took charge of an extensive and beautiful museum, in which I found occasional opportunities of making myself in some degree aquainted with objects which I might not otherwise have been able to examine. The late Mr. Wilson, Janitor of the University, who dealt extensively in birds, also allowed me to examine the specimens that passed through his hands. After remaining several years in this place, I thought it expedient to retire; and continued my observations in the fields, supporting myself by labours in the closet [writing at a desk rather than field work]."[1]

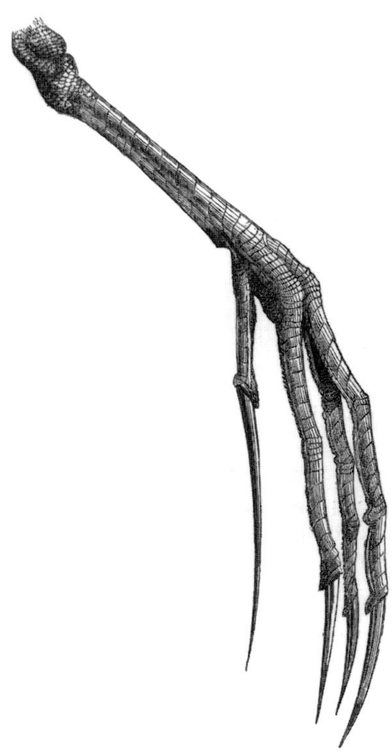

9 Foot of wattled jacana, *Jacana jacana*; 'Brazilian jacana', *Parra jacana* from *A History of British Birds*, vol. 4 (1852), p. 515

Just what MacGillivray meant by 'mineralogical speculation' is a mystery. When he began studying medicine in Aberdeen in 1814 one of his teachers was George Barclay, MD, a physician at the Aberdeen Infirmary and Lecturer on Surgery at King's College in Old Aberdeen and at Marischal College in the centre of the city of Aberdeen. Barclay was just three years older than

MacGillivray but was greatly respected as a physician and although MacGillivray studied medicine for just a year, it is clear that he and Barclay became close friends. Barclay's father-in-law, Walter Berry, lived in Edinburgh and had a strong interest in mineralogy, so it may well have been Barclay who advised him to go there in the late autumn of 1819.

By the summer of 1820 MacGillivray was back at North-town. Perhaps he had gone back to collect minerals, perhaps he had just gone home, but it was there on 29 September that he married Marion McCaskill; he was twenty-four, she was just seventeen. Whatever the "mineralogical speculation" was, it did not make his fortune, and just how he supported himself and his new wife for the next two to three years is not known in detail. He seems to have spent most of his time in Edinburgh, making small amounts of money by assisting at classes, from translations and from articles in newspapers and journals, but it must have been a difficult time. He is known to have moved between Edinburgh and Aberdeen because the MacGillivrays' first son, John, who later became a distinguished naturalist in Australia, was born in Aberdeen in December 1822. A few months later MacGillivray's name appeared in the *Memoirs of the Wernerian Natural History Society* for the first time when the secretary read a communication from him describing two varieties of *Nuphar lutea* (the yellow water-lily) that he had found in the Corby Loch, near Aberdeen.[2] Over the next few years there was a succession of papers published in the society's journal; they show the extent of his interest in the natural world, with several papers on the specific characters of birds,[3] a major paper on gulls,[4] a description of a new species of duck-billed platypus,[5] an account of the molluscs and barnacles of Harris,[6] a description of the climate and geology of the same island[7] and a paper on a new species of water vole from Aberdeenshire.[8]

MacGillivray's first regular appointment came in 1823 when he became assistant and secretary to Professor Jameson in Edinburgh. Robert Jameson (1774–1854) was one of the leading scientists of the day. He trained as a surgeon in Leith but studied geology and mineralogy at Freiberg in Germany under Abraham Gottlob Werner. Jameson was appointed to the Regius Chair of Natural History in Edinburgh in 1804, a chair he occupied for fifty years until his death. He founded the Wernerian Natural History Society and the *Edinburgh Philosophical Journal*, acting as its editor for many years. MacGillivray was made responsible for looking after Jameson's museum, a substantial one containing some 40,000 specimens of rocks and minerals, 10,000 fossils, 8,000 birds and many thousands of insects and other specimens. Working with such a large and varied collection must have been a delight for MacGillivray, giving him an extraordinary opportunity to confirm and develop his interest in natural history, especially in ornithology. This was also a time when museums were changing from collections of mere curiosities into places of serious scientific study.

Jameson may have been a scientist of national stature but not everyone who attended his classes was impressed by them. Charles Darwin, drawn to Edinburgh by the reputation of its medical teaching, attended Jameson's classes in 1825 and recorded his impression of them in his autobiography:

> "During my second year in Edinburgh I attended Jameson's lectures on Geology and Zoology, but they were incredibly dull. The sole effect they produced on me was the determination never as long as I lived to read a book on geology or in any way to study the science."[9]

The effect was not a permanent one because, of course, Darwin later regained an enthusiasm for geology and did some classic work on the subject. While he was in Edinburgh he also met MacGillivray:

> "From attending Jameson's lectures I became acquainted with the curator of the museum, Mr. MacGillivray, who afterwards published a large and excellent book on the birds of Scotland. He had not much the appearance and manners of the gentleman. I had much interesting natural-history talk with him, and he was very kind to me. He gave me some rare shells, for I at that time collected marine molluscs, but with no great zeal."[10]

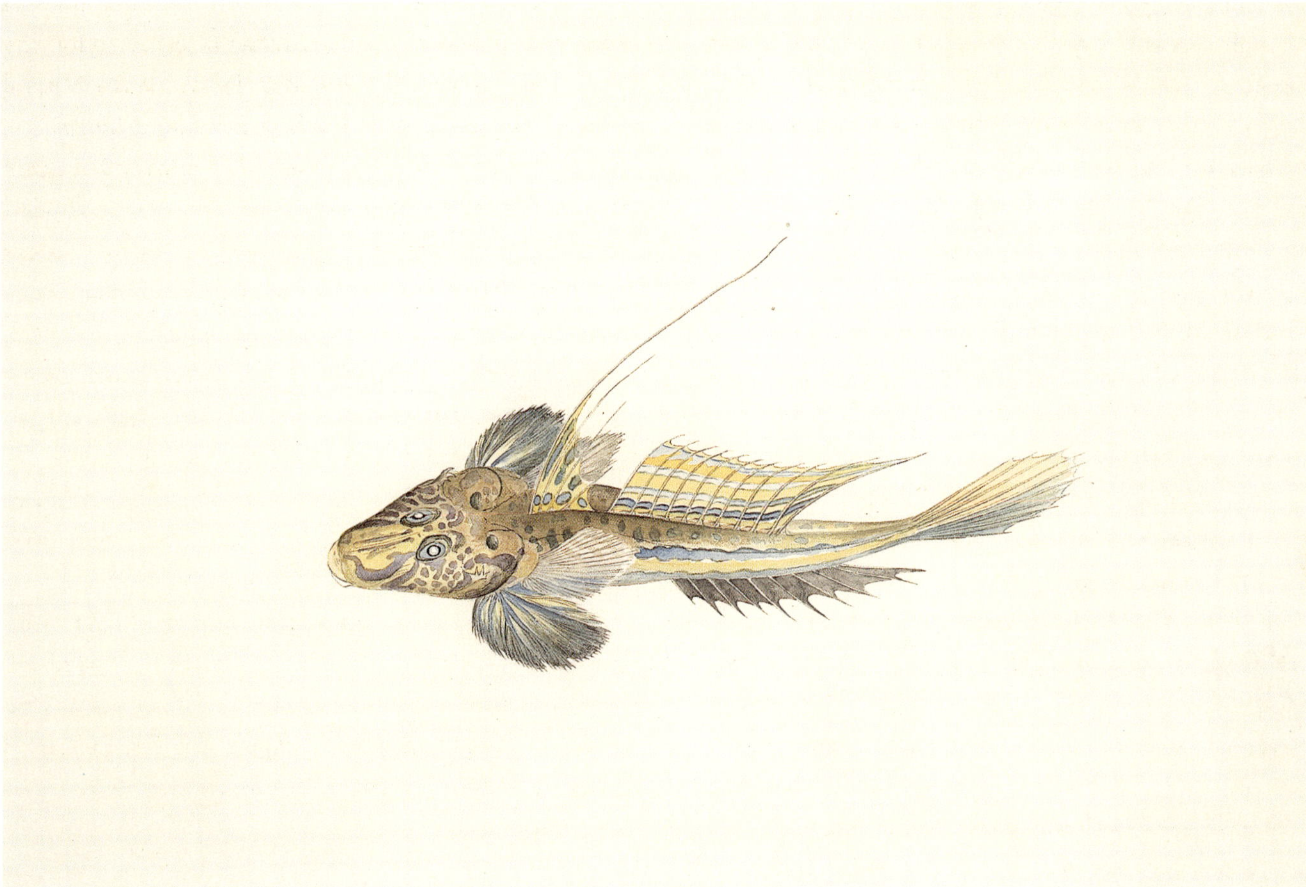

PLATE 22 Dragonet *Callionymus lyra*

RHYNCHASPIS CLYPEATA. THE BLUE-WINGED SHOVEL-BILL.

SHOVELLER. BLUE-WINGED SHOVELLER. BROAD-BILL. RED-BREASTED SHOVELLER.

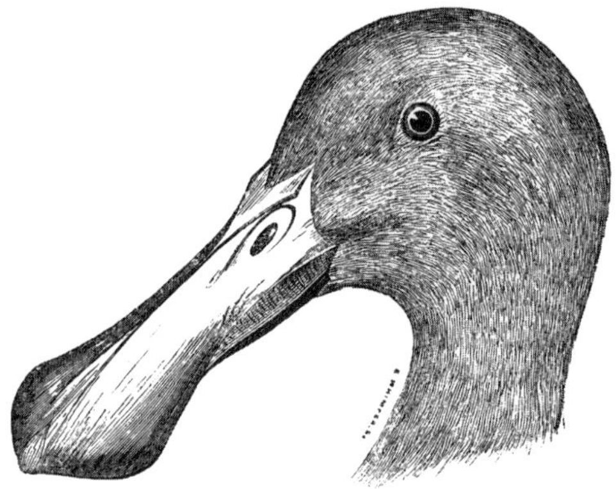

FIG. 64.

10 Shoveler *Anas clypeata*; 'blue-winged shovel-bill', *Rhynchaspis clypeata* from *A History of British Birds*, vol. 5 (1852), p. 74

Darwin and MacGillivray could scarcely have had more different upbringings and it is not surprising that the Scot was not 'gentlemanly', but there is no doubt that Darwin later had the greatest respect for his work. In *The Descent of Man* there are numerous references to MacGillivray's observations on birds and he refers to him as "the accurate MacGillivray".[11]

In 1826, MacGillivray, for some reason thought it 'expedient to retire'.[12] Problems were appearing for Jameson's museum. In its early years Jameson alone had gathered the collection together but subsequently both the University and the Government had donated specimens. Questions of ownership arose, along with questions about the museum's purpose; was it simply to be used as part of Jameson's natural history class, was it available for all of the University or was it a public and national institution that belonged to the Crown? Jameson could be an awkward man and MacGillivray had a streak of obstinacy in his make-up, so it is not too hard to imagine them falling out in the difficult times and MacGillivray taking himself off, back to Aberdeen or to Harris.

Wherever it was that he went to, he surely left Edinburgh for several months, because it was at this time that Audubon made his first visit to Edinburgh and it is inconceivable that the two of them would not have met if they had both been there. Just what MacGillivray did for the next few years, with his "labours in the closet",[13] is largely a mystery but money was coming from somewhere because by 1829 there were five children to support. Although he had no regular job, he must have settled some of his differences with Jameson because he did editing and translation work for the *Edinburgh Philosophical Journal* and wrote a regular weekly natural history column in the *Edinburgh Literary Gazette*. He was also finding time to publish scientific articles, although these would not have brought in any money. Somehow he also found the time and resources to publish his first book, a completely revised edition of W. Withering's *A Systematic Arrangement of British Plants*, published in 1830.[14] The original version was published in four volumes in 1776[15] and had been the standard text on British botany for a generation. MacGillivray's edi-

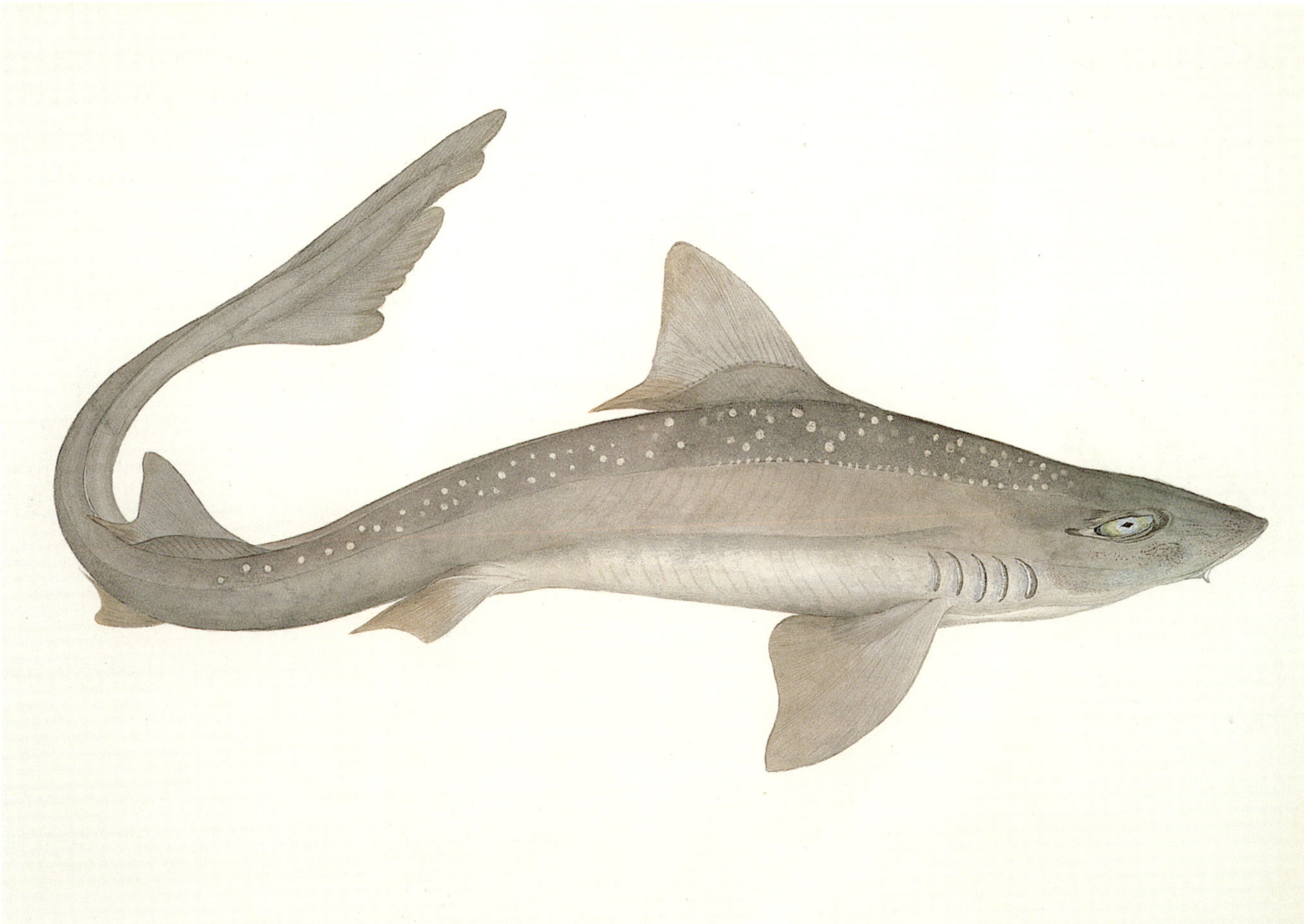

PLATE 23 Starry smooth hound *Mustelus asterias*
[*Mustela laevis.*]

tion was abridged into a single version, intended for use in the field:

"Its object is to induce the young to betake themselves, when occasion offers, to the fields and woods, the mountains and shores, there to examine for themselves the rich profusion of nature, and instead of vaguely admiring the diversified scenery of a district, to be able to mark its individual and minutest features."

The book was very successful and eight editions were published in the next twenty years, although, somehow, as with all of the other books he was to write, MacGillivray never seemed to be able to make any money out of it.

He was also beginning to make enemies, men of position who were able to use their influence against him in later years. One of them was Sir John Richardson (1787–1865) the Arctic explorer and naturalist, a man who fell out with MacGillivray in a squabble over the name of a seagull. In 1823 two Royal Navy ships, *Hecla* and *Fury*, were exploring in the northern part of Hudson Bay, searching for the elusive North-West Passage. The expedition was under the command of William Parry; James Clark Ross was on the *Hecla*, responsible for looking after the natural history collections. In June he shot and collected an unknown species of gull, a second specimen of which was collected later. When the expedition returned to Britain, Captain Parry gave the natural history specimens to the then Dr Richardson, for him to identify and write up the material. There was only one specimen of the gull in the collection by the time the material got to him but Richardson realised that the gull was new to science. However, before he could describe it, MacGillivray published a brief account of the new bird and named it *Larus roseus*, the Roseate gull. Somehow, one of the two specimens had found its way into Jameson's collection and MacGillivray included it in a review of the genus *Larus*.[16] He added in a footnote that the name was *pro tempore*, given to a new species of gull which was to be given its proper designation by Dr Richardson. Unfortunately zoological nomenclature is governed by strict rules of priority and MacGillivray's name for the gull, having appeared in print first, was the name it had to be. It is not clear what MacGillivray's motives were. He must have known about the rules of precedence, perhaps he was under pressure from Jameson who might have wanted to add another type specimen to his museum, but whatever the reason Richardson was upset by it all. Six years later, in his *Fauna Boreali-Americana* he wrote that here was a bird of which only two specimens had been collected, but for which there were two different scientific names and two different common names![17] Richardson had been with Sir John Franklin on his first two Arctic expeditions and later led the search for Franklin's lost third expedition. He was a Fellow of the Royal Society and a leading naturalist of the day, a powerful man to have as an enemy.

So, in Edinburgh, in October 1830, MacGillivray was thirty-four, with a large family, little money and no settled job: a man who was obsessed by the natural world, and driven by the ambition to make his name in one small part of it, in ornithology, and about to meet a man with the same ambition, John James Audubon.

NOTES

1 MacGillivray (1836), pp. 3–4.
2 MacGillivray (1822).
3 MacGillivray (1823).
4 MacGillivray (1824).
5 MacGillivray (1826).
6 MacGillivray (1827).
7 MacGillivray (1830).
8 MacGillivray (1830).
9 The notes left by Darwin about his life were published, as a complete autobiography, for the first time in 1958, edited by his granddaughter, Nora Barlow (p. 53).
10 *Ibid.*, p. 53.
11 Darwin (1871), p. 466.
12 MacGillivray (1836), p. 4.
13 *Ibid.*, p. 4.
14 MacGillivray (1830).
15 Withering (1776).
16 MacGillivray (1824).
17 Richardson and Swainson (1831).

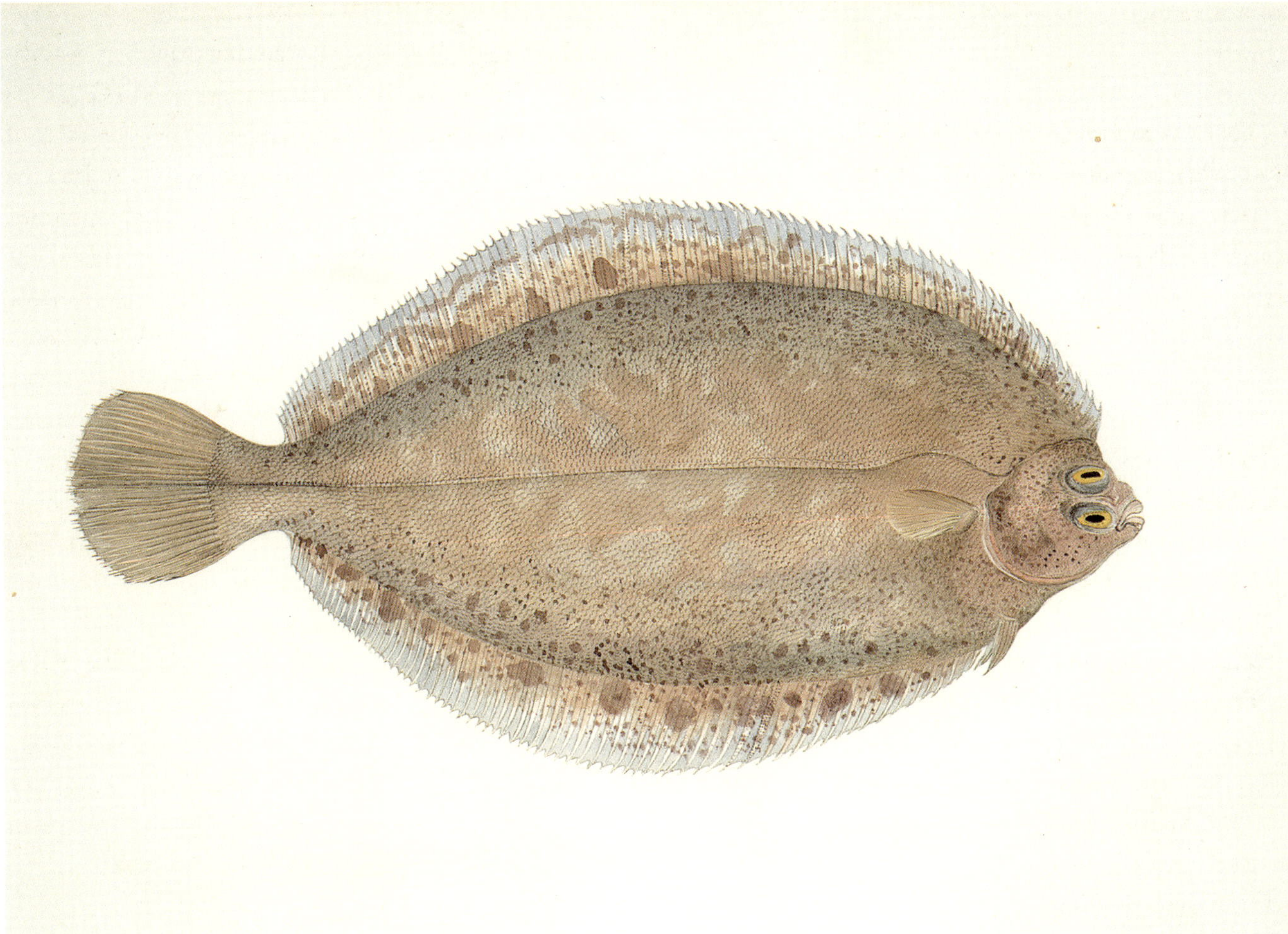

PLATE 24 Lemon sole *Microstomus kitt*
[*Platessa microcephala.*]

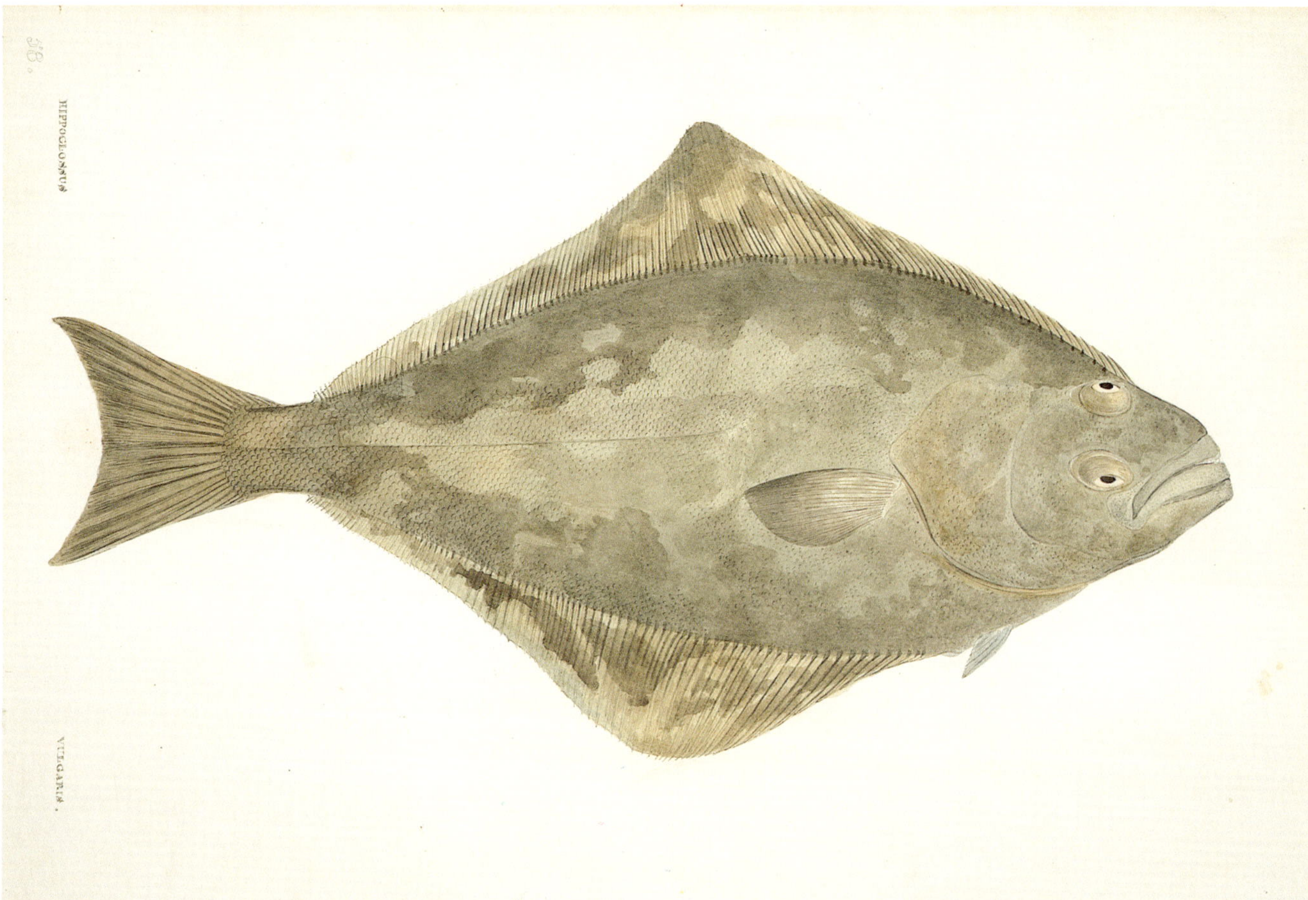

PLATE 25 Halibut *Hippoglossus hippoglossus*
[*Hippoglossus vulgaris.*]

The Path to Edinburgh

John James Audubon

Audubon's visit to Edinburgh in 1830 was the second time he had been to the city. He came there first in October 1826 as part of a tour around several cities in Britain, a tour in which he was looking for an engraver and printer to produce the first of the plates for *The Birds of America* and was also looking for subscribers to the set of paintings. The story of Audubon's life has been told many times so only the details relevant to his friendship with MacGillivray are outlined here.[1] The ambition and plan to produce *The Birds of America* was born out of his failure as a businessman. He was born in 1785 in Haiti, the illegitimate son of Jean Audubon, a French sea captain from Nantes, and Jeanne Rabin, a servant girl, from the same town. She died a few months after his birth and four years later Jean Audubon returned to France, where the young Audubon and a half-sister were brought up by his father and his wife, who adopted them as her own. In 1803 Captain Audubon sent his son to the United States to manage his plantation at Mill Grove near Philadelphia and at the same time to learn English and avoid conscription into Napoleon's army. The young Audubon showed little inclination for farming and spent his time collecting birds and drawing them. In 1806 he married Lucy Bakewell, who had been born in England, the daughter of a neighbour at Mill Grove. The next few years saw a succession of business ventures and failures, and he made his living where he could, drawing portraits, teaching drawing and French, and as a taxidermist at the Western Museum in Cincinnati, but all the time he was building up his collection of bird paintings. These were admired by the staff at the museum, and encouraged by this, his plans for *The Birds of America*, an idea he had nurtured for many years, began to take shape. For six years from 1820 he travelled extensively, by boat and on foot, down the Ohio and Mississippi rivers, from Florida to Labrador, only occasionally returning to New Orleans where Lucy was supporting herself and their children as a teacher. When his portfolio of drawings was large enough he visited Philadelphia and New York looking for a publisher, but all his efforts met with failure and he realised he would have to look further afield, to Europe. Leaving Lucy and his family to fend for them-

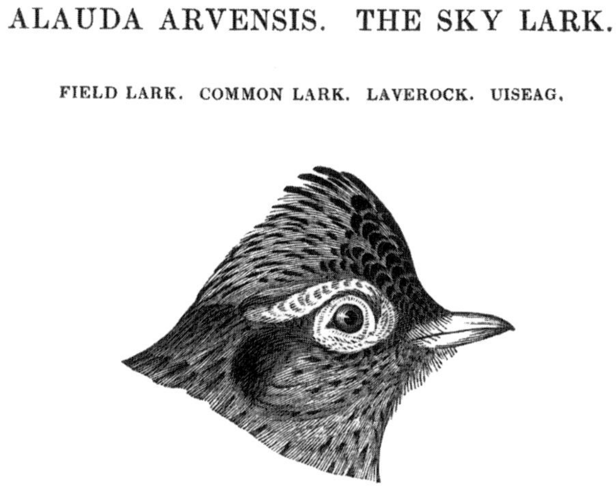

11 Skylark *Alauda arvensis* from *A History of British Birds*, vol. 2 (1839), p. 163

selves as best they could, he set sail for England in June 1826.

His first port of call was in Liverpool where he showed his paintings and drawings, some 225 of them, at the Royal Institution. He was an outstanding success, on the second day more than 400 people came to see his work, and he became something of a showman, acting the frontiersman, dressing in a wolf-skin coat, and being invited almost daily to speak to some elegant Liverpool gathering. After a few weeks he moved on to Manchester where his welcome was very different. Few people came to see his exhibition and those that did were not very interested. Audubon himself did not much care for Manchester; he thought it "a miserably laid out place, composed of an astonishing number of small dirty, narrow, crooked lanes, where one cart can scarce pass another, and the smokiest I ever was in. The funnels raised from the manufactories to carry off the smoke, appear in hundreds in every direction". MacGillivray had formed much the same opinion of the city a few years earlier when he passed through on his walk to London. A few weeks later, on 25 October Audubon arrived in Edinburgh where he was to stay until April of the following year.

Audubon was given a warm welcome by Edinburgh. He had a letter of introduction to Patrick Neill, a printer and naturalist and a member of the Royal Society of Edinburgh and the Wernerian Society. He advised Audubon to see the engraver William Home Lizars. Lizars was no stranger to bird paintings; he was already engaged on engraving the plates for Prideaux John Selby's *Illustrations of British Ornithology*[2] and for Sir William Jardine's *Illustrations of Ornithology*[3] but Audubon's paintings took him by surprise. In his journal Audubon describes how nervous he felt when he showed Lizars his first drawing, but his nervousness was quickly dispelled:

"Mr. Lizars, quite surprised, exclaimed, "My God, I never saw anything like this before!" ... Mr. Lizars was so astonished that he said Sir Somebody [Sir William Jardine] must see them, that he would write immediately, (and so did he), that Mr. Selby must see them and to him also he wrote. And, going as it grew dark, he called upon a Mr. W. Heath, a great artist from London, who came immediately to see me."[4]

Lizars immediately offered to engrave five plates for him, and the first of these, perhaps the most famous of them, the Wild Turkey, was completed at the end of November. The impact of this plate and the exhibition of Audubon's other paintings at the Edinburgh Royal Institution were nothing short of sensational and they became the talk of the city. Audubon was made an honorary member of the Royal Scottish Academy and several other learned societies. John Syme painted his portrait, dressed in a wolf-skin coat with a gun cradled in his arms, a portrait that now hangs in the White House collection; the phrenologist George Combe made a cast of his head; he dined out every night with the best of Edinburgh society; he met Sir Walter Scott, who was then at the height of his literary fame – the city had never seen anything like the "American woodsman". Audubon's

PLATE 26 Starry ray *Raja radiata*

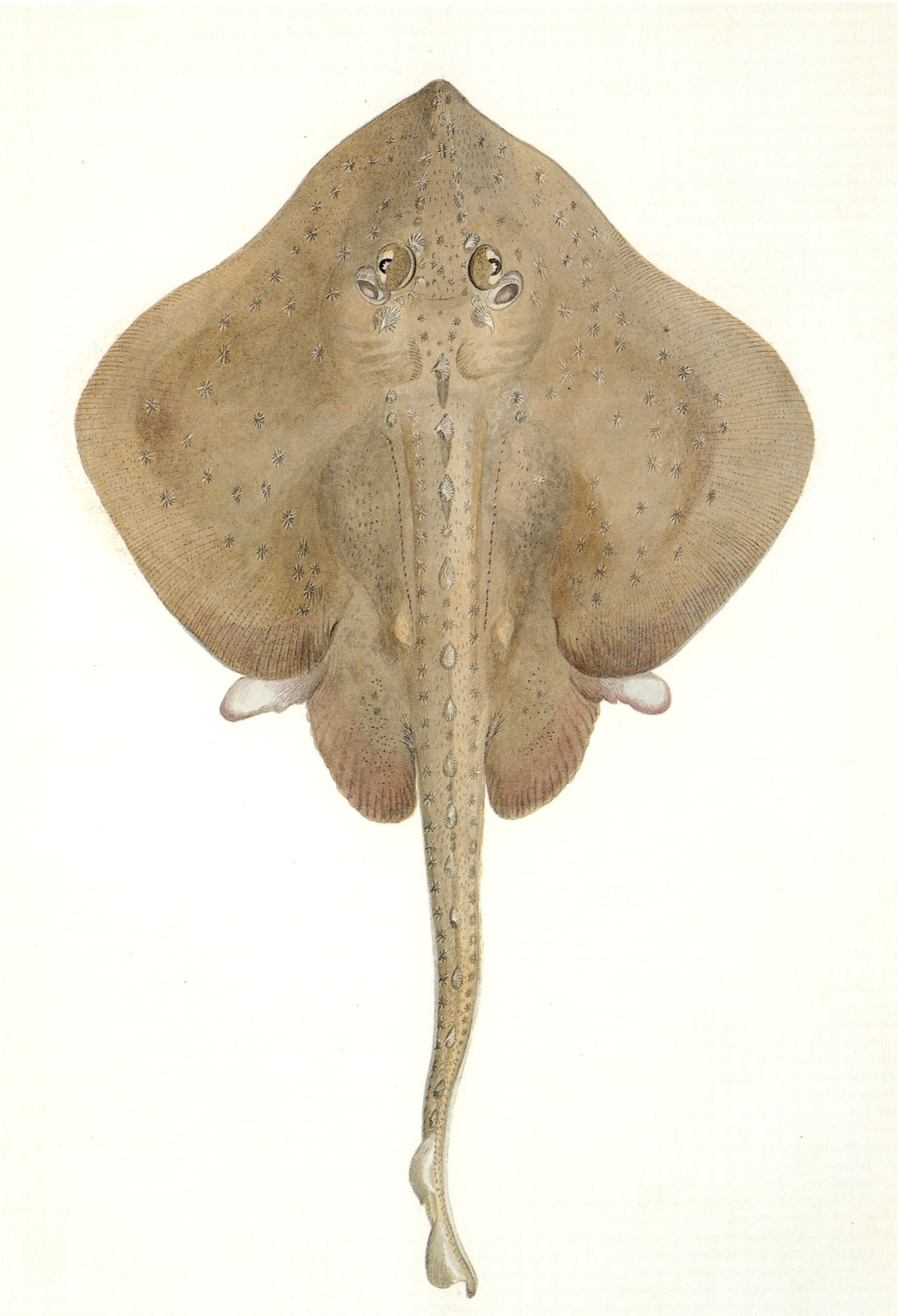

BUBO MAXIMUS. THE GREAT EAGLE-OWL.

GREAT HORNED OWL. GREAT EARED-OWL. GREAT OWL. ATHENIAN OWL. GRAND DUKE AND DUCHESS.

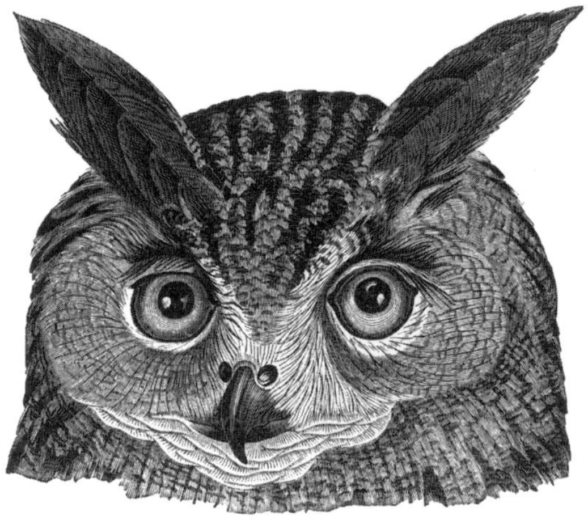

FIG. 243.

12 Eagle owl, *Bubo bubo;* 'Great eagle-owl', *Bubo maximus* from *A History of British Birds,* vol. 3 (1840), p. 428

paintings were dramatic because of their large size, double elephant folio, approximately 40 × 30 inches, but also because of their style. For the first time birds were depicted in positions and against backgrounds that made them look alive and full of movement, feeding, fighting or flying. In the prospectus for *The Birds of America* Audubon himself described how his paintings were the first to show birds in their natural habitats:

"The Author has not contented himself, as others have done, with single profile views, but in very many instances has grouped his figures, so as to represent the originals at their avocations, and has placed them on branches of trees, decorated with foliage, blossoms and fruits, or amidst plants of numerous species. Some are seen pursuing their prey through the air, searching for food amongst the leaves and herbage, sitting on their nest, or feeding their young; whilst others, of a different nature, swim, wade, or glide in or over their allotted element."[5]

Audubon's gun was almost as important to him as his brush, he regarded it as a poor day in the field if he shot fewer than a hundred birds. Most of his paintings were done from specimens that he had hunted and killed, often shooting many individuals for each painting. The dead birds were then arranged in lifelike positions using wires and pins. He also used different media – oils, watercolour, pastel, crayon, pen and ink – to achieve the effect he wanted. Before Audubon, it was commonplace for artists to paint from dried skins and from the work of taxidermists, and their representations looked stiff and immobile. Audubon had seen some of Selby and Jardine's paintings when he first met Lizars and was not impressed by them, writing in his journal, "I conceive my Johnny [his son] can do as good".[6]

Later on when the two men met Audubon and saw his paintings, they became very conscious of the difference between his style and theirs, but he willingly agreed

PLATE 27 Thornback ray or roker *Raja clavata*
[*Raja.*]

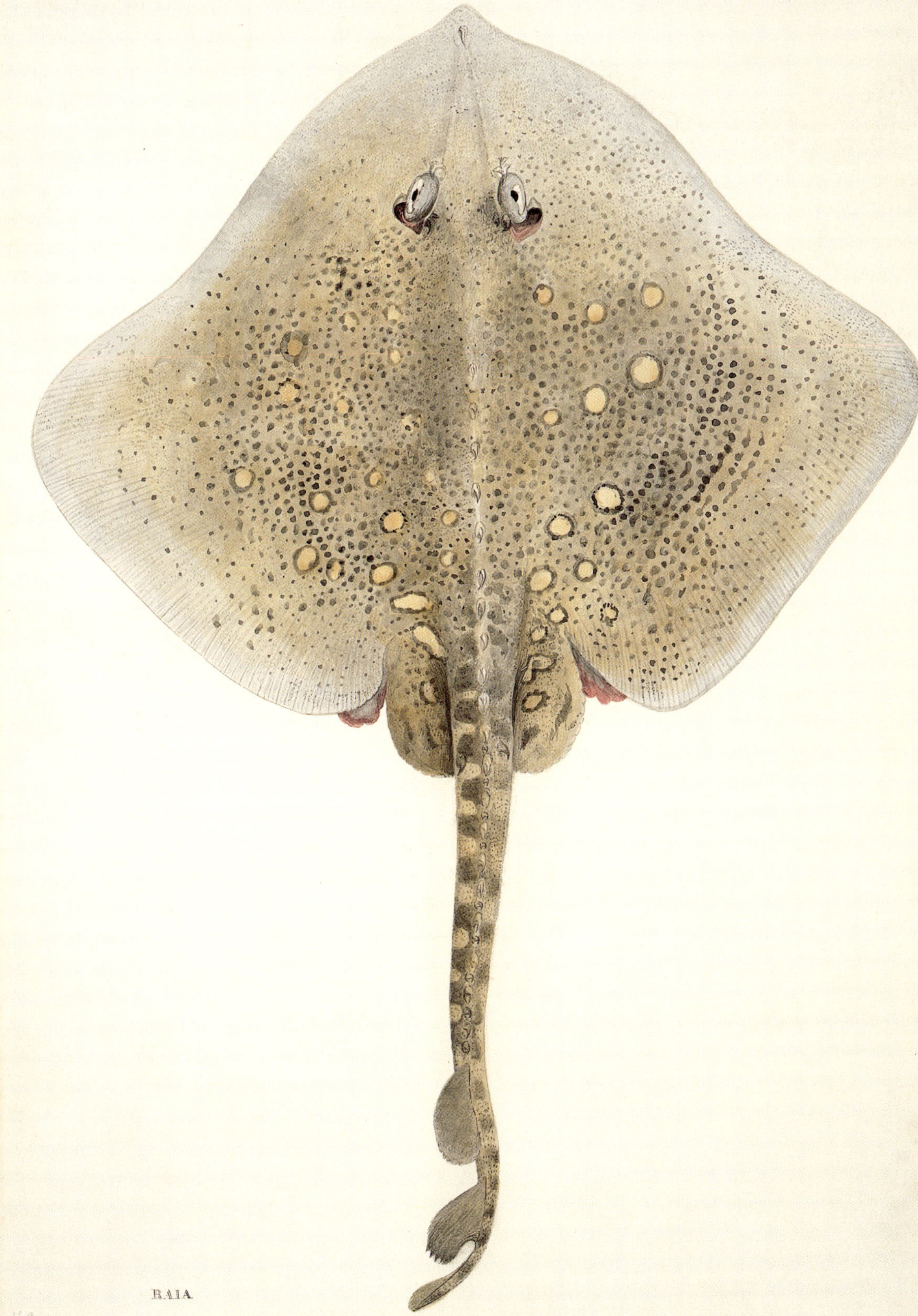

RAIA

to share his methods with them. When the three of them met in Edinburgh he gave them a demonstration:

"It was just nine, the morning fine and beautiful ... The hotel was soon reached, and I was with my friends; they had brought Ducks, Hawks, and small birds for me to draw. After breakfast we all went to my room, and I showed these gentlemen how I set up my specimens, squared my paper, and soon had them both at work drawing a Squirrel. They called this a lesson ... They worked very well indeed, although I perceived at once that Mr. Selby was more enthusiastic, and therefore worked faster than Sir William; but he finished more closely, so that it was hard to give either the supremacy. They were delighted, especially Mr. Selby, who exclaimed, 'I will paint all our quadrupeds for my own house'. They both remained with me till we could see no more."[7]

By the spring of 1827 the production of *The Birds of America* was well under way and Audubon published a prospectus for the work, announcing that the paintings would be issued in parts of five, priced at two guineas a part, with five parts each year. He left Edinburgh for London in May 1827, taking in Newcastle, York and Leeds, as well as Manchester and Liverpool again on the way. Soon after he arrived in London he received the news that Lizars' colourists had gone on strike, with just ten of the plates completed. This could have been disastrous for the whole project but Audubon quickly engaged another engraver, Robert Havell. At first he planned to use Havell simply to colour the prints from Lizars but soon decided to transfer the whole process to Havell's London shop. In fact, Havell's work was technically better and had the added advantage of being cheaper as well. Robert Havell was fifty-eight and it was his son Robert Havell junior who took over most of the work, with the final plates for *The Birds of America* published in June 1838, the last of 435 plates and 1065 figures.

Apart from his successful meeting and partnership with Havell, Audubon got off to a bad start in London. He had arrived there at the wrong time of year and although he had many letters of introduction to eminent people in science, the arts and society generally, the summer season had started and he found no one at home. He spent his time drawing and painting to sell pictures for the money he needed for Havell, but the market was for works in oils, his least favourite medium: "My birds in water-colours have plumage and soft colours, but in oils – alas!" He also found London too big and sophisticated and the city never took to him in the way that Edinburgh had. His life took on a routine of painting pictures to sell, supervising Havell's engravers and colourists and searching for subscribers. He was forever short of money and the prospect of bankruptcy and failure was never far away; he was also missing Lucy and his family. Nevertheless he stayed in London for nearly sixteen months before leaving for Paris, again in search of more subscribers, and then returning to America in April 1829, three years after he had left there.

Just a year later, Audubon was back in England, this time with Lucy, with more paintings for Havell to work on, and with a large collection of bird specimens. The summer was spent in London working with Havell, painting pictures for sale, persuading lapsed subscribers to rejoin and, all the time, searching for new ones. He returned to his beloved Edinburgh in October 1830, where, for the first time he met the man who was to become his lifelong, and, probably, his best friend, William MacGillivray.

NOTES

1 There are many accounts of Audubon's life; the material in this chapter has been taken from Herrick (1938).
2 Selby (1821–33).
3 Jardine and Selby (1826–43).
4 Audubon, M.R. (1897), vol. 1, p. 153.
5 Audubon (1827).
6 Herrick (1938), vol. 1, p. 362.
7 *Ibid.*, vol. 1, p. 363.

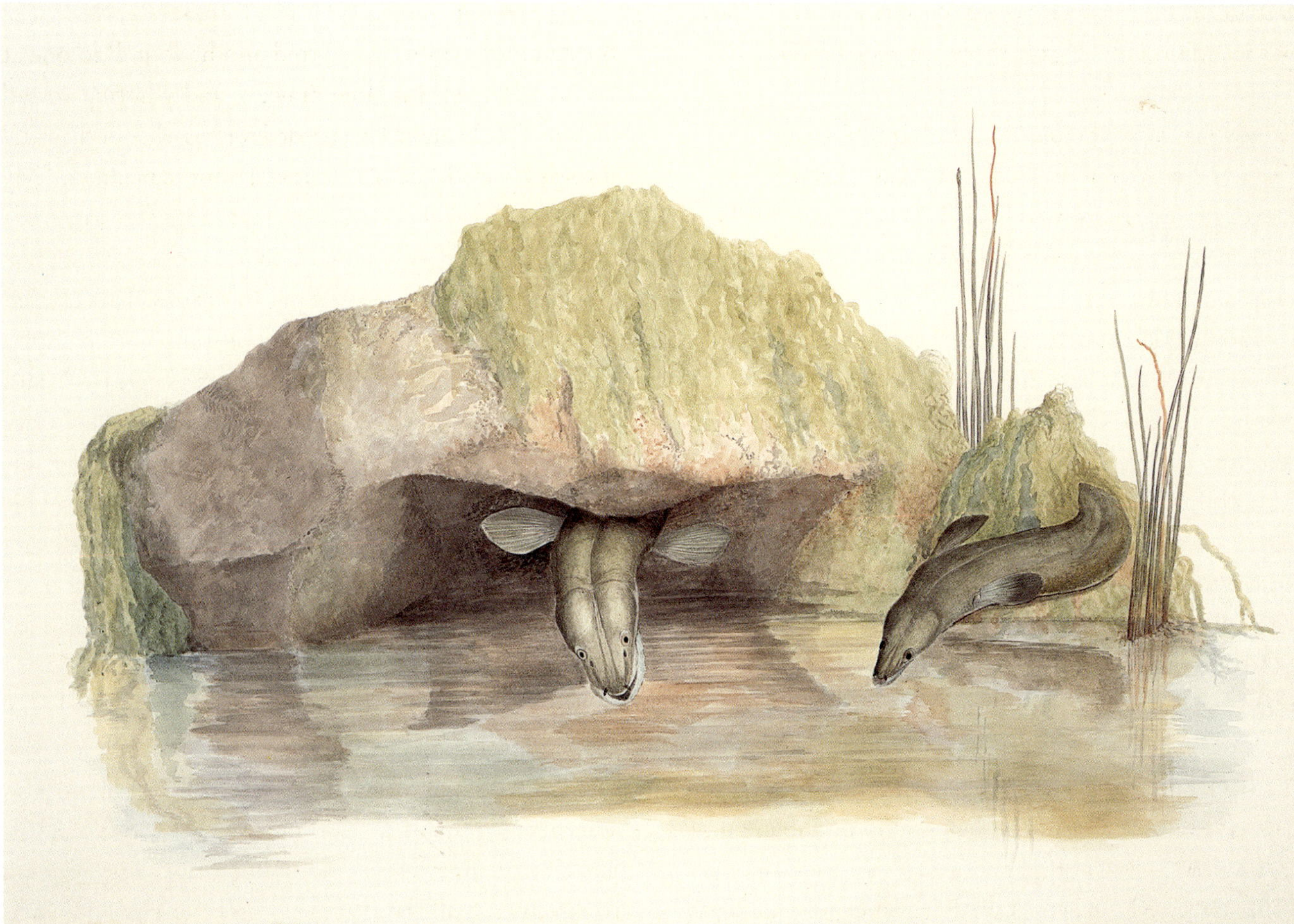

PLATE 28 Eel *Anguilla anguilla*
MacGillivray drew these eels as different species *Anguilla latirostris* and *A. acutirostris;* these two species are no longer regarded as separate from *A. anguilla.*

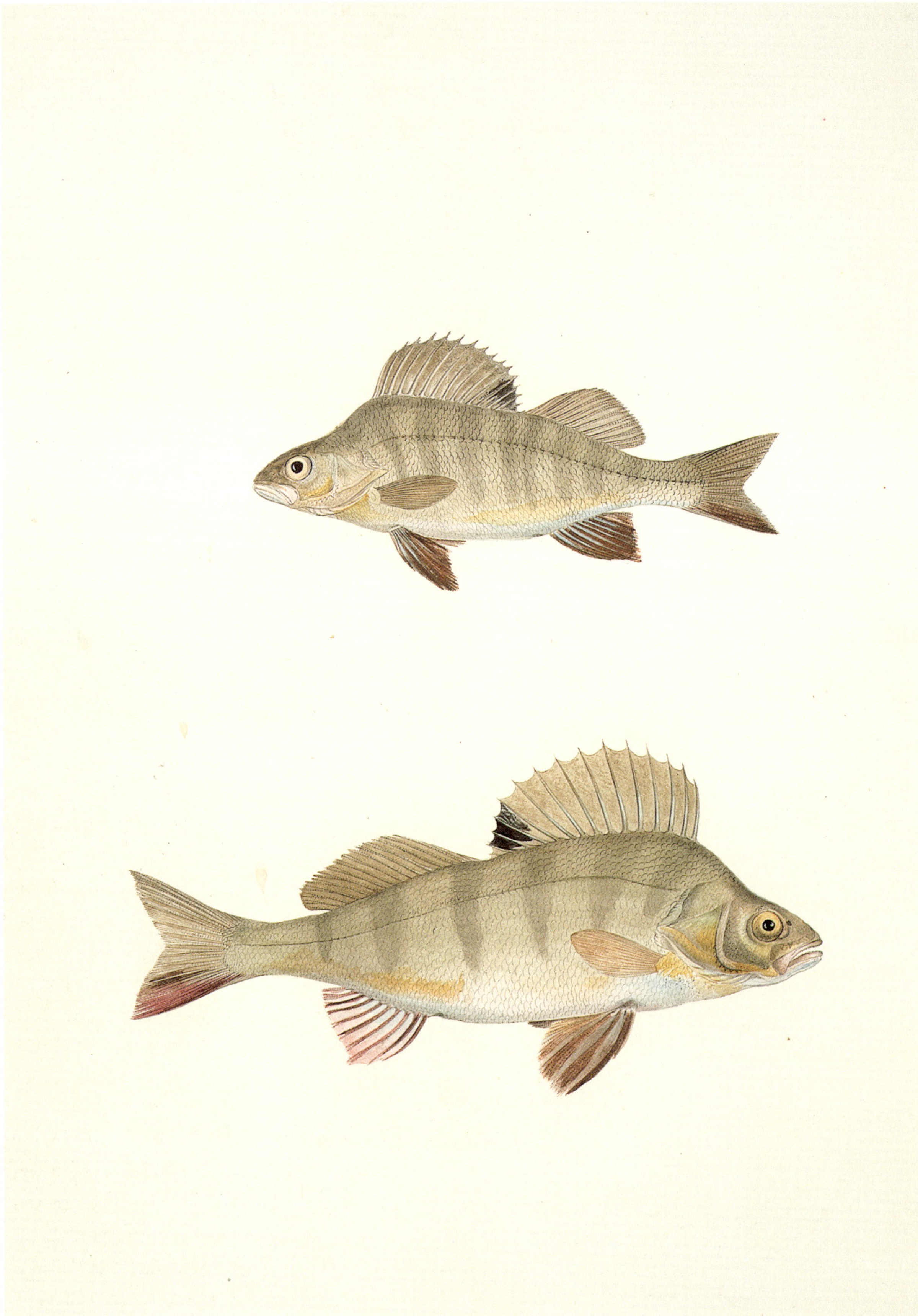

The 1830s

The Ornithological Biography

When Audubon came to Britain on his first visit he already had in mind a text, a letterpress, to go with *The Birds of America.* He had ambitions to be known as more than an artist, he wanted recognition as a naturalist. Although Audubon was content to exploit the woodsman image to promote his paintings, he realised that this inevitably had an impact on the way his other contributions to ornithology would be received. He was also at a disadvantage compared to naturalists with formal university training in systematics and anatomy. His knowledge came from his experience with living birds in their natural environment, not from the lecture room, museum or library. While Audubon was in Edinburgh in 1827, he presented several papers to the Wernerian Society, papers which were published in the *Edinburgh New Philosophical Journal.* One was about the ability of rattlesnakes to climb trees,[1] something dramatically illustrated in his plate of a family of mocking birds defending their nest against an attacking snake with fangs bared. When the paper and the plate reached America, Audubon was severely criticized by ornithologists who were convinced that rattlesnakes never climbed trees. He was also criticized for another paper that suggested that the Turkey-buzzard could find its prey using a sense of smell.[2] Although Audubon was vindicated on both scores, the experience made him suspicious and slightly disdainful of the cabinet naturalists, men with a more sophisticated education but with little experience of the natural world. In October 1826, one of his friends from Liverpool, Edward Roscoe, knowing that Selby, Jameson and several colleagues were planning a major ornithological work, suggested that Audubon should think of collaborating with them. What he thought of this is recorded in his journal:

> "I think if my work deserves the attention of the public it must stand on its own two legs, not on the reputation of men superior in education and literary acquirements, but possibly not so in the actual observations of Nature at her best, in the wilds, as I certainly have seen her."[3]

PLATE 29 Perch *Perca fluviatilis*

Later, of course, Audubon became close friends with Selby and showed him how he drew his birds. Even though he felt his work should "stand on its own two legs", Audubon recognized that he did not have the academic background to classify and describe many of the birds that he had painted and enlisted help where he could. For example, in June 1827 in London, he met up with his friend from Philadelphia, Charles Lucien Bonaparte, and in just one evening he helped Audubon name nearly fifty new species, a feat that must surely stand as a taxonomic record. It was always Audubon's intention to publish a text to accompany *The Birds of America*:

"I shall publish the letterpress in a separate book, at the same time with the illustrations, and shall accompany the descriptions of the birds with many anecdotes and accounts of localities connected with the birds themselves, and with my travels in search of them."[4]

The reason for his plan for separate publication was because he had been advised by Lizars that if the letterpress and the paintings were published together, the British copyright law at the time would have required him to give eleven copies of the work to the Stationer's Office, something he felt he could not afford to do. Audubon avoided giving copies of *The Birds of America* to the Stationer by not publishing a title page for it and indeed claiming that it was not a book, but a series of prints. The publication of the letterpress had been promised to subscribers in the prospectus, but by the end of 1830 Havell would have produced the first hundred plates and there was no sign of it. When Audubon returned to England in the spring of that year, this time accompanied by his wife Lucy, the letterpress was becoming a priority. In October he wrote in his journal:

"I know that I am a poor writer, that I can scarcely manage to scribble a tolerable English letter, and a not much better one in French, though that is easier to me. I know I am not a scholar, but meantime I am aware that no man living knows better than I do the habits of our birds; no man living has studied them as much as I have done, and with the assistance of my old journals, and memorandum-books which were written on the spot, I can at least put down plain truths, which may be useful and perhaps interesting, so I shall set to at once. I cannot however, give scientific descriptions, and here must have assistance."[5]

He looked for assistance to a friend he had made on his first visit to England, the naturalist William Swainson. They had visited Paris together in 1827, Swainson had been an enthusiastic reviewer of the first of Audubon's plates and the two had corresponded regularly. Audubon wrote to Swainson from Manchester:

"I am desirous to hear from you if you can have the time to spare and the inclination to bear a hand in the text of my work, by my furnishing you with the ideas and observations which I have and you add the science which I have not! If it would suit you and Mrs. Swainson to take us as boarders for a few months when being almost always together I could partake of your observations and you of mine. I would like to receive here your ideas on this subject and if possible what you would expect from us as remuneration. My first volume will comprise an introduction and one hundred letters addressed to the reader referring to the 100 plates forming the first volume of my illustrations. I will enter even on local descriptions of the country, adventures and anecdotes, speak of the trees and the flowers, the reptiles or the fishes and the insects as far as I know.

In the event of my living with you we will furnish our own wines, porter or ale."[6]

Swainson's reply was prompt, turning down flat any idea that the Audubons might come and stay with him, even when bringing their own drink: "First, as to boarding with us, you do not know probably, that this is never done in England." He also insisted that his scientific contributions should be clearly separate from Audubon's narrative descriptions and demanded that his name should appear on the title page as a co-author. These

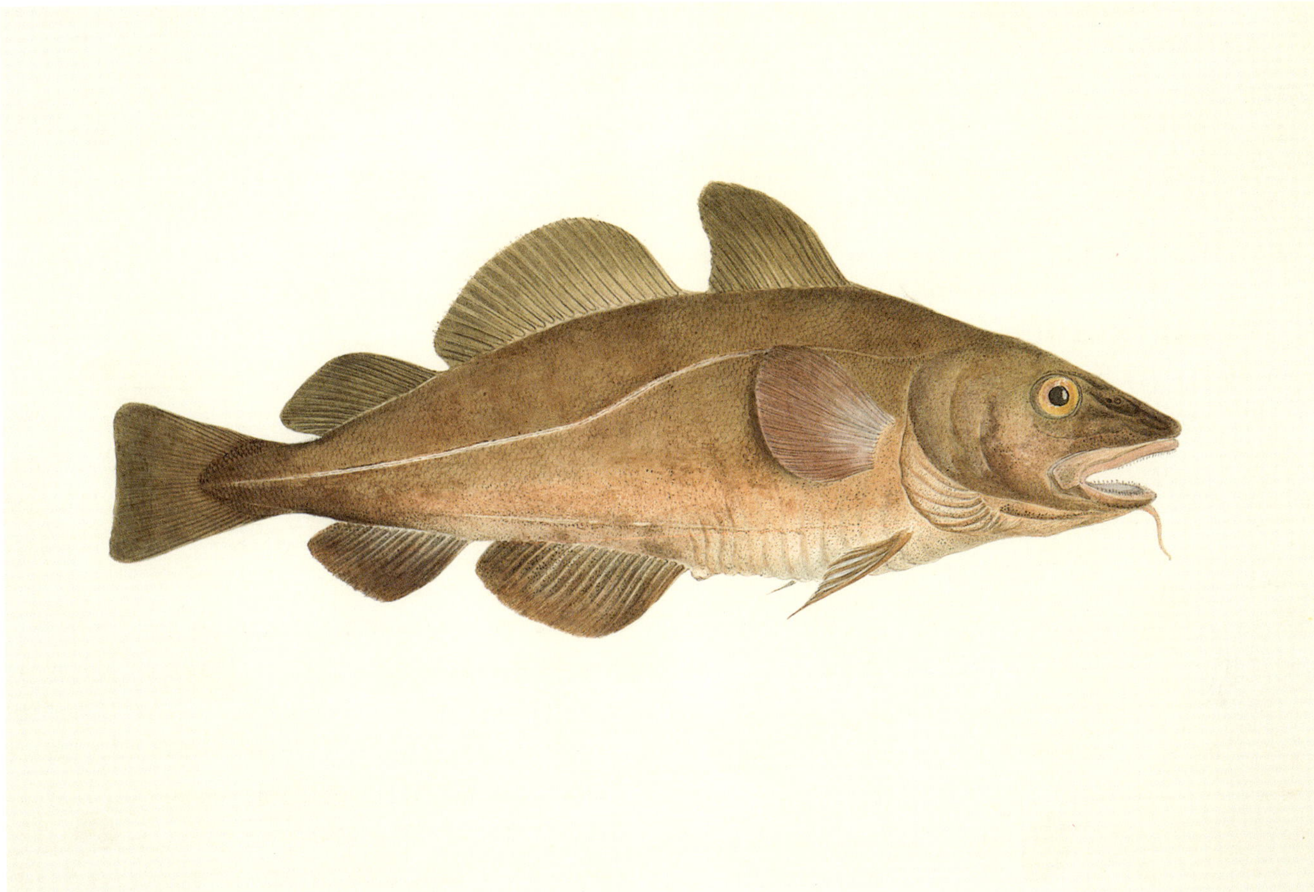

PLATE 30 Cod *Gadus morhua*

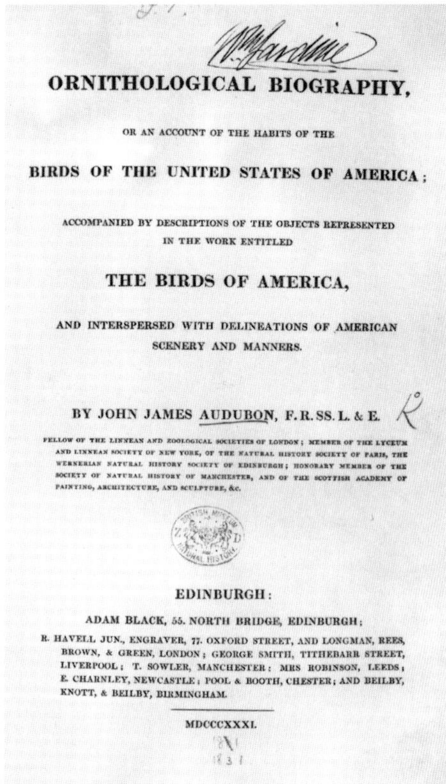
ORNITHOLOGICAL BIOGRAPHY,

OR AN ACCOUNT OF THE HABITS OF THE

BIRDS OF THE UNITED STATES OF AMERICA;

ACCOMPANIED BY DESCRIPTIONS OF THE OBJECTS REPRESENTED IN THE WORK ENTITLED

THE BIRDS OF AMERICA,

AND INTERSPERSED WITH DELINEATIONS OF AMERICAN SCENERY AND MANNERS.

BY JOHN JAMES AUDUBON, F.R.SS.L. & E.

FELLOW OF THE LINNEAN AND ZOOLOGICAL SOCIETIES OF LONDON; MEMBER OF THE LYCEUM AND LINNEAN SOCIETY OF NEW YORK, OF THE NATURAL HISTORY SOCIETY OF PARIS, THE WERNERIAN NATURAL HISTORY SOCIETY OF EDINBURGH; HONORARY MEMBER OF THE SOCIETY OF NATURAL HISTORY OF MANCHESTER, AND OF THE SCOTTISH ACADEMY OF PAINTING, ARCHITECTURE, AND SCULPTURE, &c.

EDINBURGH:

ADAM BLACK, 55. NORTH BRIDGE, EDINBURGH;

R. HAVELL JUN., ENGRAVER, 77. OXFORD STREET, AND LONGMAN, REES, BROWN, & GREEN, LONDON; GEORGE SMITH, TITHEBARN STREET, LIVERPOOL; T. SOWLER, MANCHESTER: MRS ROBINSON, LEEDS; E. CHARNLEY, NEWCASTLE; POOL & BOOTH, CHESTER; AND BEILBY, KNOTT, & BEILBY, BIRMINGHAM.

MDCCCXXXI.

13 The title page of Audubon's *Ornithological Biography*

demands, and the amount of money that he asked for, were too much for Audubon and he withdrew his request. This may have been no bad thing for ornithology; Swainson was one of the most zealous advocates of the day of the Quinarian system, a classification based on the supposed properties of the number five. The quinarians claimed that all organisms could be arranged into groups, depicted as five interlinked circles, and each circle divided into another set of five. The system is now regarded as a foolish one but in the context of its time it was popular. Swainson and other quinarians believed that as God had placed species on the earth, then he might have done so with numerical precision. It was to be another three decades before the Quinarian system and every other fanciful form of classification were swept away by Darwin and *The Origin of Species*.

In the absence of Swainson, when Audubon arrived in Edinburgh in October he was still without help with his letterpress. He turned for advice to another old naturalist friend from his first visit to the city, Professor James Wilson:

"... to ask if he knew of any person who would undertake to correct my ungrammatical manuscripts, and to assist me in preparing the more scientific part of the 'Biography of Birds'. He gave me a card with the address of Mr. W McGillivray sic, spoke well of his talents, and away to Mr. McGillivray I went. He had long known of me as a naturalist. I made known my business, and a bargain was soon struck. He agreed to assist me, and correct my manuscripts for two guineas a sheet of sixteen pages, and I that day began to write the first volume."[7]

At the time MacGillivray had no settled job, his family was growing, there were now six children, and two guineas a sheet was probably welcome, even though it was much less than the twelve guineas a sheet Swainson had asked for. Whatever MacGillivray's original motive in taking on the work, it became much more than simply a financial one. The collaboration between the two men grew into a deep and lasting friendship. In the next nine years five volumes of the *Ornithological Biography*[8] were published, followed by a single volume synopsis, more than 3000 pages of text and detailed descriptions of nearly 500 species. There were also ninety-eight detailed anatomical drawings, all done by MacGillivray. Today, the *Ornithological Biography* has been largely forgotten, overshadowed by the fame of the paintings that it accompanied, but it remains a monumental piece of work, the foundation stone of American ornithology.

Once embarked upon the text, Audubon and MacGillivray worked at a furious rate through the winter of 1830, spurred on by the news that at least two editions of Alexander Wilson's *American Ornithology* were being planned, one by Jameson, another by Jardine. Somehow Audubon found the time to write letters to his children as well:

"Writing now became the order of the day. I sat at it as soon as I awoke in the morning, and continued the whole day long, and so full was my mind of birds,

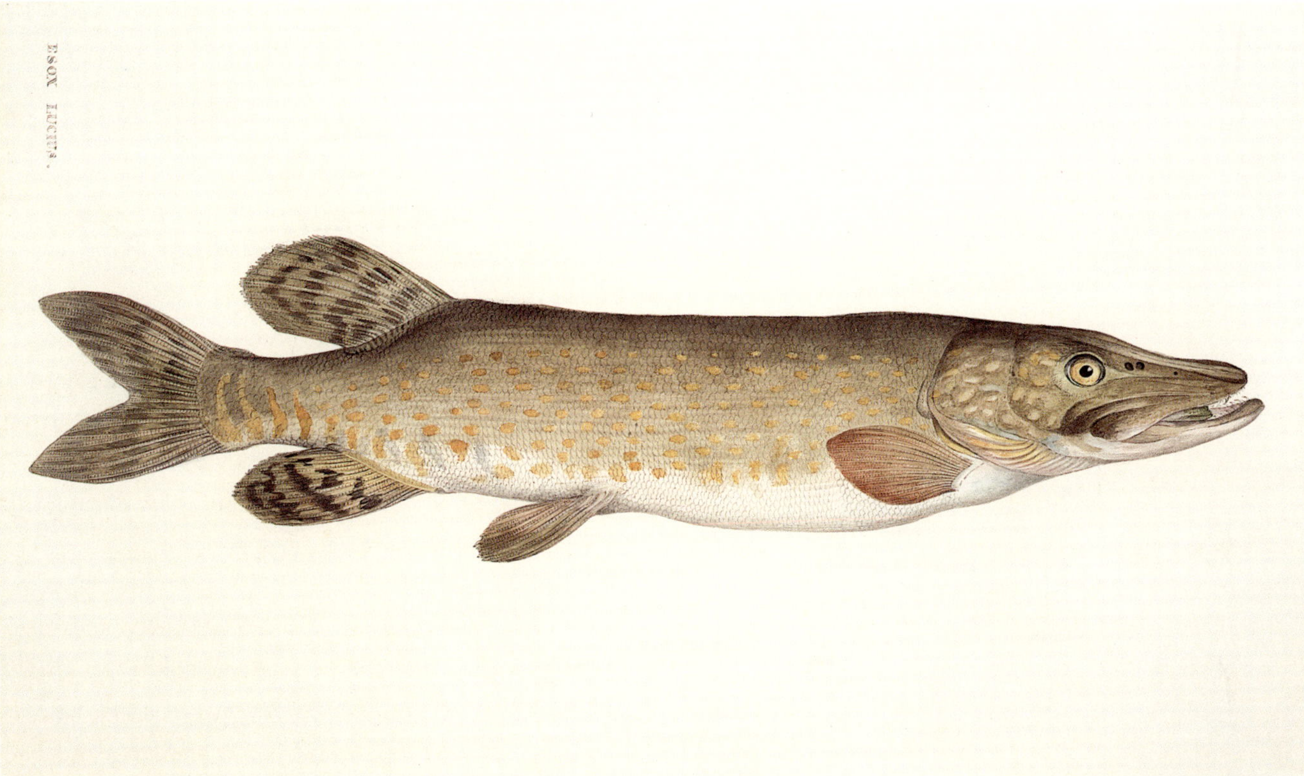

PLATE 31 Pike *Esox lucius*

and their habits, that in my sleep I continually dreamed of birds. I found Mr. MacGillivray equally industrious, for although he did not rise so early in the morning as I did, he wrote much later at night (this I am told is a characteristic of all great writers); and so the manuscripts went on increasing in bulk, like the rising of a stream after abundant rains, and before three months had passed the first volume was finished."[9]

There were difficulties in finding a publisher and Audubon had to bear the costs of publication himself but the book appeared in April 1831. A few months later with the first 100 plates of *The Birds of America* completed and the first volume of the *Ornithological Biography* receiving favourable reviews, Audubon decided that the time had come to return to North America to collect more birds and, a harder task, more subscribers. A month or two later, in September, MacGillivray was appointed as Conservator of the Museum of the Edinburgh Royal College of Surgeons, his first secure position since his appointment as Jameson's secretary and assistant eight years previously, and a position from which he was to be able to continue his work with Audubon.

It was more than three years before Audubon returned to Edinburgh. In June 1834, with Lucy and his son, John, he arrived in England, laden down with specimens, paintings and notes for volume 2 of the *Ornithological Biography*. From London he wrote at once to MacGillivray to enlist his help again, and received a prompt answer:

"I am glad to hear of your safe arrival, which I did not expect so soon, and pleased to find you in good health and high spirits. As you have the kindness to inquire respecting myself and family, I am happy to inform you that we are all very well, contented and busy. My head and hands are quite full – abundance of work and sufficient pay – time to ramble now and then for the purpose of hammering rocks, pulling plants, and shooting birds.

You say you have accumulated a mass of materials which you are desirous of seeing in print, and propose that I should revise it as before. I shall be glad to do so, if you please, and willing that you should confer the benefit on another, if you find it expedient. As to the terms, let them be such as you please with respect to money; but as time is valuable to me, I should like that arrangements be made so as to prevent unnecessary loss of it, by letting me have manuscripts, books, &c. in due array.

The skins of which you speak I apprehend cannot be disposed of here to any great extent; but I believe shells might be sold to advantage and bring higher prices than in London.

You ask if I draw Birds yet, with a view to publish. My answer is that I dissect, describe and draw Birds, Quadrupeds, whales, reptiles, and fishes, with a view of astonishing the world, and bettering my condition. I have about a hundred drawings, all the size of life, excepting two dolphins. But I have determined nothing yet respecting publication. Some time ago a friend of mine called on Mr. Havell with a letter in which I desired that person to engrave for me a few of my drawings, for the purpose of being exhibited at a meeting of naturalists. I had no answer, and so Mr. Havell can go to Jericho, or elsewhere, as he likes; but further your correspondent saith not.

I am decidedly of the opinion that, although you should continue the publication of the Ornithological Biography, you might bring out various other works which could not fail to be popular; for example, a biography of yourself, and sketches of American scenery. But of these matters it is impossible to speak to purpose unless I had the pleasure of seeing you, a pleasure which I hope I shall have at the time of the general assembly of the naturalists."[10]

This letter is a valuable insight into MacGillivray's character, his lack of interest in anyone's opinion of him or his work, his willingness to speak his mind and his lack of concern for money, but it is hard to believe that he was quite as indifferent as he made out to the idea that someone else should take over the revision of Audubon's notes. In the event a satisfactory arrangement was made between the two men and the work began,

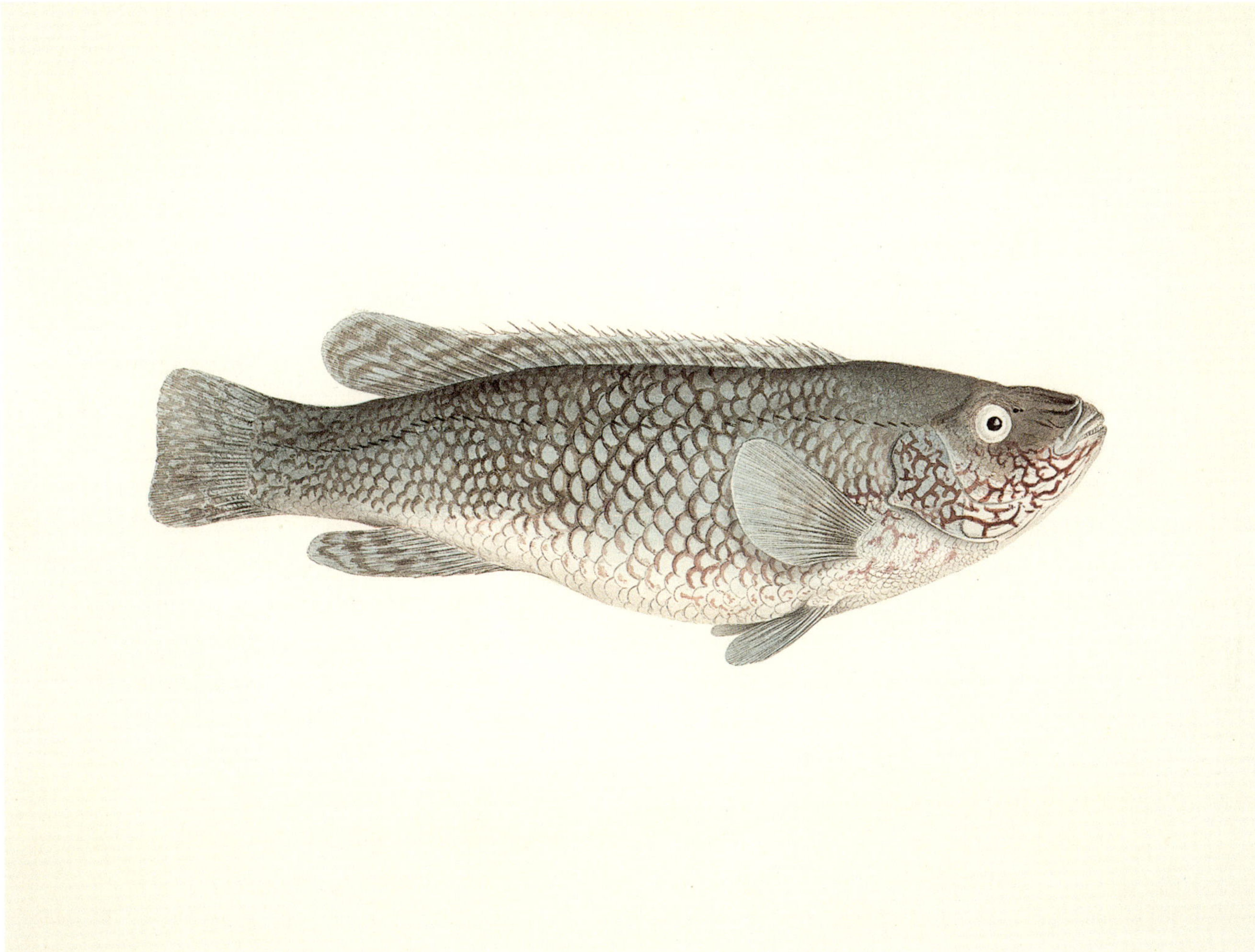

PLATE 32 Ballan wrasse *Labrus bergylta*
[*Labrus maculatus.*]

Audubon sending material to Edinburgh throughout the summer.

By the time Audubon and his family arrived in Edinburgh in October, MacGillivray had completed the revisions of the notes he had sent him. The material was sent to the publishers and the second volume of the *Ornithological Biography*, 585 closely printed pages, appeared before Christmas. The two men immediately plunged into work on the third volume, working at a frantic rate, especially MacGillivray who was still in his post at the Royal College of Surgeons. In a letter to her sons in America, Lucy Audubon wrote:

"Nothing is heard but the scratching of the pen; your father is up and at work before dawn, and writes without ceasing all day. Mr. MacGillivray breakfasts at nine each morning, attending the Museum four days in the week, has several works on hand besides ours, and is moreover, engaged as a lecturer in a new seminary on botany and natural history. His own work progresses slowly."[11]

Lucy Audubon was almost as busy as the two men because she wrote out a copy of the entire manuscript of each volume to send to the United States to secure the American copyright. The third volume was published towards the end of 1835. The work on *The Birds of America* was further ahead; by the summer of 1836 Havell had engraved half of the plates for the fourth and final volume and it was time for Audubon to return to America once again, to draw and collect the specimens for the fifty or so plates that remained to be done. He wanted to show some of the new specimens from the western side of the continent. The ornithologists Thomas Nuttall and John Kirk Townsend had collected birds from the West Coast, specimens they had sent back to the Philadelphia Academy of Sciences. When Audubon asked to see them he was allowed a brief look at them but was refused permission to draw them – MacGillivray was not the only one to have made enemies along the way! The brief look was enough for Audubon to realise that there were about forty new species, specimens that he simply had to get access to if *The Birds of America* was to be complete. He managed this when he met Nuttall in Boston and arranged to buy duplicate specimens, ninety-three skins, from him. He spent the winter in Charleston drawing the specimens, and then set off to explore Florida and Texas. More specimens arrived from the west, this time from Townsend, and in the summer of 1837 it was time to return to England again, to finish the great work. It was an anxious time for him, many subscribers had withdrawn, others were unhappy at the ever-increasing numbers of plates they had to pay for as he figured new species, and he spent a frantic year in London until, on 20 June 1838, the last plate was printed. At the end of the project there were just 161 subscribers who stayed with Audubon until the end, 82 in America and 79 in Europe. The sense of relief at the end of the project must have been remarkable, but there was not time to rest on his laurels, since there were still two volumes of the *Ornithological Biography* to be done, and the Audubon family moved once more to Edinburgh, where writing again became the order of the day.

The two men worked at an extraordinary rate. The fourth volume of the *Biography* appeared in November; just a few days later the printing of the fifth began and it was published, all 704 pages of it, in May the following year. Almost immediately a synopsis of all five volumes followed, a catalogue of 491 species, fifty-two of which were new. This work was widely acknowledged to have been written entirely by MacGillivray. He still had his museum position and was working on a number of his own books, and although he and Audubon had become great friends, the sheer pressure and pace of the work occasionally strained their relationship, as this piece from one of MacGillivray's notebooks shows:

"The two ornithologists

A large room, in which are a heap of birds' skins and a long table covered with others arranged in lines. Mr. Audubon seated, and transcribing references to authors. Mr. MacGillivray enters with a portfolio.

Audubon, pretending to be very busy, and not looking up, How are you?

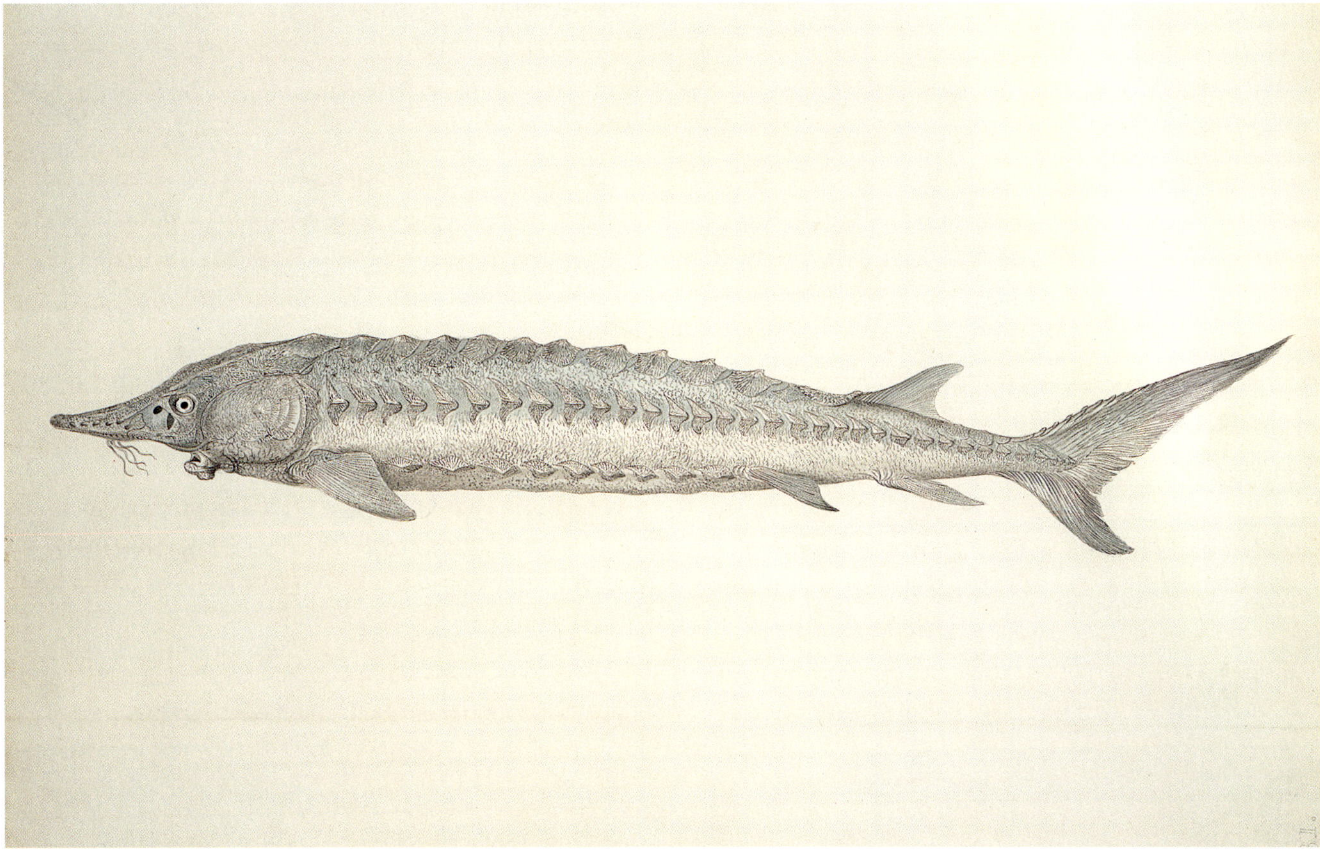

PLATE 33 Sturgeon *Acipenser sturio*

MACG Pretty well.

AUD I will be done presently.

MacG stands until he is done.

AUD Well what do you think of the Buntings now? Have we none in America?

MACG I don't care about Buntings: I have given up thinking about them. Sits down, opens his portfolio and arranges his papers. I wish, if you please, to begin at the other end of the series, and take the Icterines, that we may better understand their connection with the Finches and Buntings, for I think they run more into the Finches.

AUD (cross) That I think is a very bad plan. It is strange to begin with the Icterines, at the wrong end.

MACG I do not intend to make them come first in the series, but only to describe them, and put them into groups or genera, we can afterwards arrange them. The Quiscali, as we agreed, are nearest to the Crows, and I wish to come backwards in order to understand the relations of the Icteri, and thus fix their position. They seem to run into the Buntings by what is called the Cow Bunting first, and then by the Rice Bird.

AUD Well, there they are. But I have not specimens here. I must go hunt for them. This is a strange plan. We were going on very well. (Goes downstairs to 'hunt' for Quiscali).

MacGillivray in the meantime takes a specimen of *Quiscalis barita*, and commences writing a generic character. Audubon arrives with a parcel of Quiscali, and lays them on the table. Searches for more in a heap on the floor, finds one, and throws it rudely on the table, finds another, and throws it with less force, but grumbling to himself.

MacG. writes on without speaking.

AUD This is very strange. These birds have slender bills, and I think are nearer to this (*Icterus baltimore*). They cannot be next in order (to the Buntings and Finches).

MACG No, but they seem nearest to the Crows, and I wish to go backwards in describing. Is it not easy to see that the Quiscali are the last in the series, and, although first described are not to be placed last in order? The Icterines are composed of the Quiscali, the group of Baltimore Orioles, then the Redwings, Starlings, then the Cow Bird and the Rice Bunting.

AUD (in a pet) It is impossible to bear this. It is really awful.

MACG Well, I will give up the plan, and take up whatever group you please. (Lays aside the paper and takes up a clean sheet). What group do you wish me to do?

AUD God bless me! This will never do. If we cannot get on with it, let it alone.

MACG Very well. What is the use of squabbling in this way? You say it is all nonsense, mere child's play. If you think so, let it alone. (Rises and throws the paper on the table).

AUD I'll have nothing more to do with it, I would not be plagued in this way for anything.

MacG goes off without speaking.

AUD Goodbye to you. I am done with you.

MacG says nothing, opens the door of the room, draws it gently after him, walks quietly to the street door, puts on his hat, opens and shuts the door very gently, and emerges into the bright sunshine. Feels very hot, but remarkably buoyant from having escaped from a disagreeable task; walks home at a smart rate, plays with one of the children, corrects two sheets of the discarded synopsis, and is very happy.

Next morning, between nine and ten, was informed that Mr. Audubon, who had gone to the low room, desired to see me. So I got out of bed and went in, somewhat grave. He said he wished me to forget what had happened, he having been so vexed and irritated by various recurrences, disappointments relative to money, and the hurry of arranging for departure, that he could not command his temper. As we had got so far with the synopsis, he thought it better that I should finish it. In short, he apologised in sufficient manner, whereupon I told him that under these circumstances, I should proceed with the work, and continue to go over daily as before."[12]

In the summer of 1839, his great work finished, Audubon returned to America for the last time and the collaboration between him and MacGillivray came to an

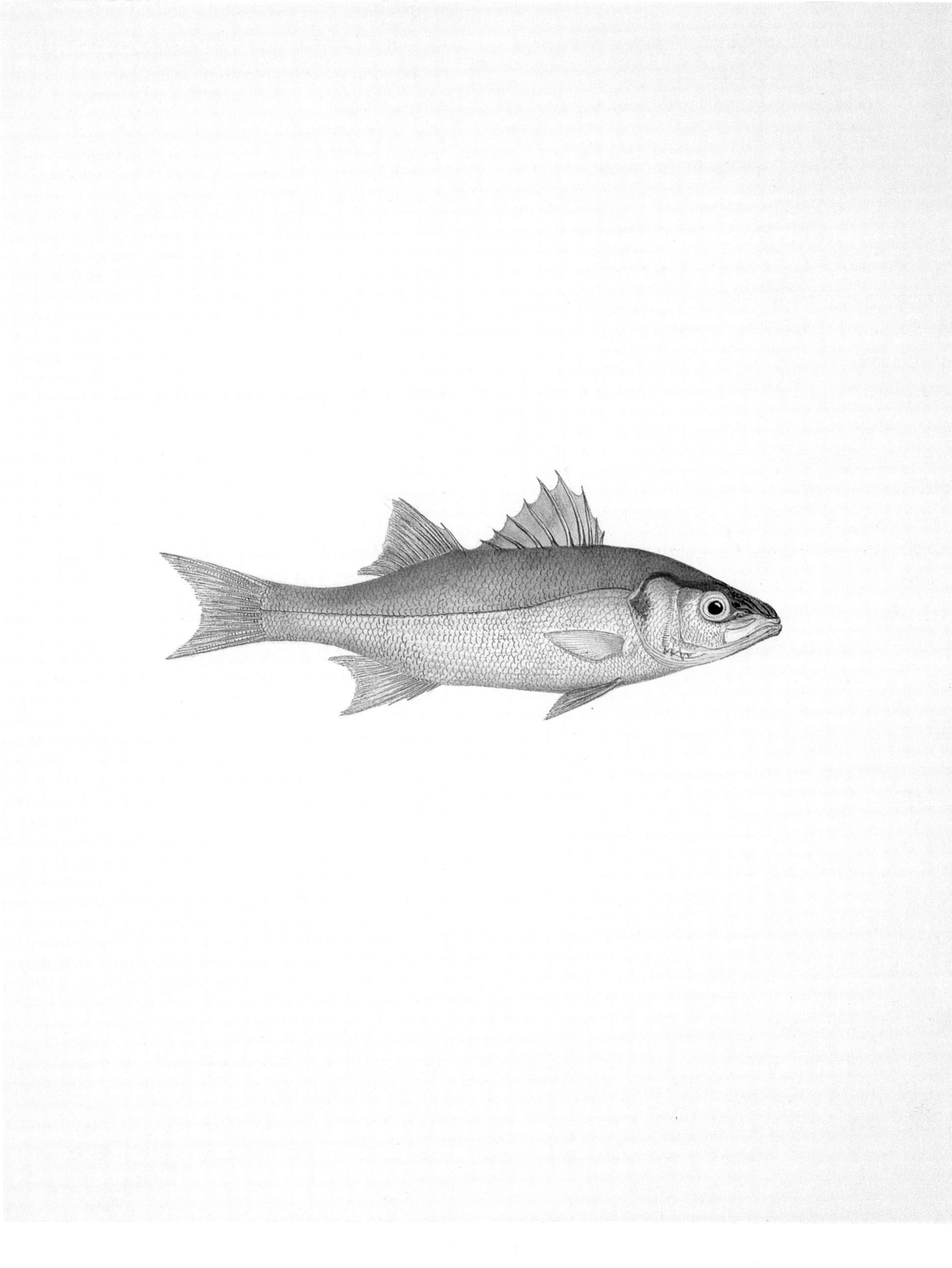

PLATE 34 Bass *Dicentrarchus labrax*
[*Labrax lupus.*]

end. Nine years earlier MacGillivray had entered into the partnership in a simple commercial agreement but his contribution became much more than that, something that has seldom been recognized. Even Audubon scarcely commented on it: in the Introduction to the first volume he acknowledged the help he received from MacGillivray in a few lines:

"There are persons whose desire of obtaining celebrity induces them to suppress the knowledge of the assistance which they have received in the composition of their works. In many cases, in fact, the real author of the drawings or the descriptions in books on Natural History is not so much as mentioned, while the pretended author assumes to himself all the merit which the world is willing to allow him. This want of candour I could never endure. On the contrary, I feel pleasure in here acknowledging the assistance which I have received from a friend, Mr. William MacGillivray, who being possessed of a liberal education and a strong taste for the study of the Natural Sciences, has aided me, not in drawing the figures of my illustrations, nor in writing the book now in your hand, although fully competent for both tasks, but in completing the scientific details, and in smoothing down the asperities of my Ornithological Biographies."[13]

Several years later, in the Introduction to the fourth volume of the *Ornithological Biography*, Audubon again acknowledged MacGillivray's help, by writing that:

"... the anatomical descriptions, as well as the sketches by which they are sometimes illustrated, have been executed by my learned friend, William MacGillivray, who in the most agreeable manner consented to undertake the labour, by no means small, of such a task, and to whom those who are interested in the progress of Ornithological science, as well as myself, must therefore feel indebted."[14]

Two mentions in 3000 pages seems little enough acknowledgement of MacGillivray's efforts, which were much more than completing the scientific details and smoothing the rough edges from Audubon's English, but he seems to have been satisfied enough. The eminent American ornithologist Elliott Coues was one of the first to give MacGillivray his due credit when he wrote about the two men in 1880:

"William MacGillivray has one very high claim upon the regard of American ornithologists; he was the source of Audubon's inspiration in all that pertains to the technic of the latter's great work. Not to put too fine a point on it, he furnished nearly all the 'ornithology' of Audubon's work, as distinguished from the portraits that the Frenchman drew either with pen or pencil. Audubon was primarily and chiefly, an animal painter, and he finally acquired no little familiarity with bird-life; but he began to paint without the slightest idea of ornithology, and never attained even mediocrity as a strict scientist. He loved warmth, color, action; he liked to exaggerate and 'embroider', and make his pages glow like a humming-bird's throat, or like one of his own marvellous pictures; he had no genius for accuracy, no taste for dull, dry detail, no care for a specimen after he had drawn it. MacGillivray supplied what was necessary to make his work a contribution to science as well as to art. In fact he wrote a great deal of Audubon's book. After Audubon had told us how his heart beat to the report of his gun, and he picked up a lovely warbler he had long sought for, but until then in vain – conveying an impression of years of solicitude about something that he probably never thought of till he stumbled on it accidentally – after all this, and the execution of a beautiful plate, MacGillivray would furnish his friend a technical name and a description. The anatomical matter of Audubon's works is probably all MacGillivray's; and the final classification and nomenclature are from the same source. It will be remembered that the names and the whole arrangement of the birds in Audubon's *Orn. Biogr.*, 1831–39, were changed in the *Synopsis*, 1839, and in the 8vo ed., 1840–44. This was entirely due to MacGillivray's hand in the matter. MacGillivray is accredited with several

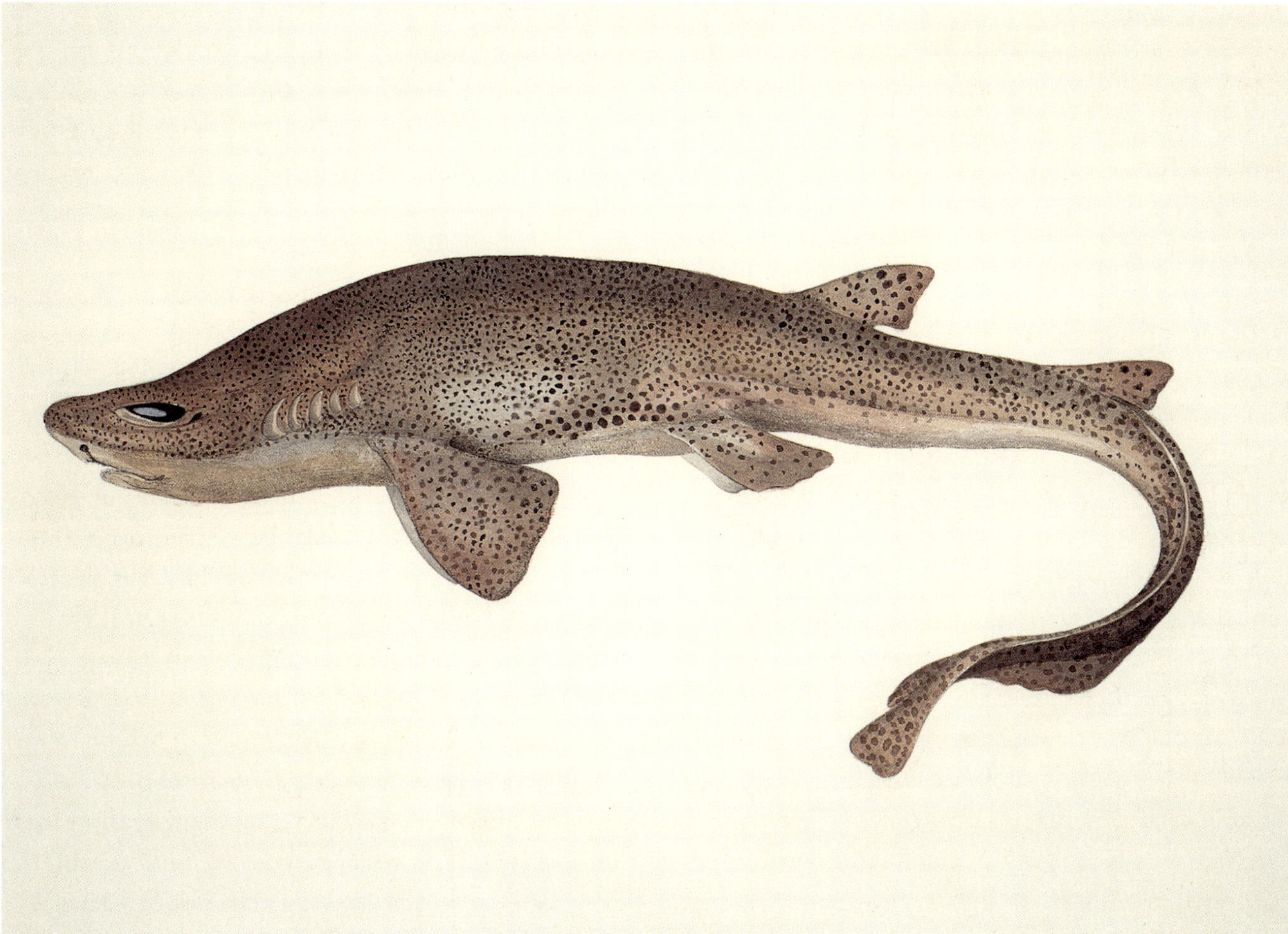

PLATE 35 Dogfish *Scyliorhinus canicula*
[*Scyllium canicula.*]

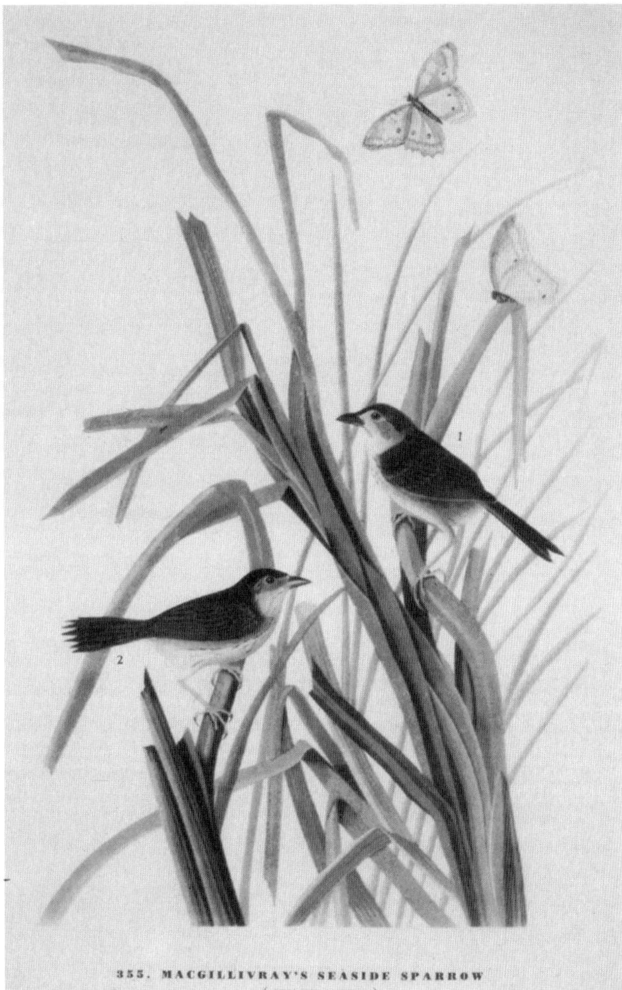

14 Audubon's painting of MacGillivray's Shore Finch, plate CCCLV in *The Birds of America*. Although Audubon described this as a new species, it had been described earlier as the Seaside sparrow *Ammodramus maritimus*, and this is the name now in use.

of the biographies in Audubon's volume; but the full extent of his joint-authorship is not generally known. There seems to have been some mutually satisfactory understanding between the two, which has never been made public. I allow these facts to go on record, not in the least to the disparagement of a brilliant and famous author, but in simple justice to a stronger, sounder, and no less agreeable ornithologist."[15]

The friendship between the two men was observed in a number of ways. When MacGillivray published the second volume of his own *A History of British Birds*,[16] he was able to describe himself, not just as a Fellow of the Royal Society of Edinburgh and a member of the Wernerian Society of Edinburgh, but also as a member of the Natural History Society of Philadelphia, of the Lyceum of New York and of the Literary and Philosophical Society of South Carolina, recognition that must have come through Audubon's influence. MacGillivray's first ornithological work, *Descriptions of the Rapacious Birds of Great Britain*, published in 1836, was dedicated to John James Audubon, "in admiration of his talents as an ornithologist, and in gratitude for many acts of friendship". One of MacGillivray's sons was christened Audubon Felix, and in a similar but longer-lasting way, Audubon named two American birds for his friend. The name of one them, MacGillivray's Shore finch, has since been changed and the bird is now called the Seaside sparrow, but the other, MacGillivray's warbler has retained its common name. Under its description in the *Ornithological Biography* Audubon wrote, "I cannot do better than dedicate this pretty little bird to my excellent friend William MacGillivray Esq. I feel much pleasure in introducing it to the notice of the ornithological world, under a name which I trust will endure as long as the species itself."

There are some more tangible indications of the friendship: in the Zoology Department Museum at Aberdeen University there are a dozen bird skins, with labels in MacGillivray's handwriting, dated between 1831 and 1838 with the words "presented by Mr. Audubon". They were discovered in 1955 buried in dust in a drawer beneath the gallery stairs, where they had probably been for perhaps nearly a century. Of the thousands of bird specimens that Audubon collected and brought to Britain, very few have survived. The collection in Aberdeen is the largest in Britain outside the Natural History Museum in London and, fittingly, one of them is a specimen of MacGillivray's Shore finch, the bird named for him by his friend. One other artefact has recently come to light, a silver snuff-box, in the possession of one of MacGillivray's great-grandchildren in Australia, engraved with the words *To his friend W. MacGillivray from J.J. Audubon.*

Although MacGillivray obviously added much to the

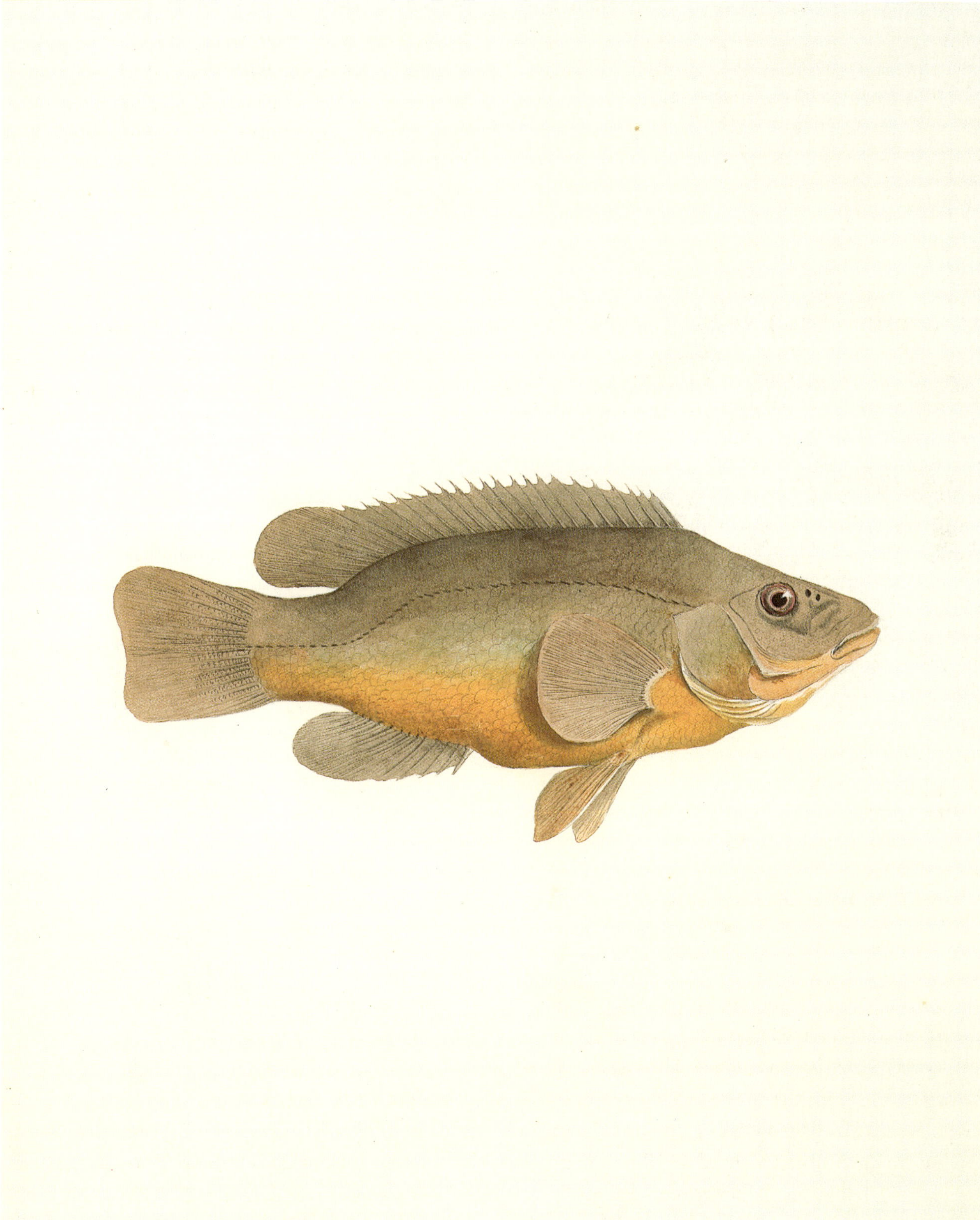

PLATE 36 Ballan wrasse *Labrus bergylta*
[*Labrus.*]

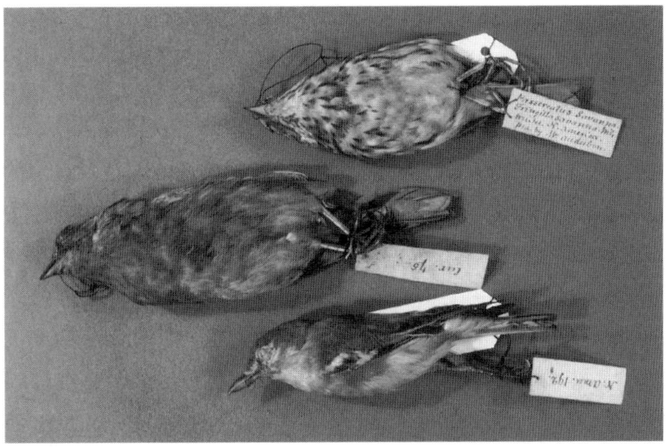

15 Three of the bird specimens given to MacGillivray by Audubon; from the collection of the Aberdeen University Zoology Department Museum

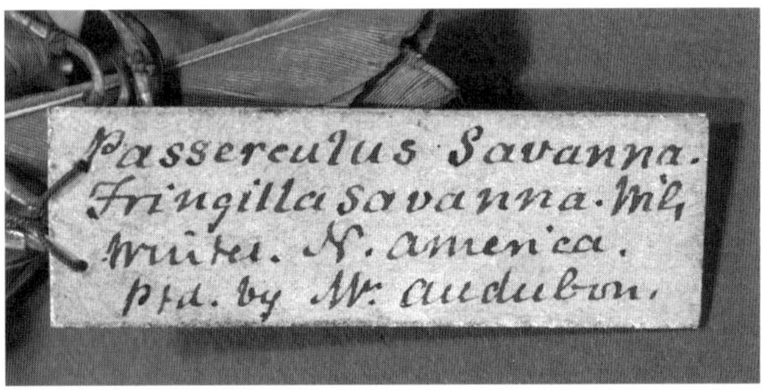

16 The label, in MacGillivray's handwriting, on one of the specimens from Audubon

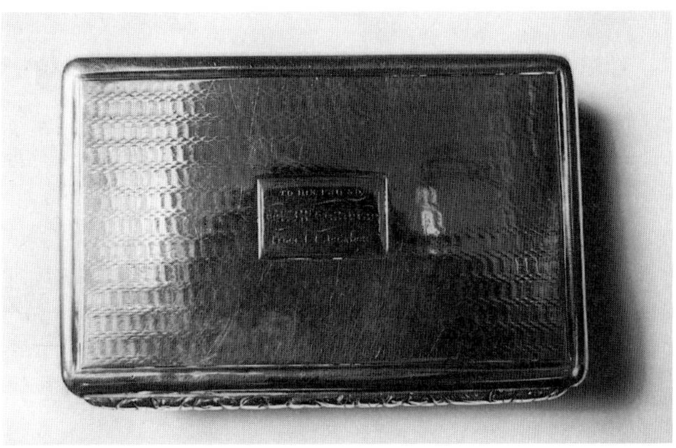

17 This silver snuff box, engraved *To his friend W. MacGillivray from J.J. Audubon,* is in the possession of one of MacGillivray's descendants in Australia. There is no reference to it anywhere in MacGillivray's or Audubon's journals, but it was probably given to MacGillivray when Audubon left for America for the last time in 1839.

Ornithological Biography, the relationship was not entirely one-sided. His own ornithological experience was greatly enriched by the opportunity to study so many American birds, and in addition he clearly learned a great deal from Audubon, the master of the art, about how to paint birds.

NOTES

1 Audubon (1827).
2 Audubon (1826).
3 Audubon, M.R. (1897), vol. 1, pp. 150–51.
4 *Ibid.*, vol. 1, p. 163.
5 *Ibid.*, vol. 1, p. 63.
6 Herrick (1938), vol. 2, pp. 101–03.
7 Harmonson (1937), p. 205.
8 Audubon (1831–39).
9 *Ibid.*, pp. 205–206.
10 Herrick (1938), vol. 2, pp. 126–27.
11 Audubon, M.R. (1897), vol. 1, p. 65.
12 The original notebook is in the Aberdeen University Library, MS 2158.
13 Audubon (1831), vol. 1, pp. xvii–xix.
14 Audubon (1838), vol. 4, p. iii.
15 Coues (1880).
16 MacGillivray (1839).

PLATE 37
Young thrushes with unfinished adult.

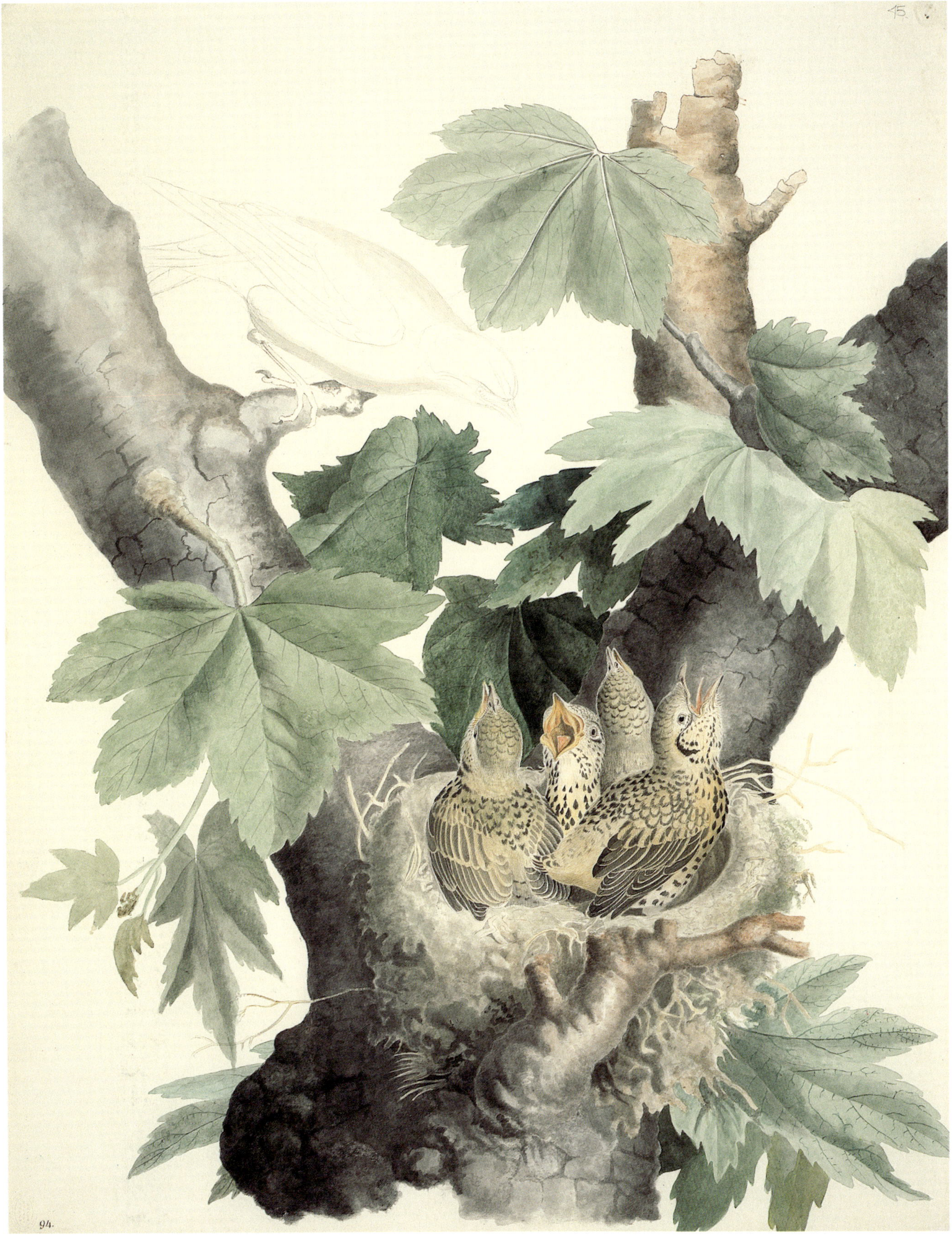
94.
15.

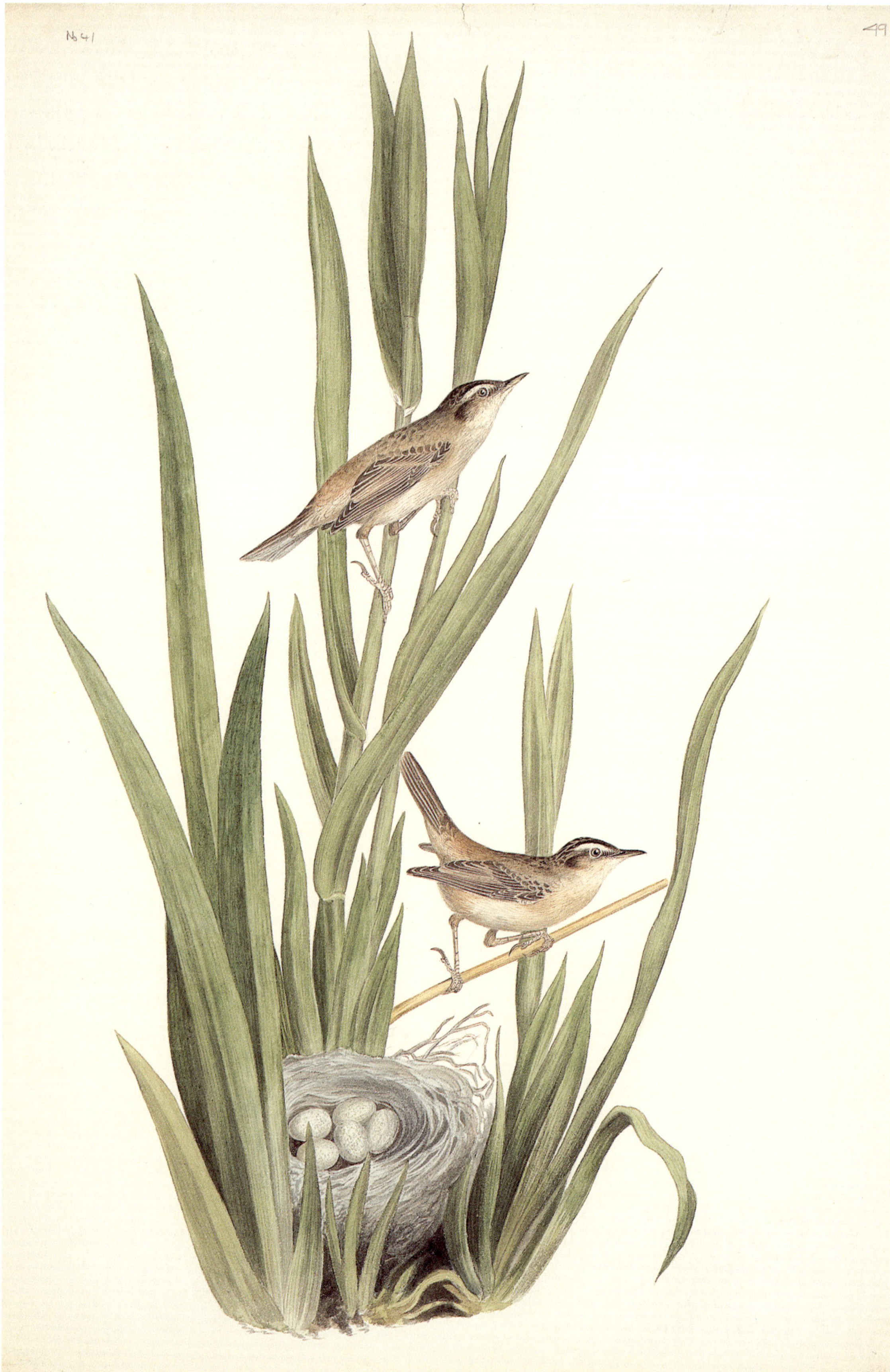
No 41
49.

The 1830s

MacGillivray's Amazing Decade

PLATE 38 Sedge warbler *Acrocephalus schoenobaenus* [Sedge Warbler. *Sylvia phragmitis.*] *Male and Female, from specimens furnished by Mr. Carfrae. Edinburgh, 9th June, 1837. W.McG.*
MacGillivray also noted the plants in the painting as *Iris pseudacoris,* the yellow iris, and *Arundo phragmites,* the common reed (now *Phragmites australis*).

The 1830s were remarkable years for Audubon; he travelled across the Atlantic six times, he explored Labrador, Florida and Texas, collecting specimens, drawing and painting them, spurred on all the time by the pressures of publishing his life's work. For MacGillivray and the amount of work he managed, the decade was even more extraordinary. At its beginning, when he first met Audubon, he was without a settled job, probably earning a little money with translation work, and perhaps some royalties from his first book, the new edition of Withering's *A Systematic Arrangement of British Plants.* In the same year, 1830, there was a second book, *Lives of Eminent Zoologists from Aristotle to Linnaeus,*[1] a book that for MacGillivray must simply have been a commercial proposition; in a similar way, in 1831, he published an edition of *Elements of Botany and Vegetable Physiology,*[2] a straightforward translation from the original French book by Achille Richard. Settled employment came in September that year when, somewhat surprisingly, he became Conservator of the Museum of the Edinburgh Royal College of Surgeons. The appointment of a man with no formal qualifications in medicine, to take charge of a museum devoted to human anatomy and pathology, was an unusual one. On the other hand he was a skilled comparative anatomist and had previously been curator of Jameson's museum, one of the largest of its kind. In 1828, three years before MacGillivray's appointment, the medical establishment in Edinburgh had been rocked by the Burke and Hare 'body-snatching' murders. The then Conservator of the Surgeons' Museum was the famous anatomist Robert Knox. He had been implicated, however unjustly, in the affair and although until then his relationship with the curators of the museum had been a very satisfactory one, things changed dramatically. Knox was ostracized by many of his colleagues and over the next two years various moves by the curators made his position untenable and he resigned. MacGillivray's appointment, from a background with no association with human anatomy, may have been seen as an exercise in public relations by the curators.

Knox must have felt bitter in having to resign. The museum he looked after was desperately inadequate and

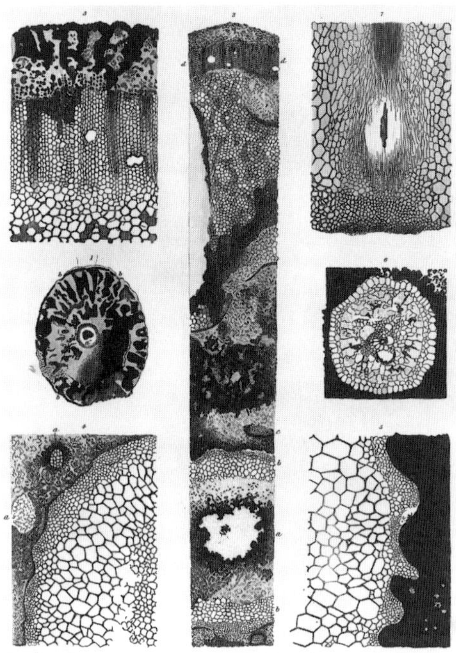

18 In 1831 Henry Witham published a book on fossil vegetables entitled *Observations*. MacGillivray did the sixteen detailed plates of microscopic sections of fossil plants, which are striking examples of his skill as a draughtsman: plate XVIII – Structure of *Lepidodendron*.

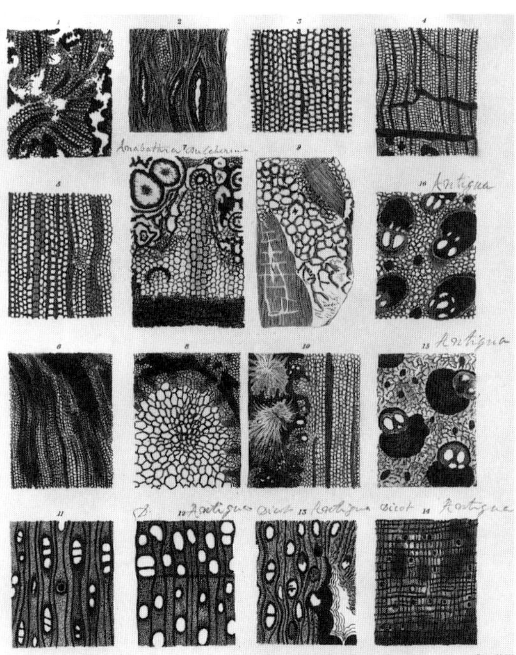

19 Another drawing by MacGillivray from Whitham's book: plate XVI – Fossil vegetables of various classes

overcrowded, indeed, one of the buildings in which most of the collection was housed had been declared unsafe. The architect William Playfair had been commissioned to design a new building and it was almost completed at the time of Knox's resignation. The task of moving the collection into the splendid building where it remains today fell to MacGillivray. Several thousand specimens were rearranged, cleaned, relabelled and placed in position in the new halls with MacGillivray doing most of the work himself, believing "that no benefit would be derived from the interference of others". The work was completed by the summer of 1832, to the obvious satisfaction of the curators. In the minutes of one of their meetings it is noted that:

"Mr. Wood said there could be but one opinion as to the general assiduity and talent which had been shown by the Conservator in the very arduous task of removing and arranging the Museum, which he had performed so much to the satisfaction of the College. He therefore begged to move that the sum of £50, together with the thanks of the College, be presented to the Conservator for the extra labour he has had in the matter."[3]

At the next meeting the motion was unanimously carried and for the next eight years that MacGillivray spent there, his relationship with the curators was a very good one. There seems to have been no conflict between the demands of his position as conservator and his continuing interest in natural history, indeed he was allowed by the curators to be absent from the museum on Saturdays, "for the purpose of allowing him to go into the country and give demonstrations on natural history".

He was also writing; there was a succession of scientific papers, seven in 1831, including one that described the plants of Deeside. From its source 4000 feet up in the Cairngorm Mountains, the River Dee runs for eighty-five miles to the North Sea at Aberdeen. MacGillivray's paper detailed the changes in the distri-

PLATE 39 Sand martin *Riparia riparia*

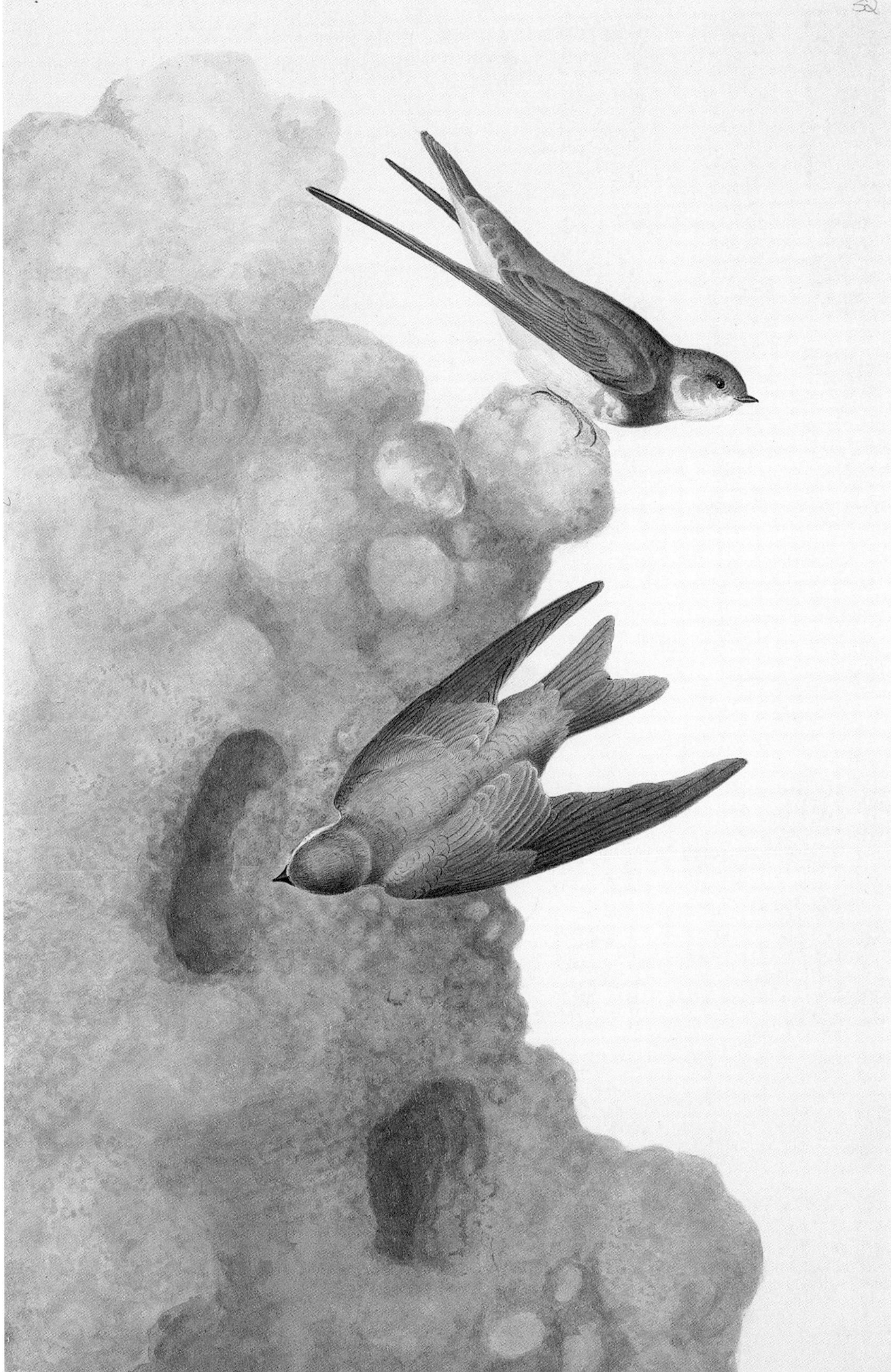

96.

bution of the different species of plants, from the alpine conditions of the mountain tops to the lower stretches of the river. This was the first time that the flora of the region had been described in a distributional way and the paper has been called the first ecological paper to be published in Britain.[4] The demands of his new job slowed down the output of scientific papers; there were just two in 1832, but there was another book, presumably another attempt to make money. This time it was an account of the travels and researches of the German explorer, Alexander von Humboldt.[5]

In the summer of 1833, the curators of the museum decided that MacGillivray should draw up a new catalogue and that it would be helpful to him if he was to visit similar museums in different parts of the country. He approached the task with his customary energy and, in the space of just under four weeks, he managed to visit twenty-four museums, as far afield as Glasgow, Liverpool, Dublin, Bristol and London. The journal he kept is not as detailed as the one kept when he first visited London, and he travelled by stagecoach rather than on foot, but it is full of sketches and brief notes on the different ways of arranging, labelling and displaying museum specimens. His comments are made with his customary candour, for example when he visited William Hunter's anatomical and pathological collection at the Andersonian Institute he found:

"... filth, dirt, and abomination; a few skeletons of quadrupeds, some skulls, and two or three hundred preparations in bottles, all disgustingly dirty and disorderly. I hope I shall not see many collections like them, otherwise I shall renounce the calling, and betake myself to geology, where if there be confusion, it is confusion with design, or to botany, where all is beauty."[6]

Moving on from Glasgow, MacGillivray went by sea to Liverpool. On finding himself beside the new railway station, he took a train to Manchester, where he stayed for half an hour, then returned. He makes no comment about this new form of transport except to say that the cuttings dug out along the track presented fine sections of the new red sandstone. The museum of the Liverpool Royal Institution held little appeal: "everything was ill-arranged, the cases ill-constructed, the ticketing bad."

He crossed the Irish Sea to find Dublin a splendid city, greatly admiring its buildings, but the people did not impress him as much:

"The Irish dialect is detestable to my ear. The people have a peculiar aspect, physically and morally bad. The lower orders are villainous in aspect, and disgustingly filthy, with a decided taste for ragged great coats."[7]

The Dublin entry also includes thoughts on the running of museums in general, and in particular on his own position in Edinburgh:

"If the Edinburgh collection were mine, and I had hands enough, and money enough to set them agoing, I could make it worthy of the nineteenth century. One of the members told me that the placing of bottles on a shelf is nothing. Truly, old one! Any person with but one eye might discover that, although it is not everything, it is yet something which may be desperately mismanaged.

Museums with too many managers must be mismanaged. Who ever heard of any great exploit emanating from ten heads, although ten thousand hands may have executed it. Did a journal with two editors ever prosper? Could two Audubons have drawn the Birds of America? If the ordination of the Museum should go contrary to my ideas, let it go to the condition in which it was when I received it. I never seriously desired the appointment, never called on a member for his vote, did not even inquire when the election was to be, and do not know who voted for or against me. Having undertaken the task, however, I am now interested in it; but, my boys, thwart a little, and you shall see that I can do without you, just as well as you can do without me.

But, more seriously, I have never been so happy in any office, and that just because I have found the members gentlemanly, considerate, and kind – with

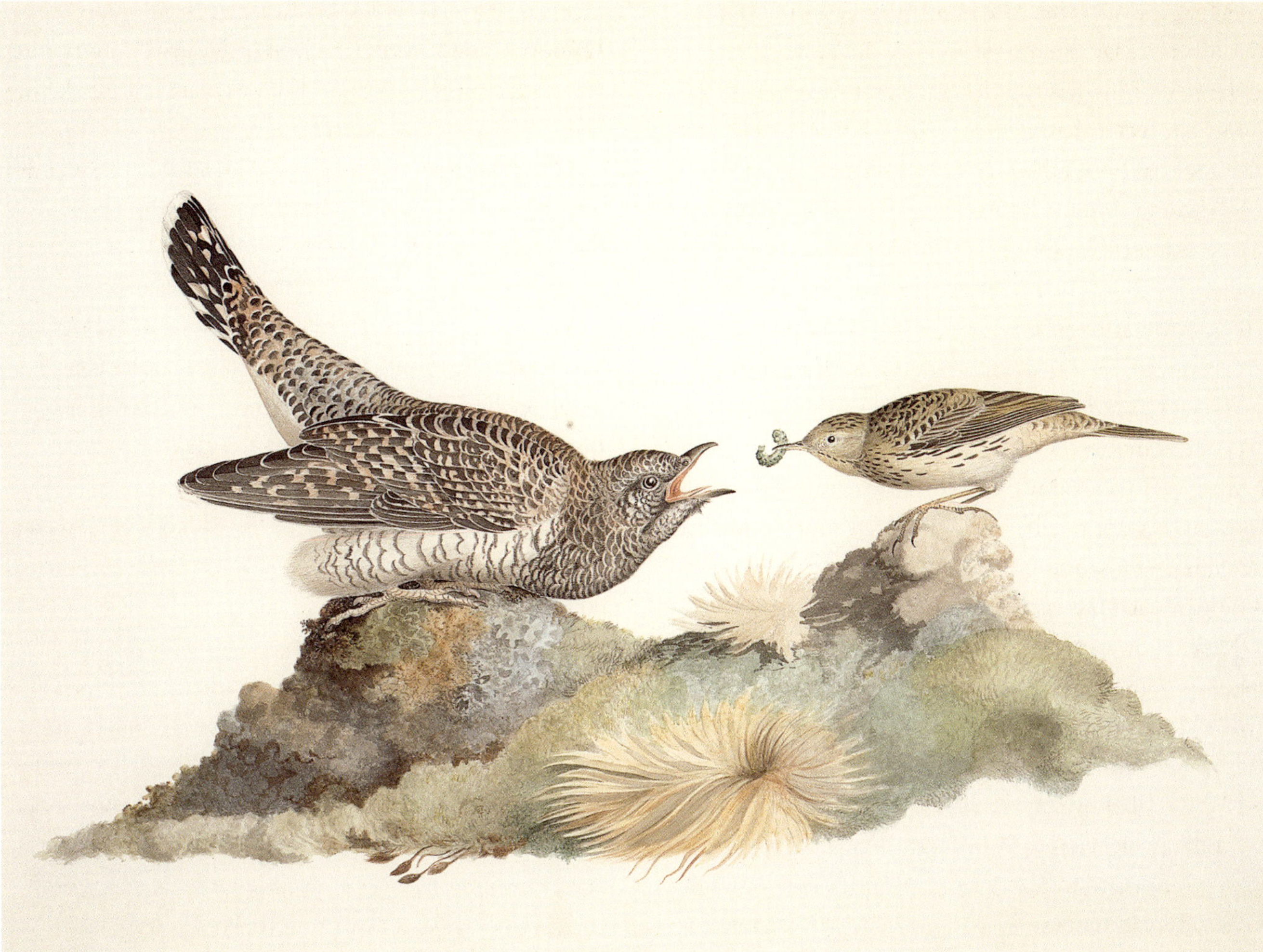

PLATE 40 Cuckoo *Cuculus canorus* and Meadow pipit *Anthus pratensis*
[Cuckoo, *Cuculus canorus* and Common Pipit, *Anthus Pratensis.*] *The former from a young individual shot at Salisbury Craigs, and presented by Mr. Hennen, Edinburgh, July. 1832. WMcG.*

few exceptions – two individuals only. I thank God that I am what I am; that although I have, and have good reason to have, a very low opinion of myself, I have yet been endowed with faculties, the exercise of which will enable me, with the guidance and protection of God, to procure a proper share of the things that belong to this life. As to the next, I have confidence in God, that, having begun, He will accomplish."[8]

Presumably, MacGillivray had no intention of letting the curators in Edinburgh read this part of his journal. It is a revealing comment on his character, exhibiting a strong belief in the correctness of his own idea, an indifference to the opinions of others, and yet a sense of modesty in his own ability, even though this was probably kept to himself. MacGillivray was never one to cultivate influence, and he never worried about making enemies, a lack of concern that was to bring him pain and sorrow in just a few years.

From Dublin he recrossed the Irish Sea to Bristol, and went by stagecoach to London. There he visited ten medical museums, was generally impressed by them, and collected ideas on labelling and presentation that he later used in his own museum.

He returned to Edinburgh by stagecoach, retracing in three days the route through Manchester and Carlisle that had taken him as many weeks on foot fourteen years before.

The minutes of the next meeting of the Royal College of Surgeons noted that the 'Curators have every reason to be pleased with the industry and intelligence displayed by the Conservator in the tour which he has made', approved of his report and appointed a clerk to assist in making out the catalogue.[9] The task was a substantial one; it was to be another year before the work was finally published. For MacGillivray the next two years were taken up with the catalogue, with helping Audubon on the *Ornithological Biography*, and with teaching, but in the corners of his time, for his own work, he was accumulating information on the birds of Britain. He had been doing this for nearly twenty years, ever since he wrote in his North-town journal "that it might not be a mad scheme to attempt the ornithology of Scotland". His first ornithological work was *Descriptions of the Rapacious Birds of Great Britain*, published in 1836. MacGillivray regarded this as his first real work, disregarding his previous translations and compilations as being 'all in the regular way of business'. The Preface to the book has some revealing comments in which he expresses his contempt for most of his fellow naturalists, the cabinet naturalists as he called them, a contempt he shared with Audubon. He wrote:

"From the professed ornithologists I expect little favour, and very certain it is that I desire none. I have observed that students of natural history follow very different paths in the acquisition of knowledge. Some are merely desirous of knowing objects by name. They learn to distinguish the skins of birds in a museum, the shells in a cabinet, and the plants in a herbarium, by fixing upon one or two characters; and they believe that the description of a species may with advantage be confined to a dozen words :- *Homo sapiens* Erectus, capite subgloboso, cauda obsoleta. It is vain to argue with such person. They hate everything that they deem superfluous, they dock their hobbies [hobby-horses] to the rump, crop their ears, and pare their hooves to the quick. It is obvious that a man who knows one plant, or one animal well, has more knowledge than one who can merely name a hundred or a thousand; and for this reason, I would urge that every student of nature should in his researches penetrate a good deal deeper than the cuticle of a plant, the scales of a fish, or the feathers of a bird."[10]

PLATE 41 Hawfinch *Coccothraustes coccothraustes*
[Common Grosbeak. *Coccothraustes vulgaris.*] *From two Females and a Young bird lent by Profr. Jameson. Edinburgh, 9th February, 1833. W.Mc.G.*

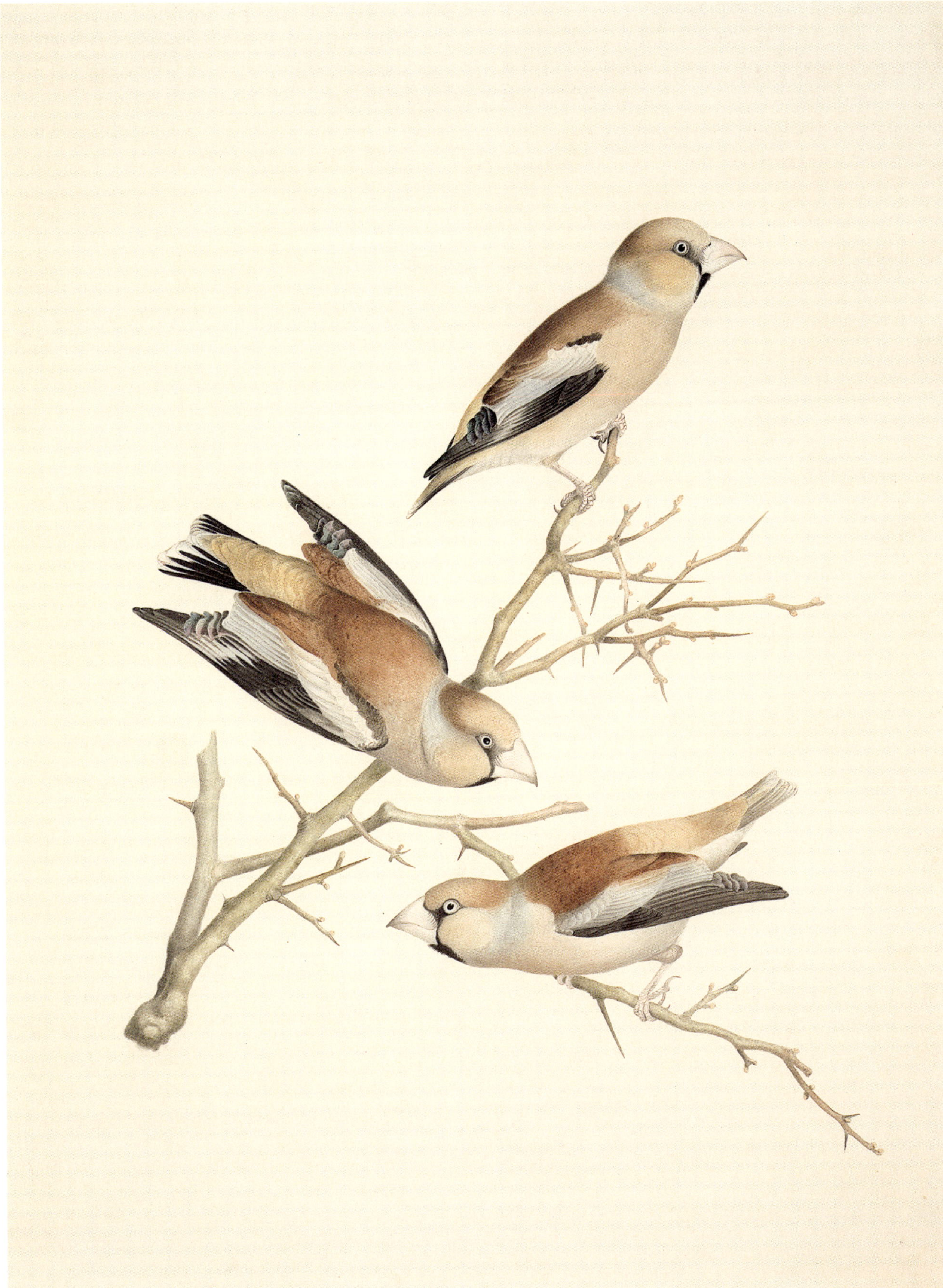

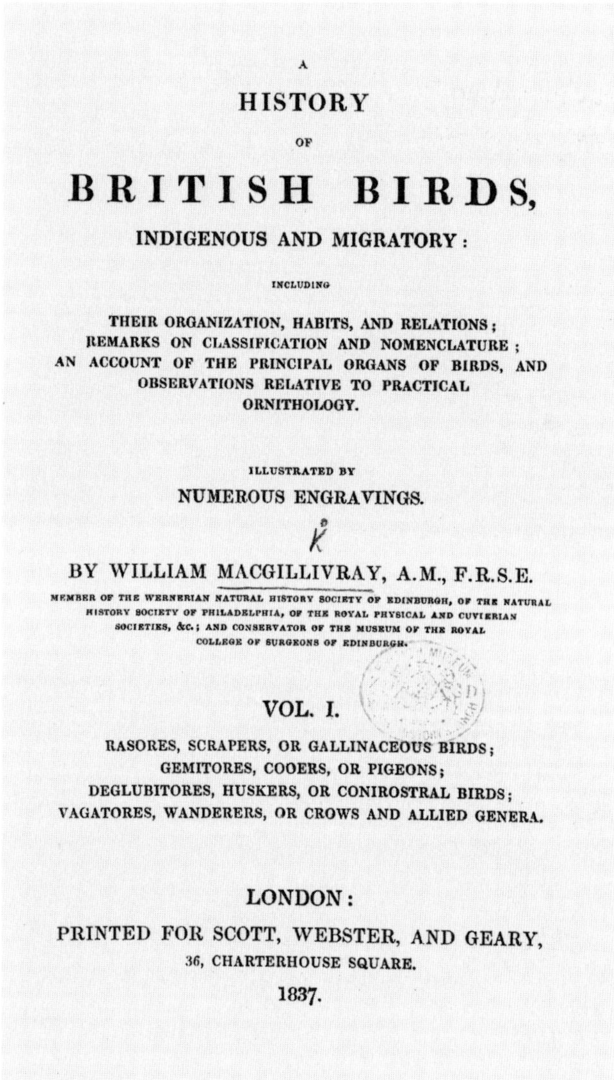
A

HISTORY

OF

BRITISH BIRDS,

INDIGENOUS AND MIGRATORY:

INCLUDING

THEIR ORGANIZATION, HABITS, AND RELATIONS;
REMARKS ON CLASSIFICATION AND NOMENCLATURE;
AN ACCOUNT OF THE PRINCIPAL ORGANS OF BIRDS, AND
OBSERVATIONS RELATIVE TO PRACTICAL
ORNITHOLOGY.

ILLUSTRATED BY
NUMEROUS ENGRAVINGS.

BY WILLIAM MACGILLIVRAY, A.M., F.R.S.E.

MEMBER OF THE WERNERIAN NATURAL HISTORY SOCIETY OF EDINBURGH, OF THE NATURAL HISTORY SOCIETY OF PHILADELPHIA, OF THE ROYAL PHYSICAL AND CUVIERIAN SOCIETIES, &C.; AND CONSERVATOR OF THE MUSEUM OF THE ROYAL COLLEGE OF SURGEONS OF EDINBURGH.

VOL. I.

RASORES, SCRAPERS, OR GALLINACEOUS BIRDS;
GEMITORES, COOERS, OR PIGEONS;
DEGLUBITORES, HUSKERS, OR CONIROSTRAL BIRDS;
VAGATORES, WANDERERS, OR CROWS AND ALLIED GENERA.

LONDON:
PRINTED FOR SCOTT, WEBSTER, AND GEARY,
36, CHARTERHOUSE SQUARE.
1837.

20 The title page of MacGillivray's *A History of British Birds*

Just why MacGillivray felt so strongly contemptuous of many of his contemporaries, or why he felt the need to express it so publicly, is not clear. Perhaps there was a lurking sense of inferiority stemming from his background, perhaps it was a strong streak of Scottish independence in his nature, but more likely, he simply knew, and in an almost obsessive way needed everyone else to know, that the natural world could only properly be studied and understood by observing it in the field. Whatever the reason, he was making plenty of enemies for himself, enemies who were to have their day soon enough.

Descriptions of the Rapacious Birds of Great Britain was in some ways a trial run for MacGillivray. For twenty years he had been planning his great work, a complete history of British birds, the culmination of his dream to one day "merit the name of ornithologist". In spite of all the other demands on his time, the first volume of *A History of British Birds* was published on 1 May 1837. It ran to more than 600 pages with detailed descriptions of nearly fifty species.[11] The book was a totally new approach to ornithology and to the classification of birds. Early attempts at classifying plants and animals tried to arrange what were seen as God's creations into some kind of order and to discover the laws by which the Creator had produced the world. The characters on which any particular system was based were subject to the personal judgement of the individual taxonomist and, in the classification of birds, these characters were most often beaks and feet. For example, Linnaeus established an order of birds "with curved beaks" that included such widely separated species as hoopoes, treecreepers and hummingbirds. MacGillivray, with his background in anatomy, looked beneath the skin, reasoning that internal structures were just as important in determining the affinities between different species. He argued that if the form of the beak was an important character then the whole of the digestive tract, the tongue, the crop, the stomach and the various caecal appendages were just as important; indeed he believed them to be more so. He had dissected and drawn the alimentary canals of hundreds of specimens, and used his knowledge of them in the classification system that he put forward. In his system he also introduced his own nomenclature, producing, without any real justification, new terms such as the Volitatores, Palpatores and Deglubitores, as well as the Cooers, Huskers and Gropers.

PLATE 42 Chaffinch *Fringilla coelebs*

Males, Female, and Young on a poplar twig. From individuals shot near Cramond. Edinburgh, 26th December, 1831.

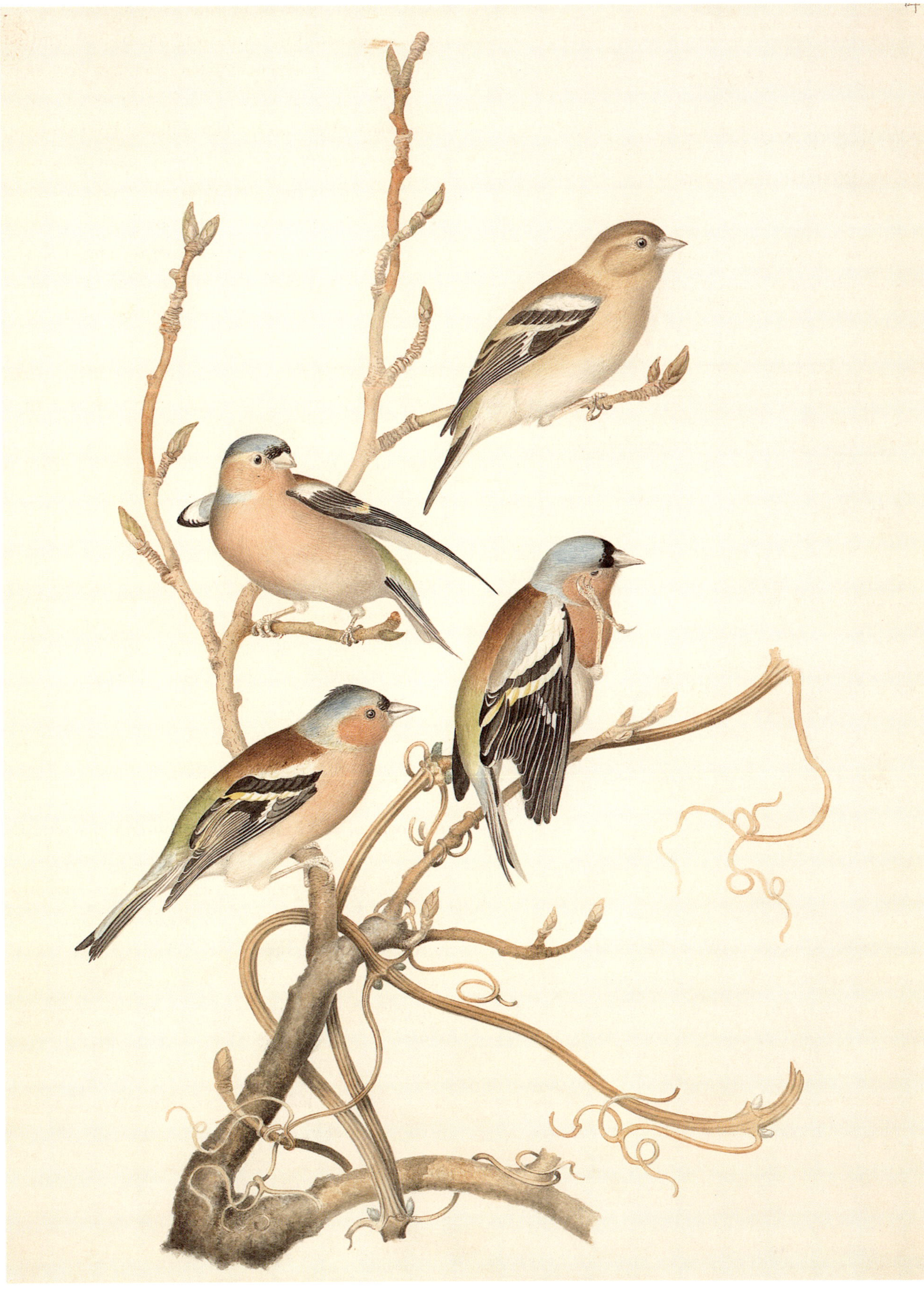

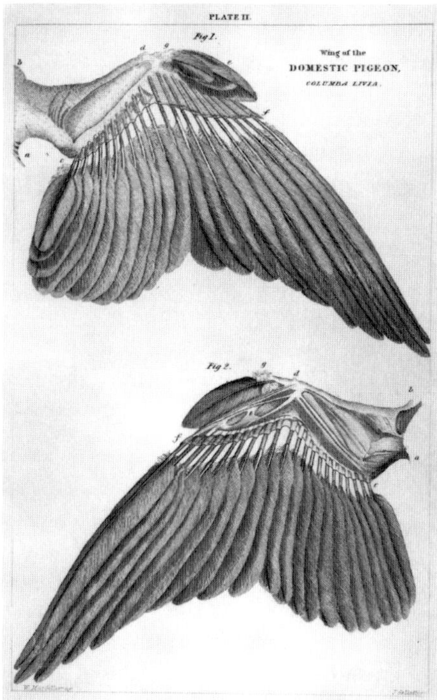

21 Wing of the domestic pigeon *Columba livia* from *A History of British Birds*, vol. 1 (1837), plate II

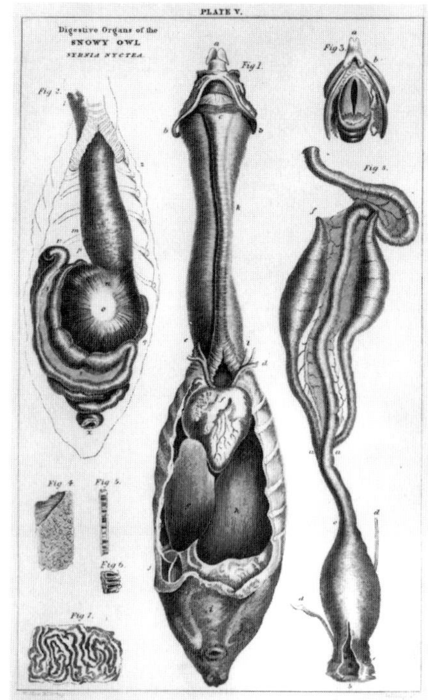

22 Digestive organs of the snowy owl *Nyctea scandiaca; Syrnia nyctea* from *A History of British Birds*, vol. 1 (1837), plate V

Not content with putting forward his own system, MacGillivray was fiercely critical of the efforts of previous authors:

"Methods spring up and die like mushrooms, and for the same reason:– they are composed of flimsy and unsubstantial materials, easily elaborated; and having no solid frame to give them stability they fall suddenly into decay, withered by the breath of criticism, which but serves to invigorate that which is possessed of real stamina."[12]

These were strong words, critical of earlier workers, and unfortunately for MacGillivray, were soon to be turned against him. His classification system had no more of a solid frame to it than earlier attempts; the foundation that taxonomy needed was to come more than twenty years later when Darwin published *The Origin of Species*, which explained the theory of evolution by natural selection, bringing some order to classification systems, basing them on evolutionary relationships rather than on appearance or structure.

A History of British Birds, however, is much more than dry anatomy or the detailed descriptions of dead skins; at the time it was published, ornithology needed knowledge of living birds, their appearance, their distribution

PLATE 43 Crossbill *Loxia curvirostra*
[European Crossbill. *Crucirostra europea.*] *From stuffed specimens lent by Mr. Macduff Carfrae, Edinburgh. Adult male and Female shot in June 1836. Young Male in winter. On a branch of* Pinus sylvestris [Scots Pine] – *planted. Edinburgh. 11th March, 1837. W.Mc.G.*

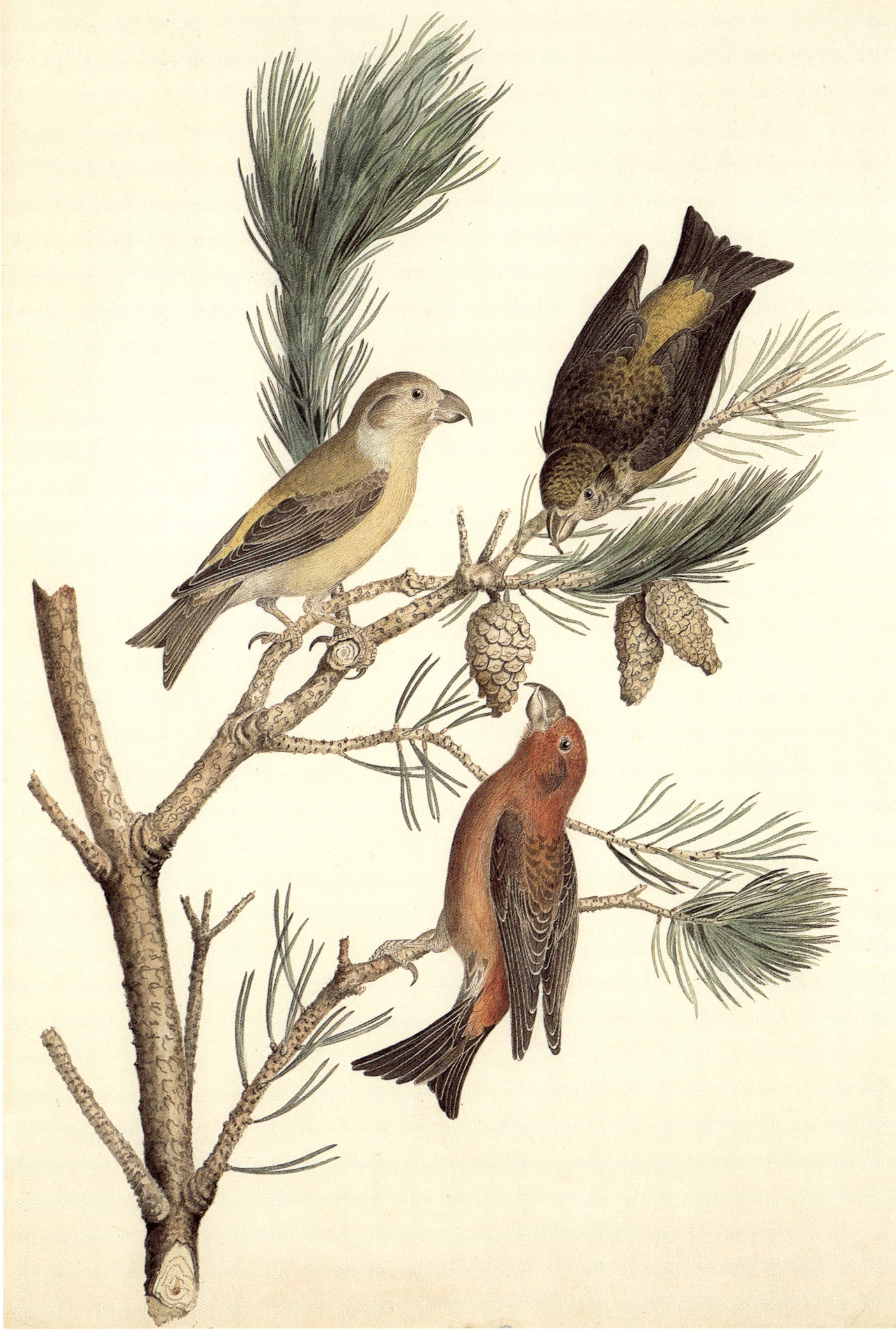
72

and their behaviour, as much as a classification system. MacGillivray's style was unique; he could describe an anatomical structure in the cold, remote language of science but on the next page could write with a warm, often affectionate manner. For example, writing about the humble House sparrow, he said:

"Rustic sparrows are always more beautiful than those residing in large towns, the latter generally having their plumage soiled by smoke and dirt. Indeed the difference is striking, and the country sparrow is really a beautiful bird, having none of that slovenly appearance which has gained for it in towns the appellation of a vulgar and dirty-looking creature. But this is equally the case with our own species; for the farm-servant or field-labourer is a cleanly, robust, and healthy animal, compared with the artisan of the city, begrimed with filth, pallid in countenance, feeble, bloated in frame, and of unenduring constitution."[13]

Interspersed with the chapters describing the various species of birds, there are "Lessons in Practical Ornithology" consisting not just of practical hints about bird-skinning and egg collecting, but of personal accounts of bird-watching excursions around Edinburgh. Reading MacGillivray today, his characteristic style has a charm of its own, but his contemporaries were less pleased by it, and by the book generally. When the reviews appeared, they were written mainly by cabinet-naturalists, men who had previously suffered the lash of MacGillivray's pen. They took their chance for revenge, well illustrated by this review:

"The History of British Birds is a thick octavo volume of 531 pages, having for its object 'to lay before the public, descriptions of the birds of Great Britain, more extended, and if possible, more correct than any previously offered.' We do not wish to appear unnecessarily critical regarding the manner in which Mr. MacGillivray has accomplished this object, but we should not act fairly to our subscribers were we to say that it is done successfully. The writing appears to us an unaffected attempt to imitate the styles of Isaac Walton and of Audubon, which, being extremely peculiar, can only be relished in the originals, and here, as in the case of similar imitations, we desiderate their freshness, and dislike the misplaced quaintness of expression. It appears trifling, while the meaning is by no means distinctly conveyed. The incidental remarks and digressions liberally dispersed throughout the volume are sometimes expressed scarcely with a kindly feeling, and seem to show an inclination to undervalue the opinions of others when a unison of ideas cannot be found.

The book is composed of two parts; the first, introductory; the second, commences the history of the birds themselves belonging to four of the orders, which our author has thought necessary to form on principles of his own, and which are doubtless excellent and admirable in the eyes of their inventor.

The introductory portion contains first 'remarks on classification systems and nomenclature' and samples of systems are given in outlines of those of Linnaeus and Vieillot. Next follows an exposition of our author's own system. This is primarily divided into four groups, sections, or sub-classes, determined by their mode of life, and they come in the place of the familiar divisions of land and water birds. They are I. Aerial birds or Volitoriae: II. Terrestrial birds or Ambulatoriae; III. Amphibious or wading birds or Grallatoriae; IV. Aquatic birds, or Natatoriae. These again are separated into no fewer than 19 Orders, each section containing four, except the second, in which seven have been placed. We cannot consider this system more simple or comprehensive than many of its predecessors, and we do not think the nomenclature

PLATE 44 Linnet *Carduelis cannabina*

[Brown Linnet. *Fringilla cannabina.*] *Two Males and a Female on* Fagus sylvaticus [beech]. *From individuals shot by W. and John MacGillivray, near Edinburgh. 1st January 1834. Edinburgh. 3rd January, 1834.*

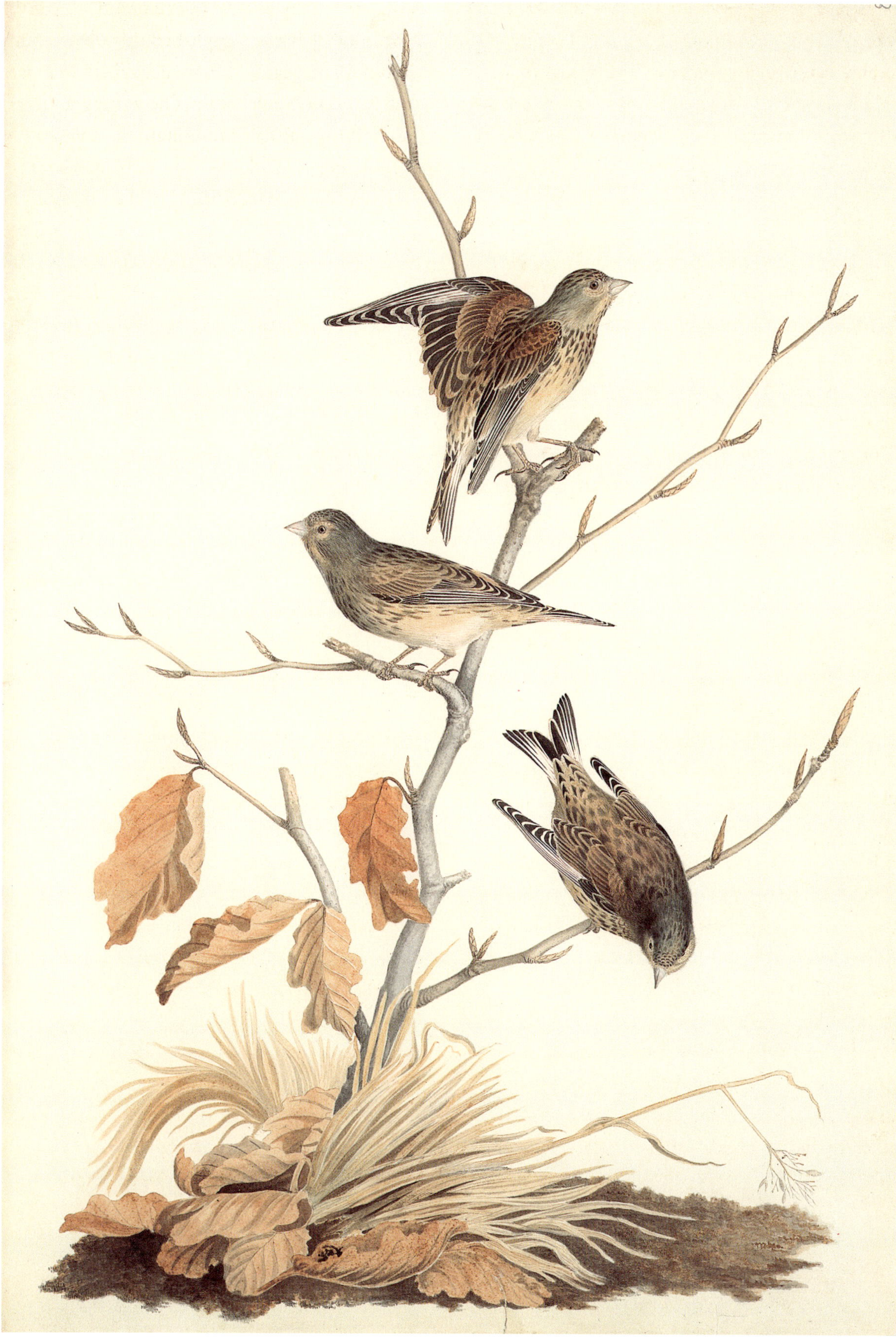

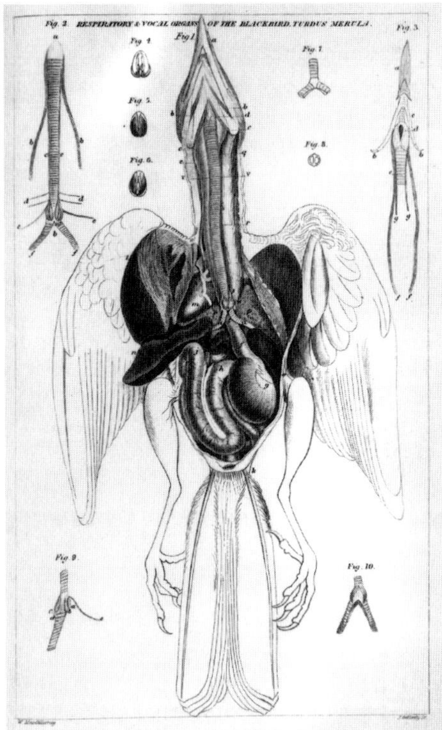

23 Respiratory and vocal organs of the blackbird *Turdus merula* from *A History of British Birds*, vol. 2 (1839), plate X

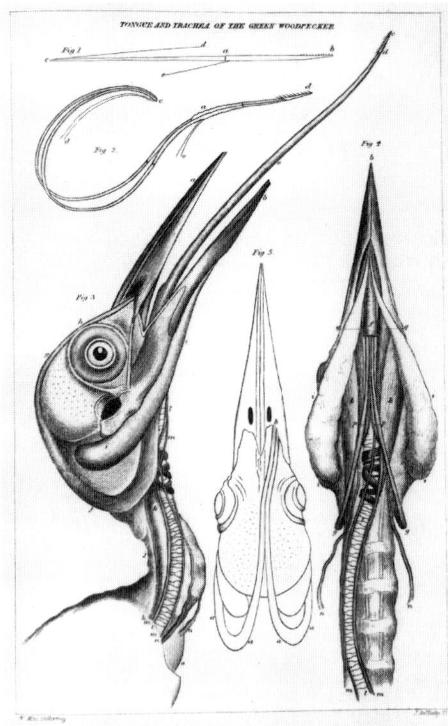

24 Tongue and trachea of the green woodpecker *Picus viridis* from *A History of British Birds*, vol. 3 (1840), plate XV

improved by the introduction of sectional, or generic titles, such as Volitatores, Deglubitores, Raptatores, Palpatores, and the rest, or in another language, of Plunderers, Cooers, Huskers, Gropers, Probers, and so on; but 'methods spring up and die like mushrooms, and for the same reason; they composed of flimsy and unsubstantial materials easily elaborated.' [How easily MacGillivray's own words were turned against him.] Of the concluding part of the introduction, 'Remarks on the structure of birds', we have a higher opinion. This part, though short, is well done. The anatomy is concisely detailed, without any of the affectedness of style which we dislike so much elsewhere, and it is illustrated by nine engravings well wrought from the pencil of the author, exhibiting views of the osteology, the muscular arrangement, and the digestive organs in the principal divisions.

The second part of the book, occupying 500 pages is devoted to the history of four of the orders 'Rasores, Scrapers, Gemitores, Cooers, Deglubitores, Huskers, Vagatores, Wanderers.' This description or historical part wants condensation; it is much too lengthened, without bringing together the information which is really of use to the student of British ornithology. It is illustrated by woodcuts of most of the parts which are essential in the system, as generic, many of which are well drawn and executed. We are treated also with 'Practical Ornithology', in Chapters

PLATE 45 Whitethroat *Sylvia communis*
[Whitethroat. *Sylvia cinerea.*] *Young in first plumage. From an individual shot on Corstorphine Hill.* Rubus idaeus [raspberry bush]. *Edinburgh, June 1831. W.Mc.G.*

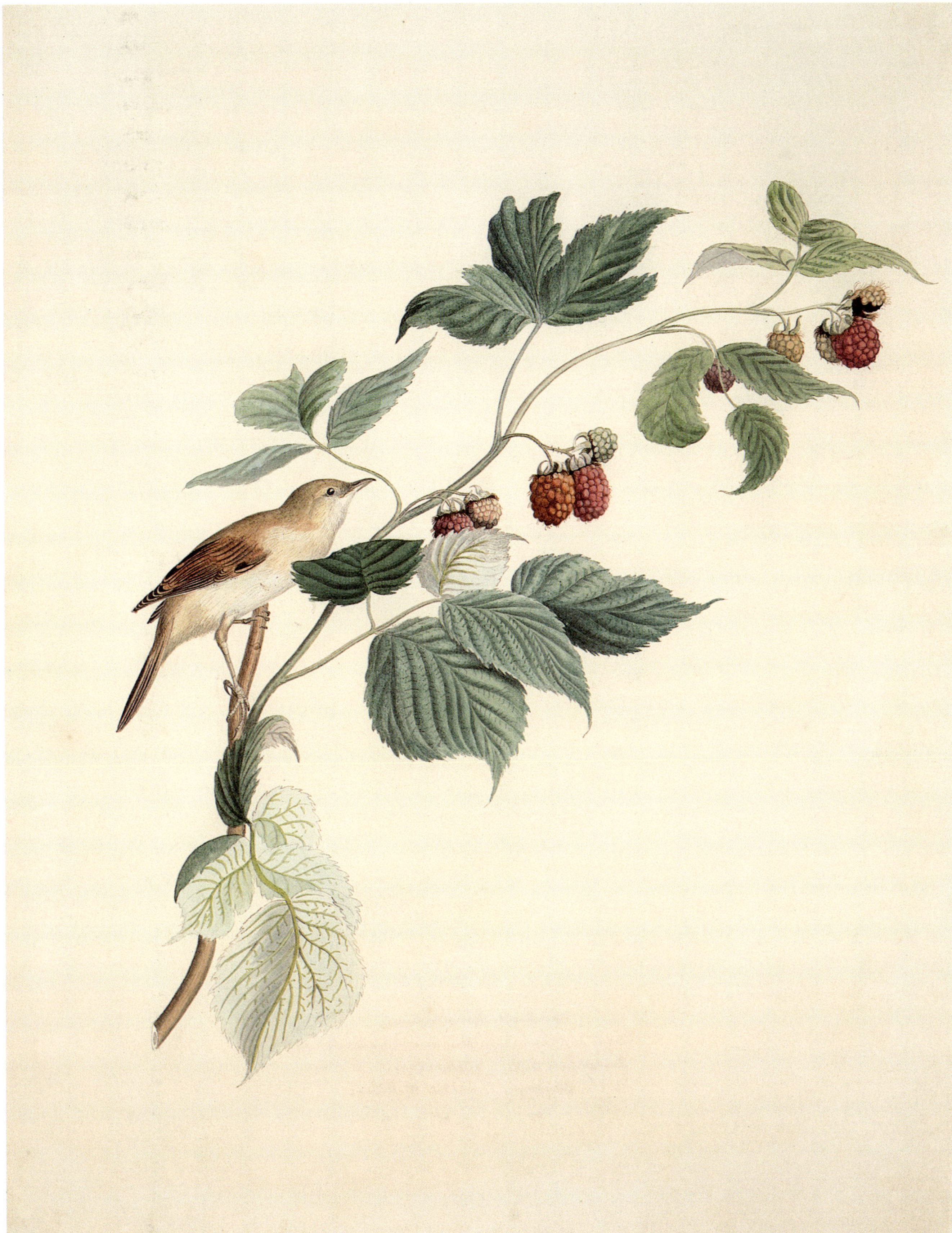

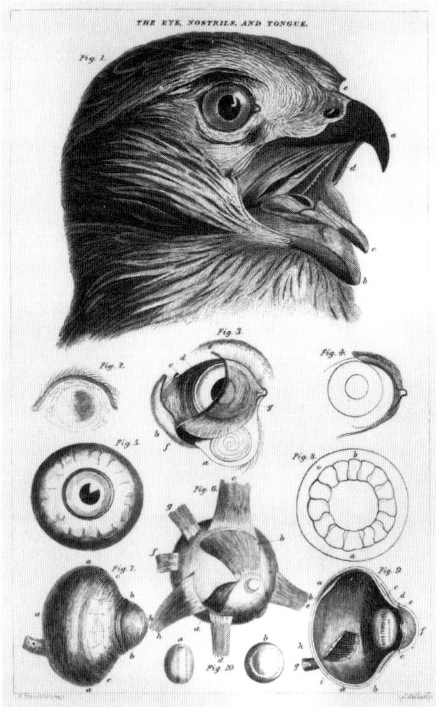

25 The eye, nostrils, and tongue of rapacious birds from *A History of British Birds*, vol. 3 (1840), plate XVII

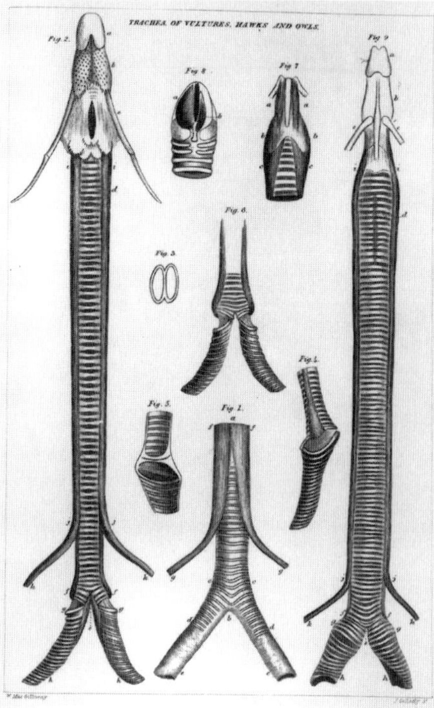

26 Trachea of vultures, hawks and owls from *A History of British Birds*, vol. 3 (1840), plate XIX

1, 2, 3, and 4, but these lesson we dislike *in toto*, both in substance and in spirit."[14]

Beneath the cool, gentlemanly language this was a devastatingly cruel review. MacGillivray's classification scheme was dismissed without a single argument being put against it, and the greatest part of the book, some 500 pages of the most detailed descriptions of British birds that had ever been published were cast aside, in half a dozen lines, as being too long. Other reviews were just as condemning, as the enemies that MacGillivray had so carelessly made took their opportunity. The effect they had on the book is well described by the ornithologist W.H. Mullens, writing in *British Birds* in 1909:

"The word went forth that MacGillivray's work was choked with anatomical details. The half-truth repelled the public. *A History of British Birds* was doomed to oblivion and the chamber-naturalists returned to their discussions in triumph. That they had incidentally broken the heart of the greatest ornithologist that this country has ever produced, that they nearly prevented the completion of one of the greatest books on British birds, was to them of course, not a matter of the least importance."[15]

Perhaps MacGillivray should not have been too surprised by the treatment handed out to him. He had often professed not to care what others thought of him,

PLATE 46 Blackcap *Sylvia atricapilla*
[Black-capped warbler. *Sylvia Atricapilla.*] *The male from a specimen shot near Edinburgh, on the 6th June 1837. and lent by Mr. Carfrae. Edinburgh, 7th June, 1837. W.Mc.G.*

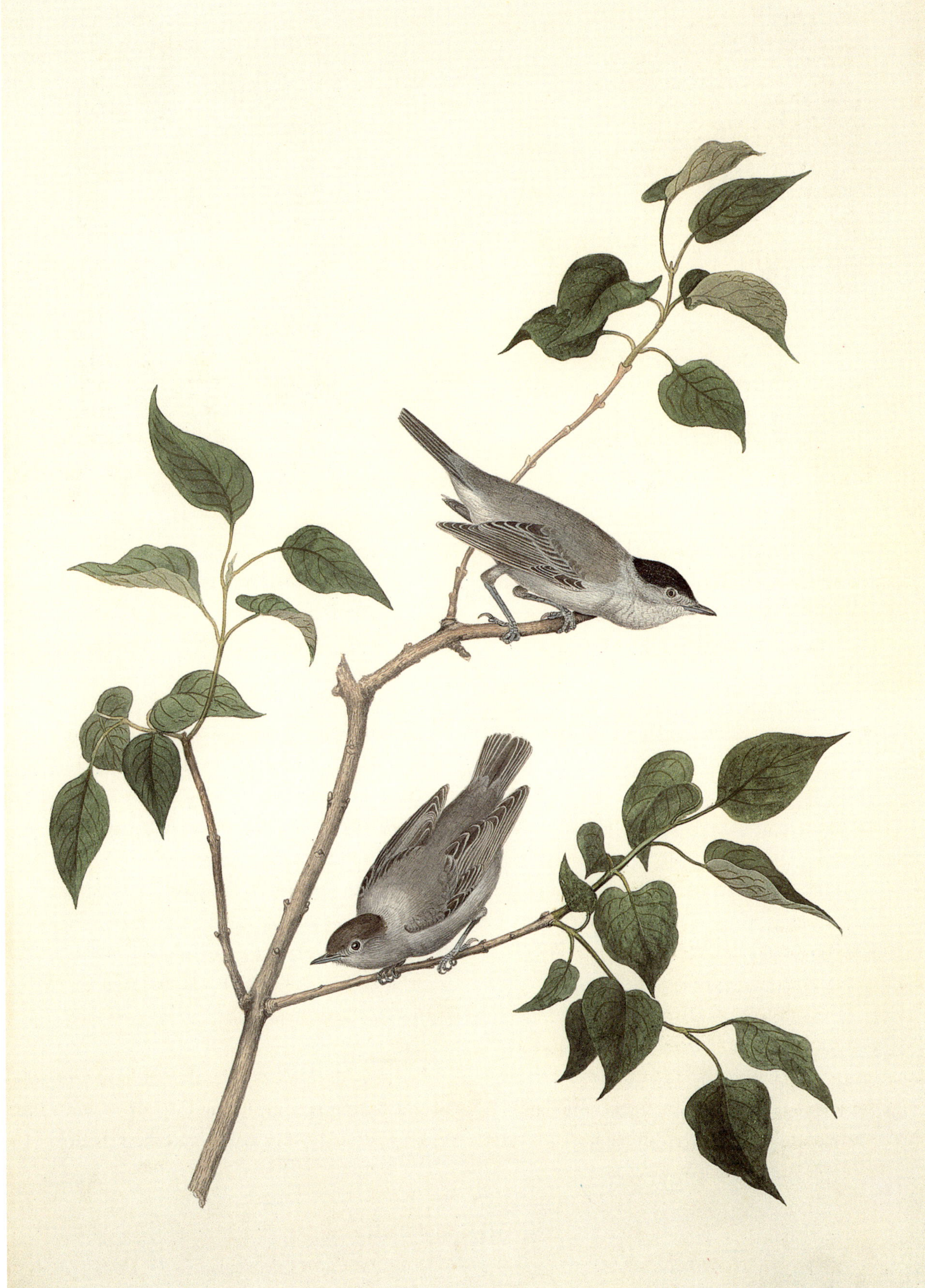

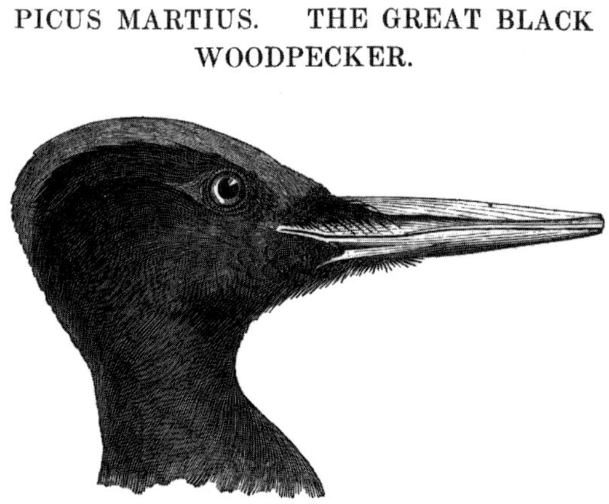

27 Black woodpecker *Dryocopus martius*; 'great black woodpecker', *Picus martius* from *A History of British Birds*, vol. 3 (1840), p. 77

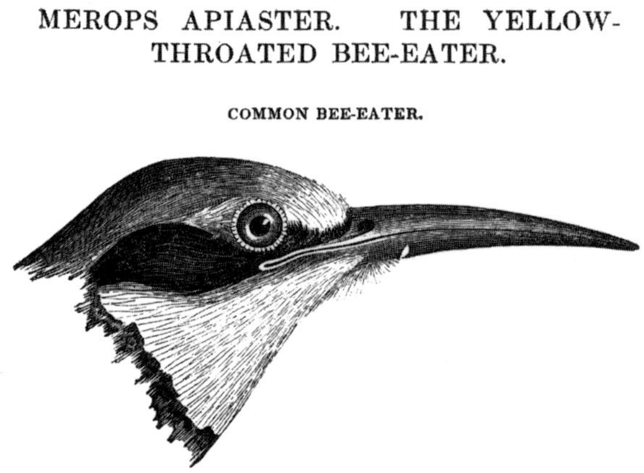

28 Bee-eater *Merops apiaster*; 'yellow-throated bee-eater' from *A History of British Birds*, vol. 3 (1840), p. 685

but *A History of British Birds* was so much a part of him and his life's work that the reception it received must have hurt deeply. He never expressed any feelings in public but in one of his notebooks, again held in Aberdeen University Library, there is this revealing piece, written in characteristic style:

"Many bright stars have risen on the horizon of our ornithological hemisphere, some to increase in brightness, others to twinkle for a season, and fade. Montagu still blazes with unshorn beams while Bewick, Selby, Wood, Blythe, Yarrell, and Jardine, clustering to form a constellation whose mingling rays send enough of light over the land to enable the benighted traveller to escape immersion in a peat marsh. Mine too has appeared among the mists of Cairngorm, the haunt of the ptarmigan and raven. There it glimmers in the north, now observed by the cold grey clouds that cling to the summit of the mouldering crags of red granite, bleached by the rains and sunshine of a thousand summers, now sending a faint light through a ragged break in the mists, now flaring with momentary effulgence and anon fading into the dark waters of Loch Avon. On Bennabuird a mightier and more massive churl interposed his broad bulk between it and the valley of the Dee, thinking thereby to prevent the natives from observing it, but a blast from the Braeriach has swept him towards the land of the Saxon and sent him howling to his gods. Yes, there it is struggling through the mists, now obscured, now twinkling, glimmering, glowing Star of the North! Will thy course be turned toward the zenith? Art thou a vapour kindled to shed a feeble light on the land, to shoot off into an eccentric path, and be at length quenched in the foul waters of human scorn. Shine on little star, and as thou risest higher, let thy rays shine brighter and let the traveller bless thy gentle light."[16]

The "twinkling, glimmering, glowing Star of the North" did shine on. Volume 2 of *A History of British Birds* appeared in 1839,[17] to be followed by volume 3 in 1840.[18]

PLATE 47 Yellowhammer *Emberiza citrinella*
[Yellow Bunting. *Emberiza Citrinella.*] *Male, Female, and Young, on a twig of* Rosa canina [dog rose]. *From individuals shot by W. MacGillivray, near Edinburgh. Edinburgh, 3rd November, 1831.*

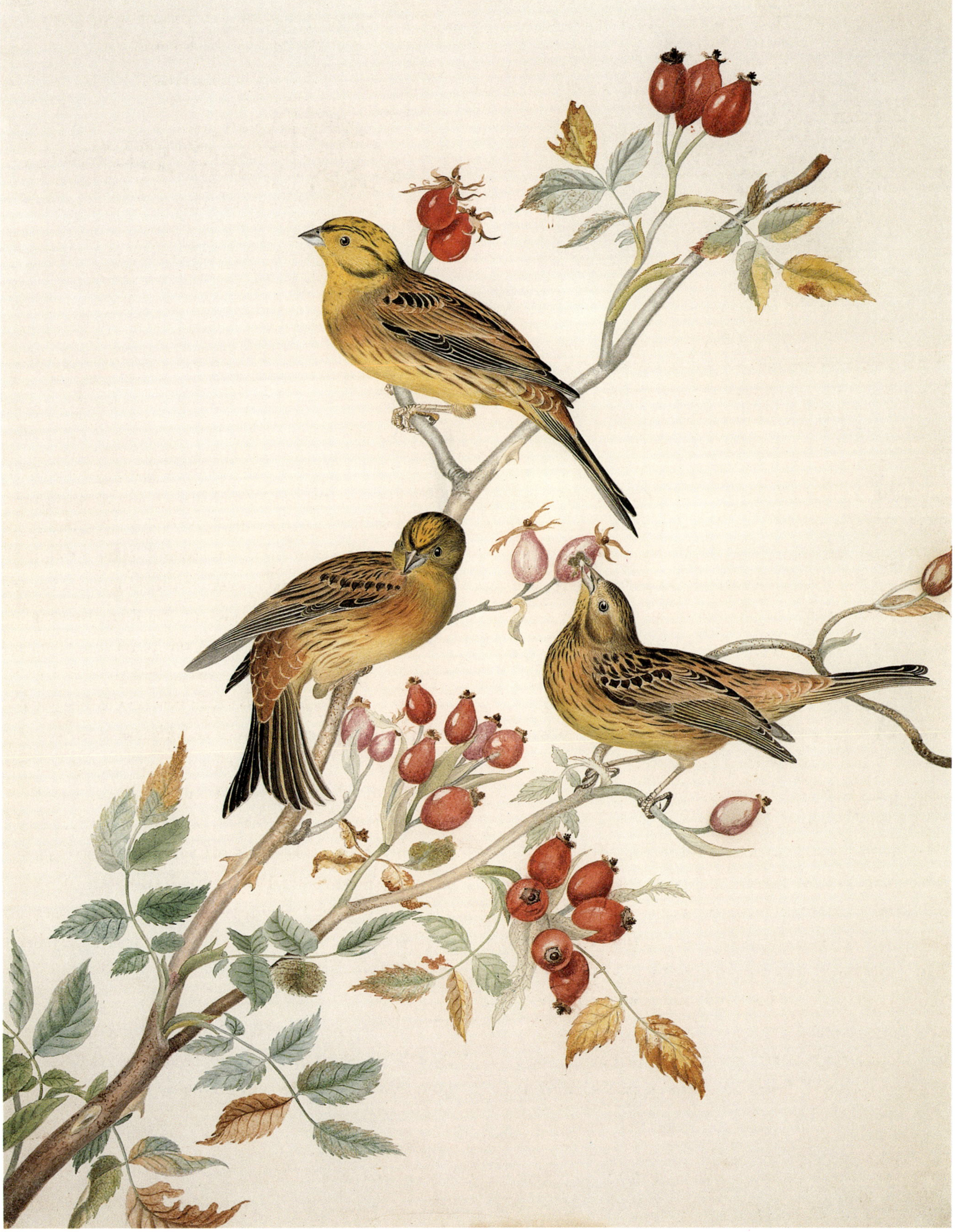

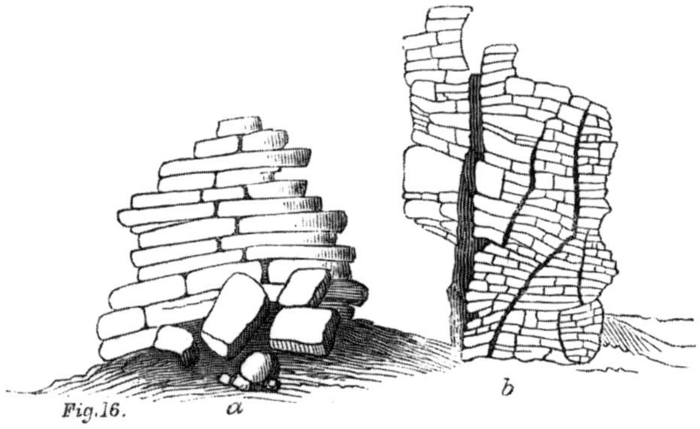

29 The structure of granite
from *A Manual of Geology*, p. 86, 1840

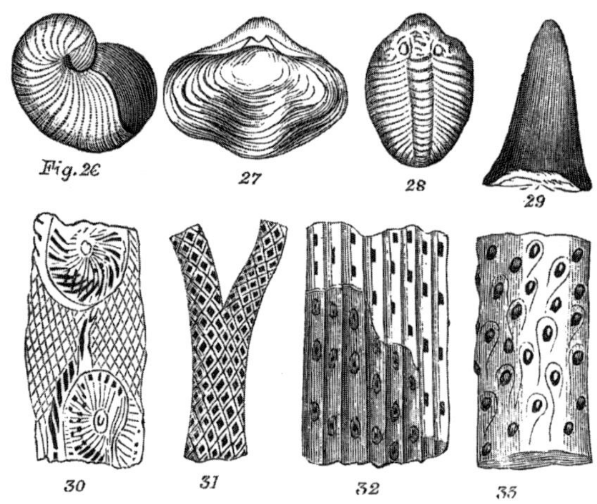

30 A variety of different shells
from *A Manual of Geology*, p. 126, 1840

Although many of the reviews were critical in a very personal way, much of MacGillivray's work was highly idiosyncratic. His classification scheme, based largely on the structure of the digestive system, had no real taxonomic basis to it and the hours and hours of work that he did, dissecting and drawing hundreds of bird intestines were largely wasted. He also had some strange ideas about the common names of birds. For example, it is hard to see a good reason for deciding to call the Redshank, the Common redshank tatler, or the Common sandpiper, the White-breasted weet-weet.

The first three volumes of MacGillivray's work were a commercial failure for his London-based publisher Scott, Webster and Geary, and MacGillivray himself did not make a penny from them. Indeed, they cost him money because, in an effort to encourage publishers to get the last volumes out, he invested some of his own money in the company, money they promptly lost for him. The two final volumes were not to appear for another twelve years. There is no information on why MacGillivray went to a London firm rather than an Edinburgh one, on how the books were advertised or how many copies of each were sold. They were big books – volume three had more than 750 pages – and MacGillivray might have been better served if they had been issued in parts, to a list of subscribers, making them more accessible to the public.

Unfortunately for MacGillivray and his publishers, as well as receiving critical reviews, the first two volumes appeared at the same time as another major work, William Yarrell's own, identically named *A History of British Birds.*[19] This was published in a series of parts, was written in a neat concise style and was illustrated with attractive woodcuts. It became the standard work on British ornithology for many years, overshadowing MacGillivray's more detailed, more scientific work.

Somewhere in this extraordinary period in his life, he also found the time in 1838 to write a volume for Sir William Jardine's *Naturalist's Library, A History of British Quadrupeds;*[20] in 1840 he wrote *A Manual of Geology*[21] and

PLATE 48 Reed bunting *Emberiza schoeniclus*

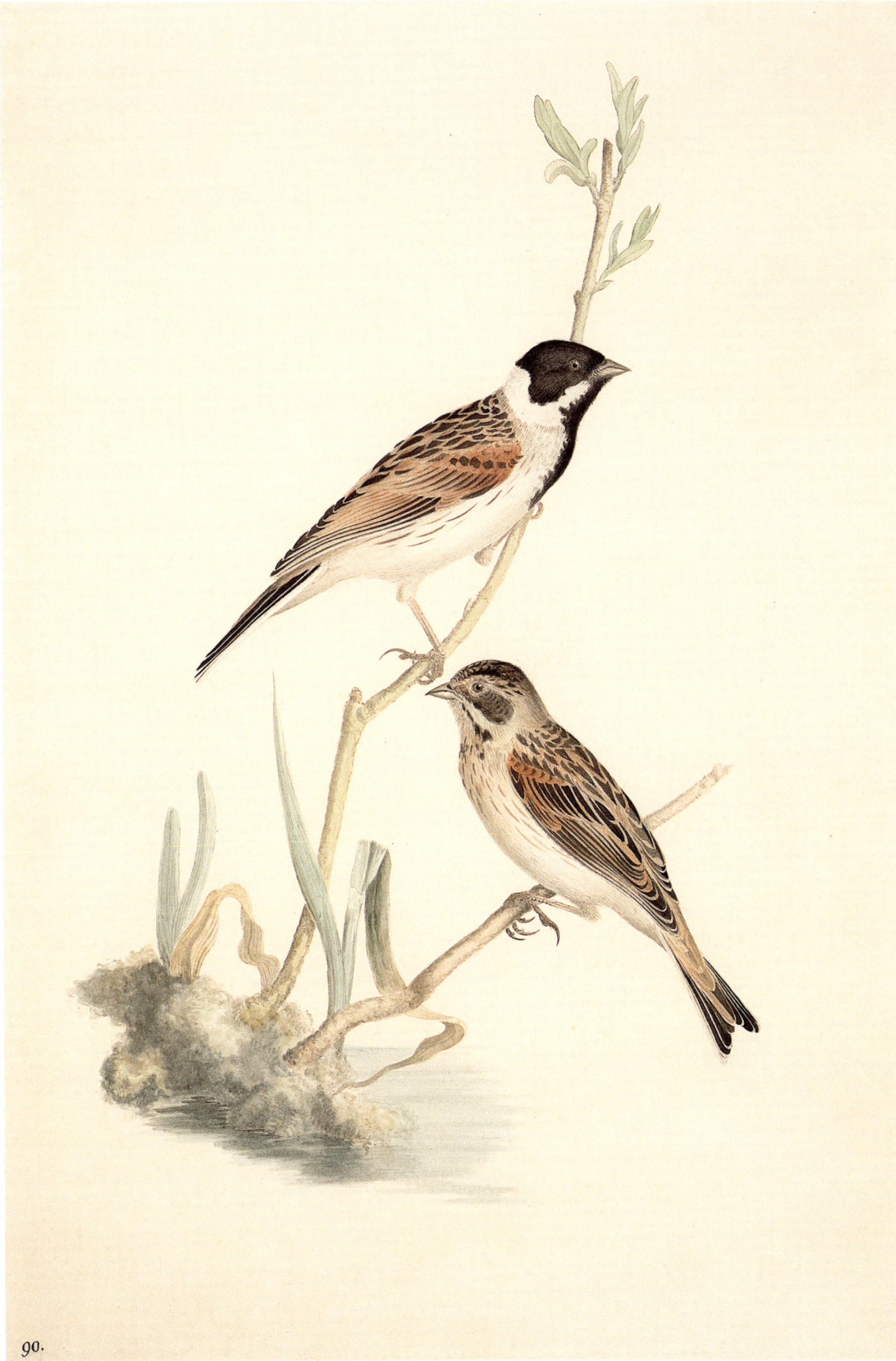
90.

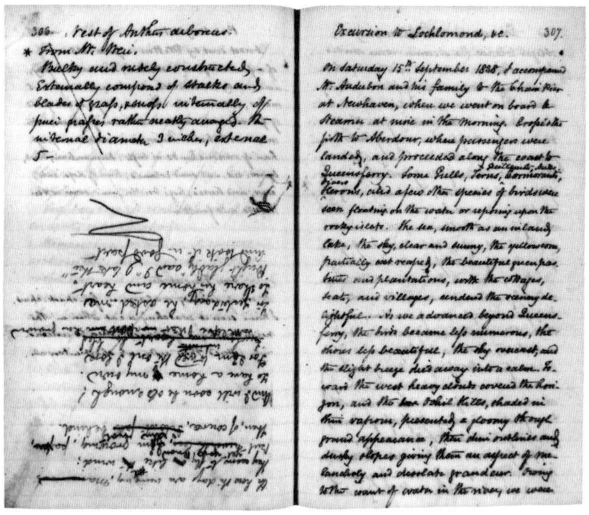

31 One of MacGillivray's working notebooks from 1838. The right-hand page is an account of an excursion to Loch Lomond with "Mr. Audubon and his family". The left-hand page has a short poem, not in MacGillivray's handwriting, written upside down. Not all of the poem is legible but it reads:

Oh how the days are winging, Ma ————,
They seem to fly like the wind;
Yet young, I know I'm growing, papa.
Then, of course, I'm not behind

And I will soon be old enough!
To have a home my own,
For I am to wed the one I love
With love that just has grown

For yesterday, he asked me
To share his home and heart,
Right gladly, said I, "I take thee"
And took it in good part

At the time this was written MacGillivray was prodigiously busy; could this be one of his daughters trying to attract his attention to tell him that she was getting engaged?

a *Manual of Botany*.[22] In the ten years from 1830 to 1840 MacGillivray wrote thirteen books of his own, the five volumes and synopsis of Audubon's *Ornithological Biography*, twenty-seven scientific papers, and compiled the new catalogue for the Royal College of Surgeons Museum. He edited the *Edinburgh Journal of Natural History and Physical Science* from its beginning in 1835 until its demise in 1840, and contributed the section on web-footed birds to the seventh edition of the *Encyclopaedia Britannica*; and he also found time to paint.

NOTES

1 MacGillivray (1830).
2 MacGillivray (1831).
3 Minutes of the Council of the Royal College of Surgeons, Edinburgh, August 1832.
4 MacGillivray (1831).
5 MacGillivray (1832).
6 The notebook describing MacGillivray's visits to various museums is in the Aberdeen University Library, MS 2158. Parts of it have been published by Robert A. Bayliss in the *Aberdeen University Review* 1983, 169, pp. 46-58, 'The 1833 Journey of William MacGillivray'.
7 *Ibid.*
8 *Ibid.*
9 Minutes of the Council of the Royal College of Surgeons, Edinburgh, August 1833.
10 MacGillivray (1836), pp. 13–14.
11 MacGillivray (1837).
12 *Ibid.*, p. 19.
13 *Ibid.*, p. 345.
14 This anonymous review of Volume 1 of *A History of British Birds* appeared in the *Magazine of Zoology and Botany* 1838, 2, pp. 267–69.
15 Mullens (1909).
16 Aberdeen University Library, MS 2158.
17 MacGillivray (1839).
18 MacGillivray (1840).
19 Yarrell (1837–43).
20 MacGillivray (1838).
21 MacGillivray (1840).
22 MacGillivray (1840).

PLATE 49 Pochard *Aythya ferina*

[Pochard. *Aythya Ferina.*] *Adult Male. From an individual bought in the market. Edinburgh, November, 1833.*

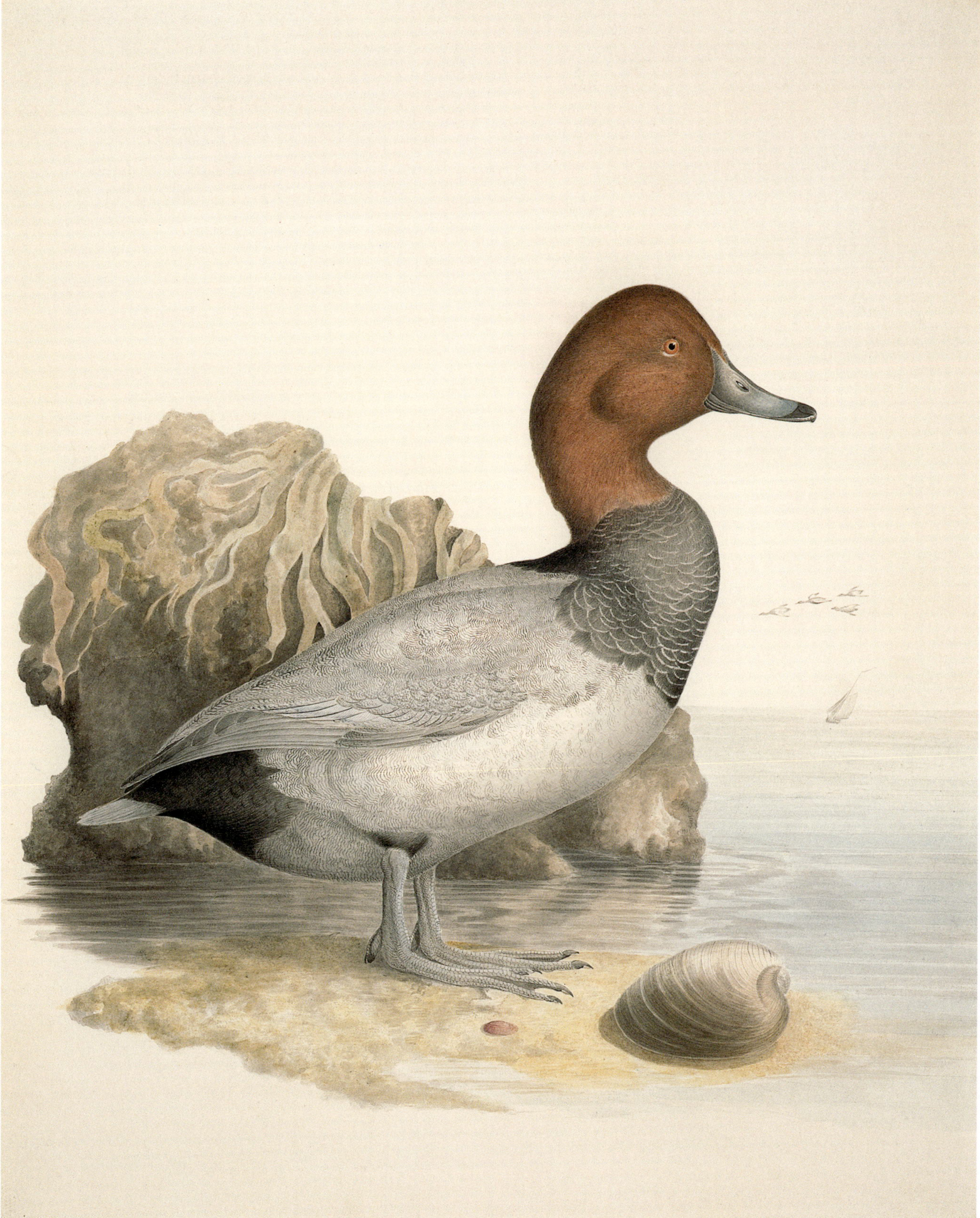

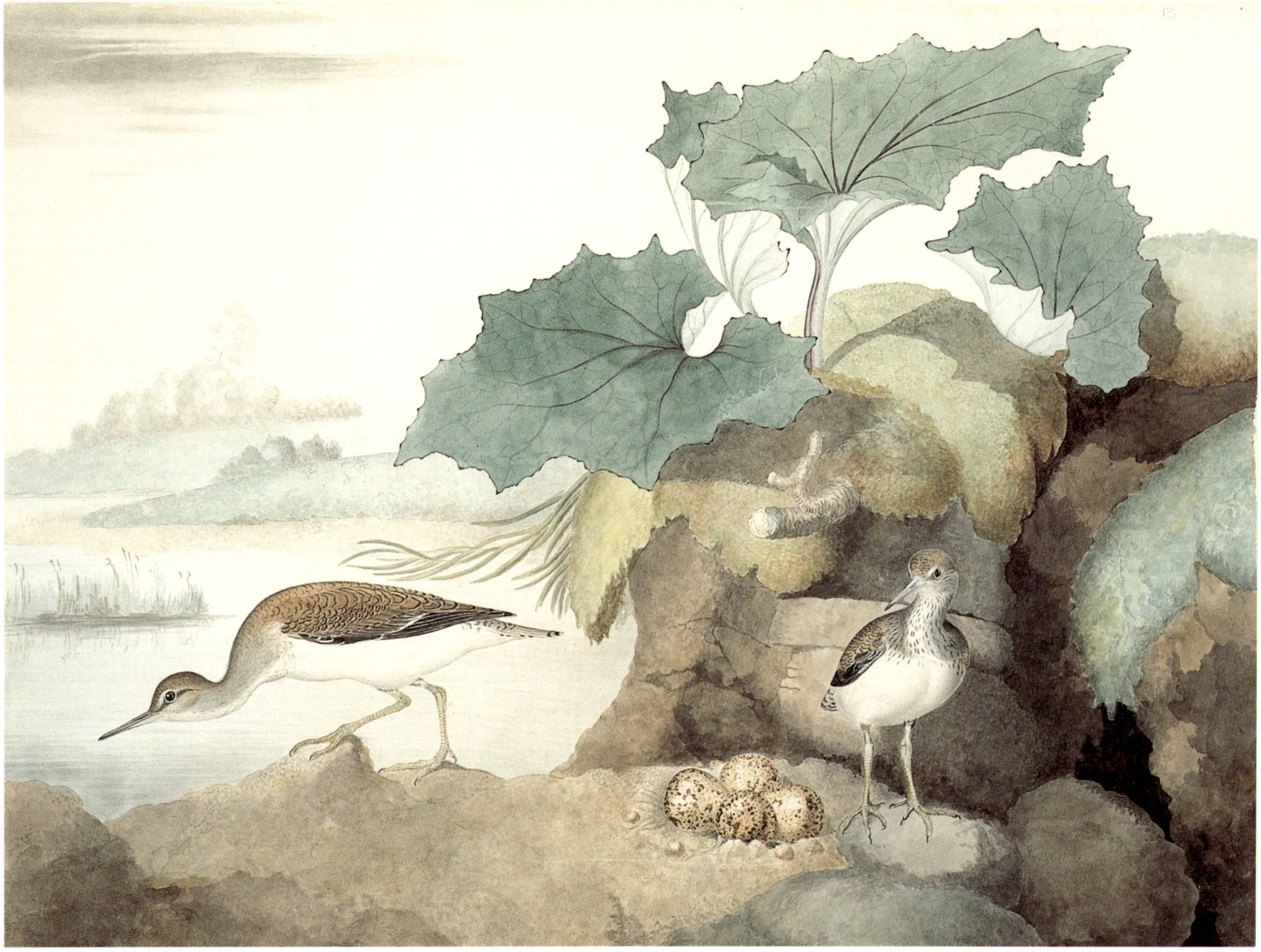

PLATE 50 Common sandpiper *Actitis hypoleucos*
[Common Sandpiper. *Totanus hypoleucos.*] *Female with eggs, and Young fully fledged. Leaves of* Tussilago farfara [coltsfoot]. *The young bird shot on the Almond. Edinburgh. Summer of 1831. W.Mc.G.*

MacGillivray's Art

Painting and drawing were always a part of MacGillivray's life. When he was just twenty-two he wrote in his North-town journal:

"For painting I have a natural genius and in as far as I have tried this art I have succeeded well. Flower drawing however is the only branch of it in which I have made considerable progress."[1]

On his walk to London he carried paints, brushes and seventeen pieces of drawing paper with him and painted landscapes that he found particularly attractive, but none of this early work has survived. The first reference to MacGillivray's natural history paintings comes from the minutes of the Wernerian Society in March 1833:

"An extensive and valuable series of highly finished representations of the indigenous animals of Great Britain, chiefly quadrupeds and birds, by Mr. MacGillivray, was also exhibited to the meeting. Professor Jameson pointed out that their peculiar excellence consisted in their combining, with great beauty of pictorial effect, a more accurate representation of the forms of the crania, as always identical in the young and old of the same species, an important particular, greatly neglected by ornithological draughtsmen; and also in there being less mannerism in the general treatment of the plumage, the characteristic form and texture of the feathers of each species being particularly attended to by Mr. MacGillivray."[2]

Although there is no direct evidence for it, the paintings shown to the members of the Society were surely some of those now held by the Natural History Museum. The Museum has 214 watercolours of mammals, fishes and birds by MacGillivray. They are well travelled, having been taken to Australia by one of his sons, Paul Howard MacGillivray, in the 1860s but returned to the Museum in 1892, presumably for safe keeping. There are 122 bird paintings, almost all of which have labels in MacGillivray's hand on the back, the earliest of which date from the early 1830s. When Audubon wrote to MacGillivray from London in 1834, he had

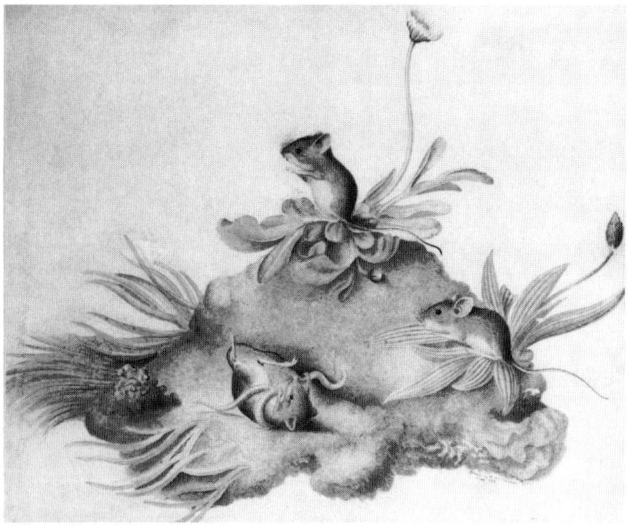

32 Harvest mice. This painting belongs to one of MacGillivray's descendants in Australia. It was used to illustrate the species in *A History of British Quadrupeds* published in 1838.

asked if MacGillivray drew birds yet 'with a view to publish' and MacGillivray clearly did. At the back of his mind there must always have been the nagging fear that once Audubon had finished *The Birds of America*, he would turn his attention to a work on British birds. MacGillivray had spent his life working towards such a work, observing, collecting, dissecting and drawing specimens; it would have been a crushing blow if his dreams had been shattered by his closest friend. These fears were expressed in another letter to Audubon in July:

"Now that your American birds are completed I suppose you will have at the European or the British. In the latter case what will become of mine? However, I have resolved, God willing, to go through with my task. I have at least twenty drawings superior to anything in the way ever seen by me, excepting always 'The Birds of America', and so good that one might look at them without disgust even after seeing yours."[3]

Soon after Audubon arrived in Edinburgh, MacGillivray wrote a strangely formal letter to him:

"I take the liberty of sending you a collection of drawings made by myself, and intended for a work on the vertebrate animals of Great Britain. The astonishing success with which you have depicted a whole class of the productions of your native land, as evinced in the incomparable delineations of your 'Birds of America', renders your opinions respecting ornithological drawings of the highest authority; and I have been anxious to submit my attempts to your decision, which, if unfavourable, will induce me to remedy my defects, or, if otherwise, will encourage me to proceed with an undertaking, which by its arduousness and extent, is precisely suited to my disposition. I shall therefore feel grateful for the expression of your ideas respecting the Drawings, and I request that you should favour me with it, you will not scruple to censure freely, should you find occasion."[4]

This letter is curious because the two men were friends, were working together and living in the same city; Audubon's reply was just as formal but must have been just what MacGillivray wanted to hear:

"I have great pleasure in affording you my opinion respecting the productions of your pencil, which you have submitted to my inspection. After examining with care and attention above one hundred coloured drawings of British Birds made by you, I am satisfied, not merely that they are minutely accurate representations of the originals, but that they display a perfect knowledge of the characteristic forms and attitudes of the different species of birds, together with a taste and execution capable of giving effect to the objects in a pictorial point of view. In short, I think them decidedly the best representations of birds I have ever

PLATE 51 Knot *Calidris canutus*

[Knot or Ash-coloured Sandpiper. *Tringa cinerea.*] *Temm* [?] *From two recent specimens presented by Mr. Macduff Carfrae, Edinburgh. Edinburgh, 12th January, 1837. W.Mc.G.*

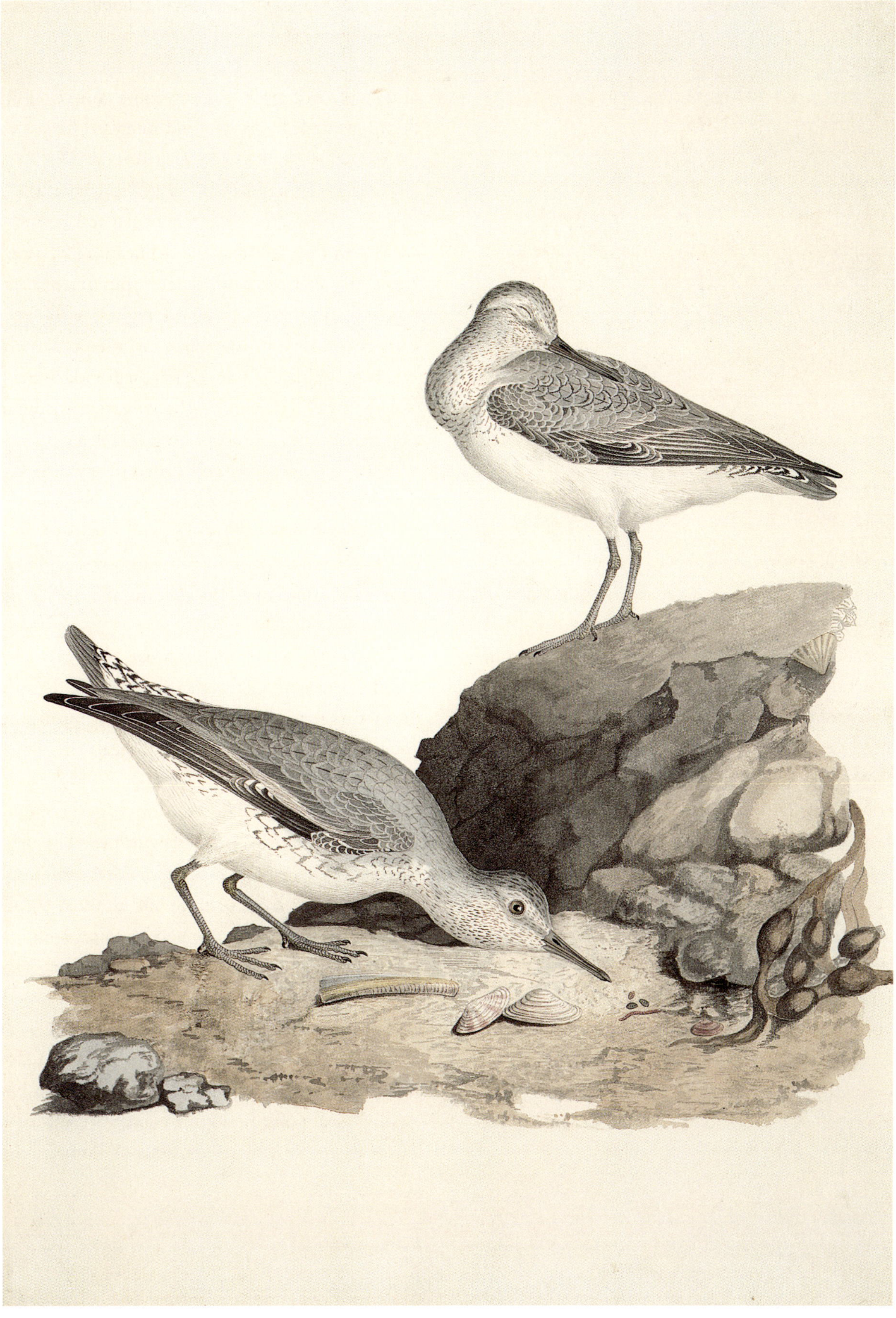

MORMON ARCTICUS. THE ARCTIC PUFFIN.

PUFFIN. POPE. SEA PARROT. COULTERNEB. GULDER-HEAD. TAMMY-NORRIE. BUIKIR. MULLET. BOTTLE-NOSE.

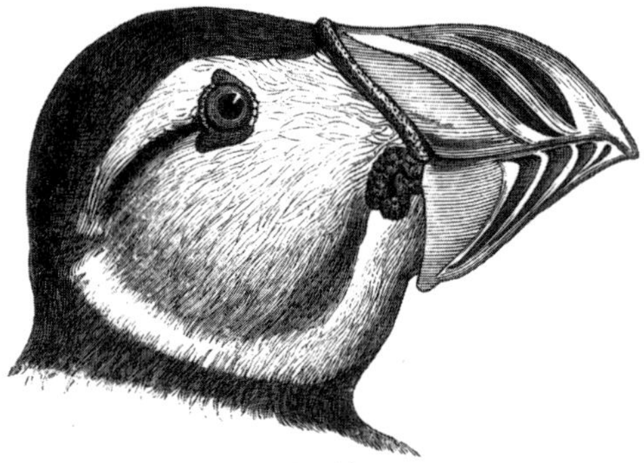

FIG. 84.

33 Puffin *Fraternula arctica*; 'Arctic puffin', *Mormon arcticus* from *A History of British Birds*, vol. 5 (1852), p. 365

seen, and have no hesitation in saying that, should they be engraved in a manner worthy of their excellence, they will form a work not only creditable to you but surpassing in splendour anything of the kind that Great Britain or even Europe has ever produced."[5]

Coming from Audubon, this was praise indeed. In volume 2 of *A History of British Birds*, MacGillivray records a conversation with Audubon which took place while resting at a public house during an excursion in the Pentland Hills to the south of Edinburgh:

"AUDUBON. Good health to you. Your Scotch whisky is excellent, I wish we had as good in America. May you prosper, and may I live to see engraved your drawings of the Birds of Britain, which I sincerely believe to be the best representations I have yet seen.

MACGILLIVRAY. You have often said so, that I must believe your partiality to the man has not deceived you into a belief that his productions are better than they really are. I wish all the world, excepting of course the authors of similar works, may agree with you. Who knows but the day may come?

AUDUBON. Be assured more strange things have happened. How little did I think when I commenced my drawings, that they should ever form a series of engravings, occupying more than four hundred sheets of double elephant folio. Hope for the best, and put me down as your first subscriber."[6]

In his heart of hearts MacGillivray must have known that these were vain hopes. The disastrous reception that the first volume of *A History of British Birds* had received meant that his dreams of having his bird paintings engraved and coloured were doomed to failure. His publishers refused to take the commercial risk and MacGillivray himself simply never had enough money. *A History of British Birds* was illustrated with steel engraved plates of skeletons and wood engraved figures of heads and feet; they are well done but in all five volumes of the work there is not a single figure of a complete bird.

It is clear from the most cursory glance that MacGillivray's bird paintings are based on Audubon's characteristic style; they are life-sized, painted against natural backgrounds and many are from fresh specimens, the labels on the back of the paintings referring to birds shot a day or two before, or purchased in the local market. The smaller birds are arranged in groups on suitable branches or foliage, while the larger birds are often vividly portrayed in action, for example, the golden eagle with a rabbit clutched in its talons (plate 18), or the raven about to feed on a dead lamb (plate 14). On the other hand, if he was painting a bird in flight that he had probably never seen alive, he was as likely as anyone else to get it wrong, for example, the wings of his storm petrel are in a very unrealistic position (plate 52). Unlike Audubon, who was a master of many different media, watercolour, oil, pastel, chalk, ink and others, MacGillivray seems to have painted exclusively in watercolour, a natural choice for painting birds and foliage, quickly with good colour and detail. At the same time it was probably the most economical medium available to him.

The only MacGillivray paintings to be published in his lifetime were some of the mammals, again painted in the 1830s, that were used in *A History of British Quadrupeds*,[7] a volume in Sir William Jardine's *The*

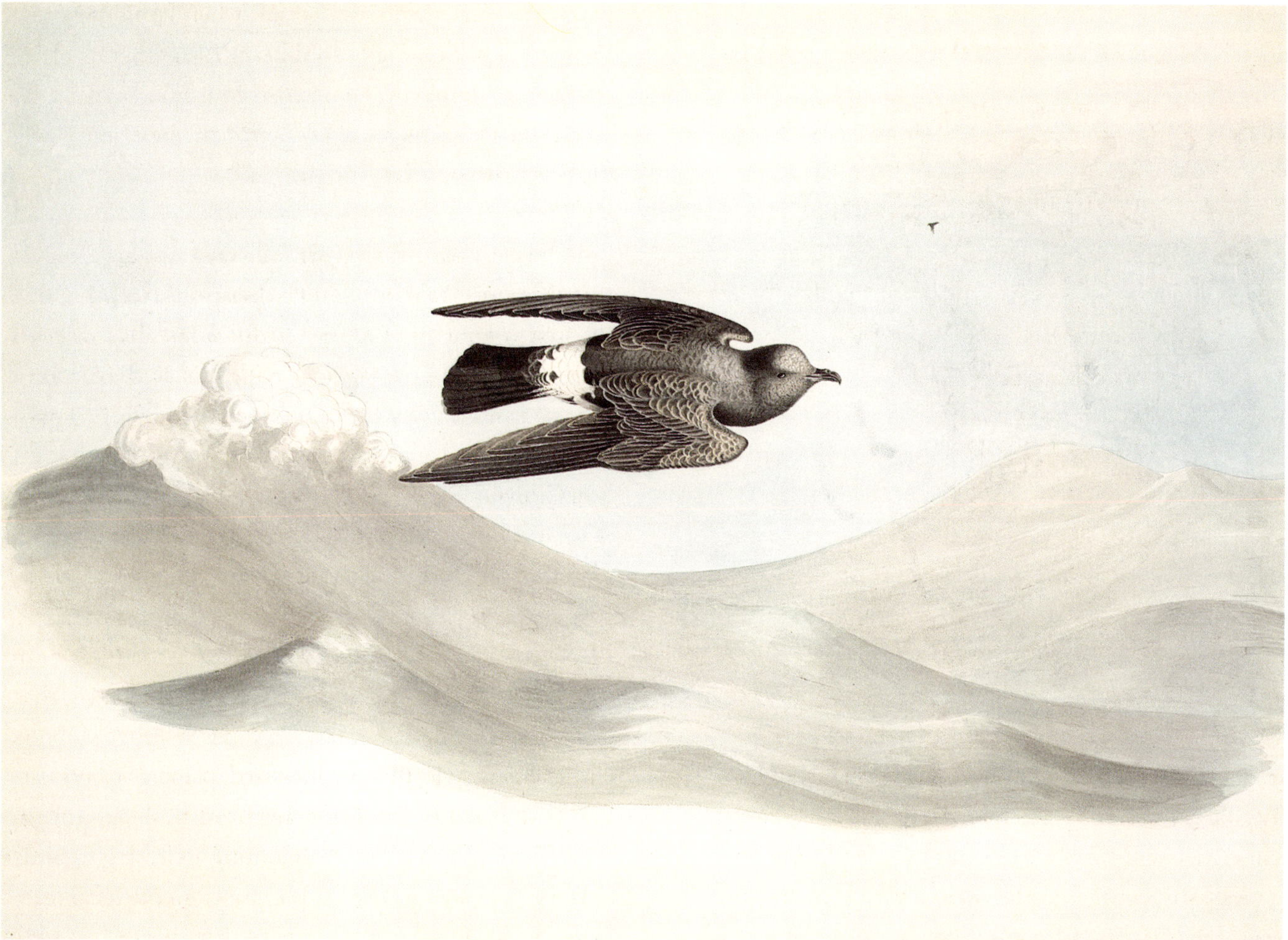

PLATE 52 Storm-petrel *Hydrobates pelagicus*
[Stormy Petrel. *Procellaria pelagica.*] *From an individual caught off the Isle of May, and lent by James Wilson Esq. Edinburgh, July 1832. W McG.*

Naturalist's Library. His fish paintings have no labels on them and there is no record of when they were painted. They may have been done in Edinburgh at the same time as the birds and mammals, or they may have been done later in Aberdeen in the 1840s, when he was preparing a book on the vertebrate fauna of the north-east of Scotland. Because his paintings were never published, MacGillivray's work and his artistic merit have never been critically evaluated and put into a historical context. His best work is surely on a par with Audubon's and is part of a transition in bird painting in Britain, from paintings of birds stuffed and set up by taxidermists, to those using freshly killed specimens, set in life-like positions with wires and pins. However, it was for others, men like Swainson, Selby and Jardine, to achieve the fame and reputation that might have come to MacGillivray if he had had the financial resources to match his talent. For an opinion on his talent, there can be no better judge than the master himself, Audubon. In the description of the MacGillivray shore finch in the *Ornithological Biography* Audubon says this:

"Another species of finch, found abundantly in the salt marshes of the Carolinas, has been discovered by my most worthy friend, Rev. John Bachman of Charleston, who has presented me with a dozen specimens of it. With his approval I have named it after a gentleman who, besides being my friend, is possessed not only of a technical, but also of a practical knowledge of ornithology, and of whom I may safely say, that he is unquestionably the best portrayer of the feathered race that I know."[8]

Audubon was not a man to give praise readily, but even allowing for the close friendship between them, he clearly thought highly of MacGillivray's paintings.

As well as his paintings, MacGillivray produced many hundreds of other drawings, for example, the originals of the heads and feet in *A History of British Birds*; in addition there must have been many anatomical drawings of the skeletons and alimentary canals of different species of birds, but it seems that none of these have survived. They remain only as woodcuts and steel engravings in his published books, examples of his skills as a draughtsman as well as an artist. The only known examples of his work outside the collection in the Natural History Museum are three paintings owned by some of his descendants in Australia.

NOTES

1 Ralph (1996), p. 127.
2 The Minutes of the Wernerian Society of Edinburgh – 26th Session, 23 March 1833, p. 465.
3 Deane (1901).
4 Herrick (1938), vol. 2, pp. 130–31.
5 *Ibid.*, vol. 2, p. 132.
6 MacGillivray (1839), p. 470.
7 MacGillivray (1838).
8 This comment by Audubon on MacGillivray's artistic ability is in the second volume of the *Ornithological Biography*, p. 285.

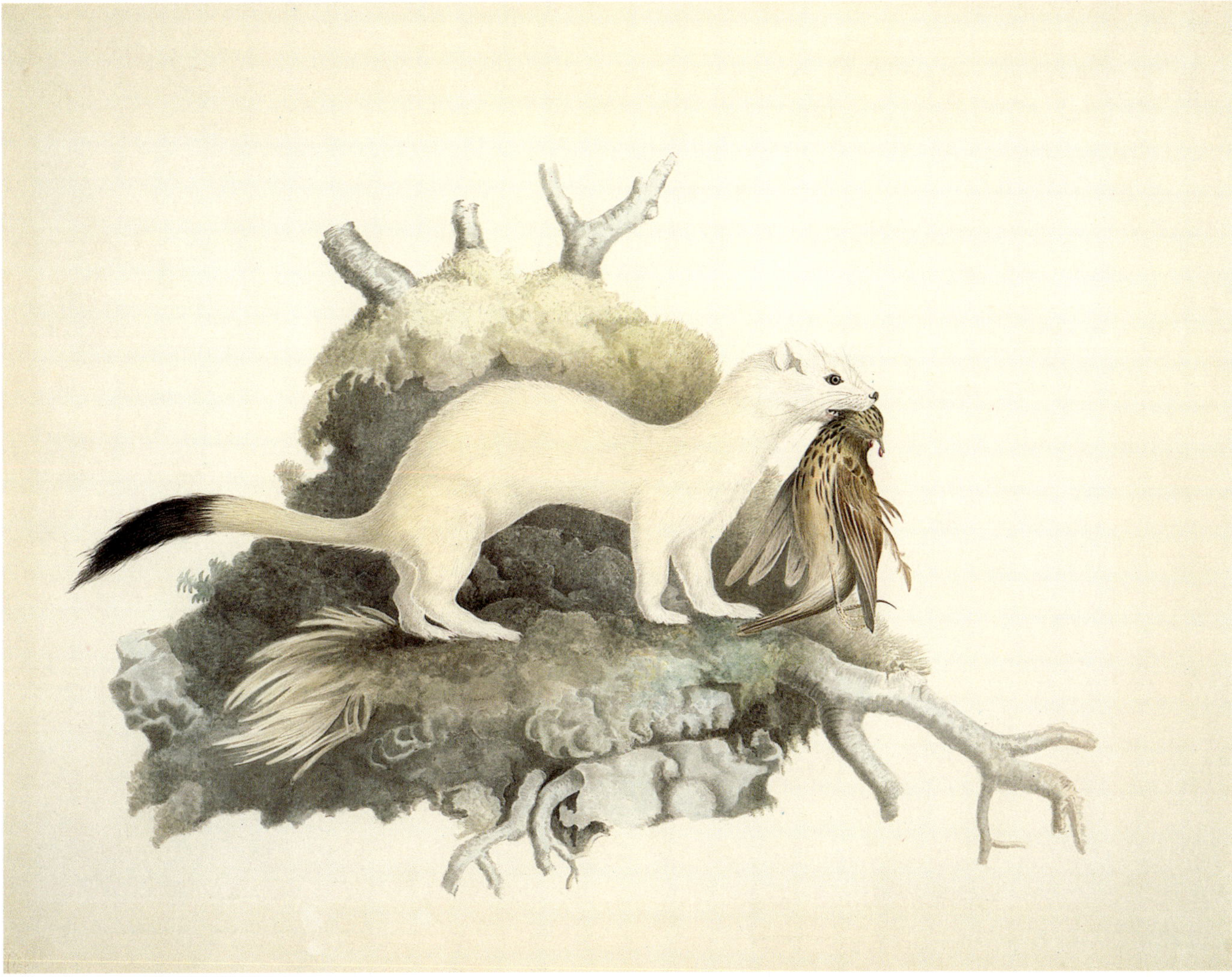

PLATE 53 Stoat *Mustela erminea* in winter coat

Ermine Adult male from a specimen presented by Mr. Ferguson of Raith. Edinburgh 22nd March 1834.

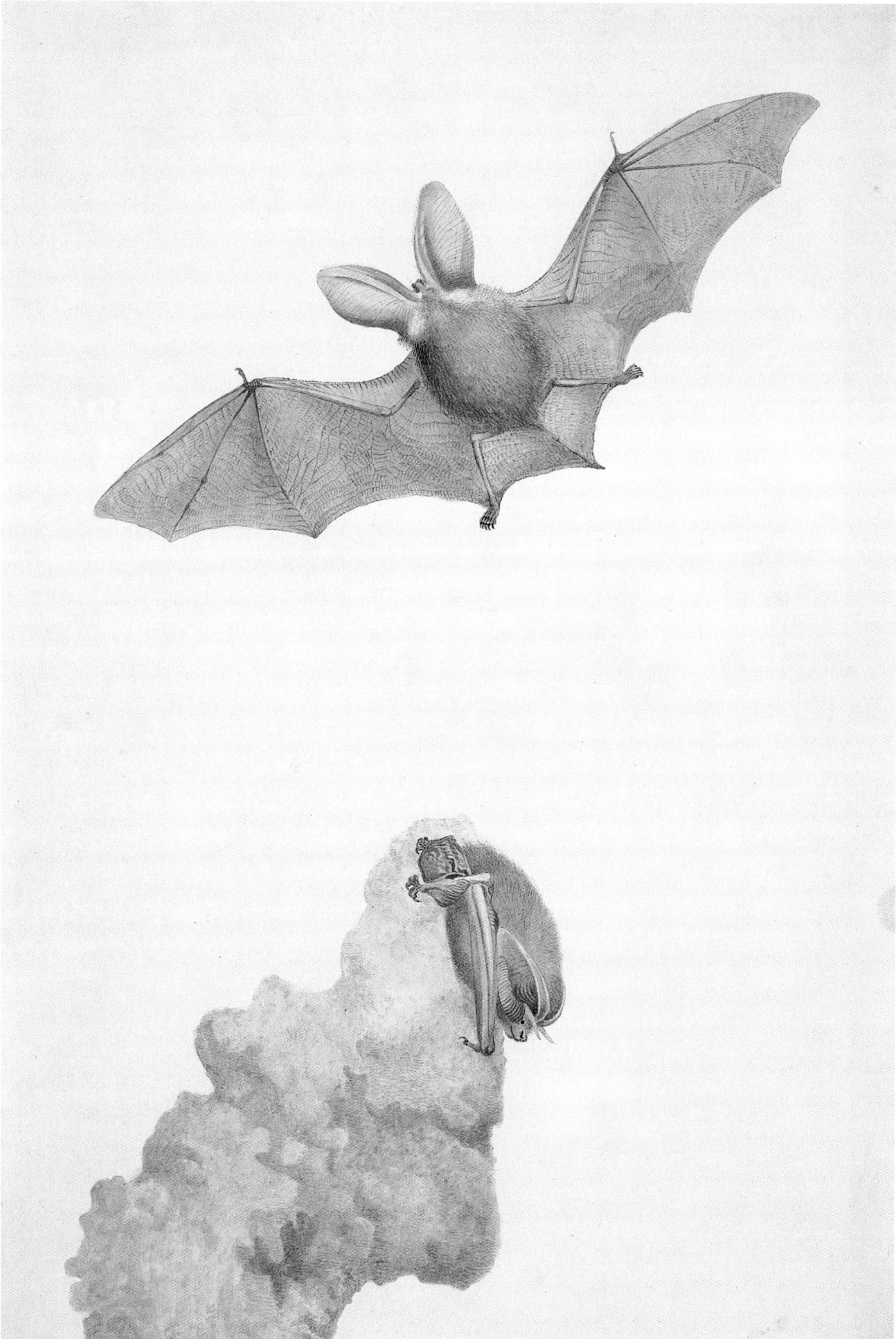
104.

Aberdeen Again

PLATE 54 Brown long-eared bat *Plecotus auritus*

By early 1841 MacGillivray was at a low ebb. The final departure of Audubon, his closest friend, affected him deeply, and Edinburgh, his home for nearly twenty years, must have seemed an empty place. The general lack of money, the destructive critical reception of the first three volumes of *A History of British Birds*, the lack of interest by his publishers in getting out the last two volumes, must have depressed him intensely. There were also occasional domestic problems, vividly expressed in a letter to his friend James Harley in January 1841:

"I have been thinking about you for weeks and yet have not until now resolved to ask your forgiveness. I have been so remiss, so perplexed, so harassed, that I have not somehow been able to thank you for all your kindnesses or answer any of your letters. My pecuniary affairs had gone wrong, I got tired of writing books, and fell to the British Birds, which do not require so much study as other subjects, as I was familiar with them to a certain extent; and in these three months I have written more than half of each of the two remaining volumes, and this merely to keep myself alive, although I can get no money for them, and cannot guess when they may be published, as the London booksellers seem disheartened by the dull sales of the rest. Five weeks ago one of the children took scarlet fever, then another, a third, a fourth, a fifth then their mother, then the youngest child got unwell with her teeth, I believe, and we had seven in bed all at once. One had a relapse, and one is still very ill. Yesterday my oldest, John, a medical student, took the fever, and now the eruption is on him. I have a sore throat myself but it may be a cold. So, we have a complete hospital, but you will give me credit for being grateful for such mercy as we have experienced. I write this merely to let you know where we are, being unable at present to discuss other matters."[1]

A few months after writing this letter MacGillivray moved on from Edinburgh in the final move of his career, back to the city of his birth, when he was appointed to the Regius Chair of Civil and Natural

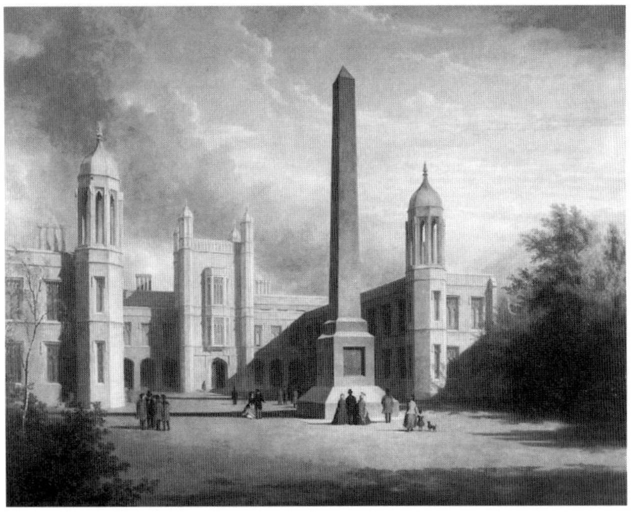

34 Marischal College by James Giles, at the time that MacGillivray was appointed to the Regius Chair of Natural History (1841)

History at Marischal College in Aberdeen. Marischal College and the rival King's College were two separate, old-established universities; King's was founded in 1495 and Marischal almost a century later in 1593, so that at one time Aberdeen had as many universities as the whole of England. The two colleges were united in 1860, into the single University of Aberdeen.

There were three other candidates for the chair. Two of them were local men, one at King's, the other already at Marischal College. The first was the Revd John Fleming, one of the foremost naturalists of the day, who was in the Chair of Natural Philosophy at King's, and teaching physics. The second candidate was John Shier who had been assistant to the Professor Davidson who had occupied the Chair of Marischal College until his death in February 1841. Davidson had been ill for some time and Shier had already been teaching the natural history and botany class for three years. The third candidate was the naturalist Edward Forbes. The men were formidable opposition for MacGillivray, as he wrote in a letter to James Harley:

"As to the Professorship, there were three candidates for it, in the field; namely Dr. Fleming, Professor of Natural Philosophy, an old naturalist, a DD and LL D, and Mr. Shier, a young naturalist, who has taught the class in question for three years, and myself. Dr. Fleming was supported by an enormous force of cavalry, infantry, and artillery. Among the great guns on his side were Buckland, Murchison, Sedgewick, Lyell, and Jamieson [Jameson]; enough to batter the most adamantine heart of an umpire. Mr. Shier was supported by the Lord Provost, Magistrates, Town-Council, and Professors of Aberdeen. Both had a splendid array of political influence. For me there were 26 testimonialists, Dr. Birkbeck in London, my bookseller Mr. Scott, who is a good shot, a single county member, backed by Mr. Weir, – and what thinkest thou? – the Divine Providence. Well, who now gained the battle? It is a Regius Professorship in the gift of the Crown – rather of Lord Normanby [Lord Normanby was the Home Secretary at the time]. Well, his Lordship said to himself thus – here is a poor fellow who has devoted himself to natural history for 25 years, with no other profession, has persevered, written books, given lectures, supported a large family. It is clear he has talent; his testimonials show that he has done his duty in the only two offices he has held; his enthusiasm will kindle the dying embers in the north. Fleming is old, and besides is provided for, Shier too young and unburdened. MacGillivray is the man. So he lays his name before Her Majesty and gives orders to make out his appointment. His Lordship has done me the honour of intimating that I have been preferred to the Professorship."[2]

MacGillivray seems to have been unaware that Forbes was a candidate; like Shier, Forbes at twenty-six may have been too young, but rejection by Aberdeen did not seriously impede his career. The next year he became Curator of the Museum of the Geological Society and Professor of Botany at King's College in London. He eventually became Professor of Natural History at Edinburgh in 1853 but sadly died after just six months in the post.

The Chair at Marischal was a Regius one, in the gift of the Crown, and this external influence may have overcome the local political infighting and tipped the balance in MacGillivray's favour. One of his most powerful

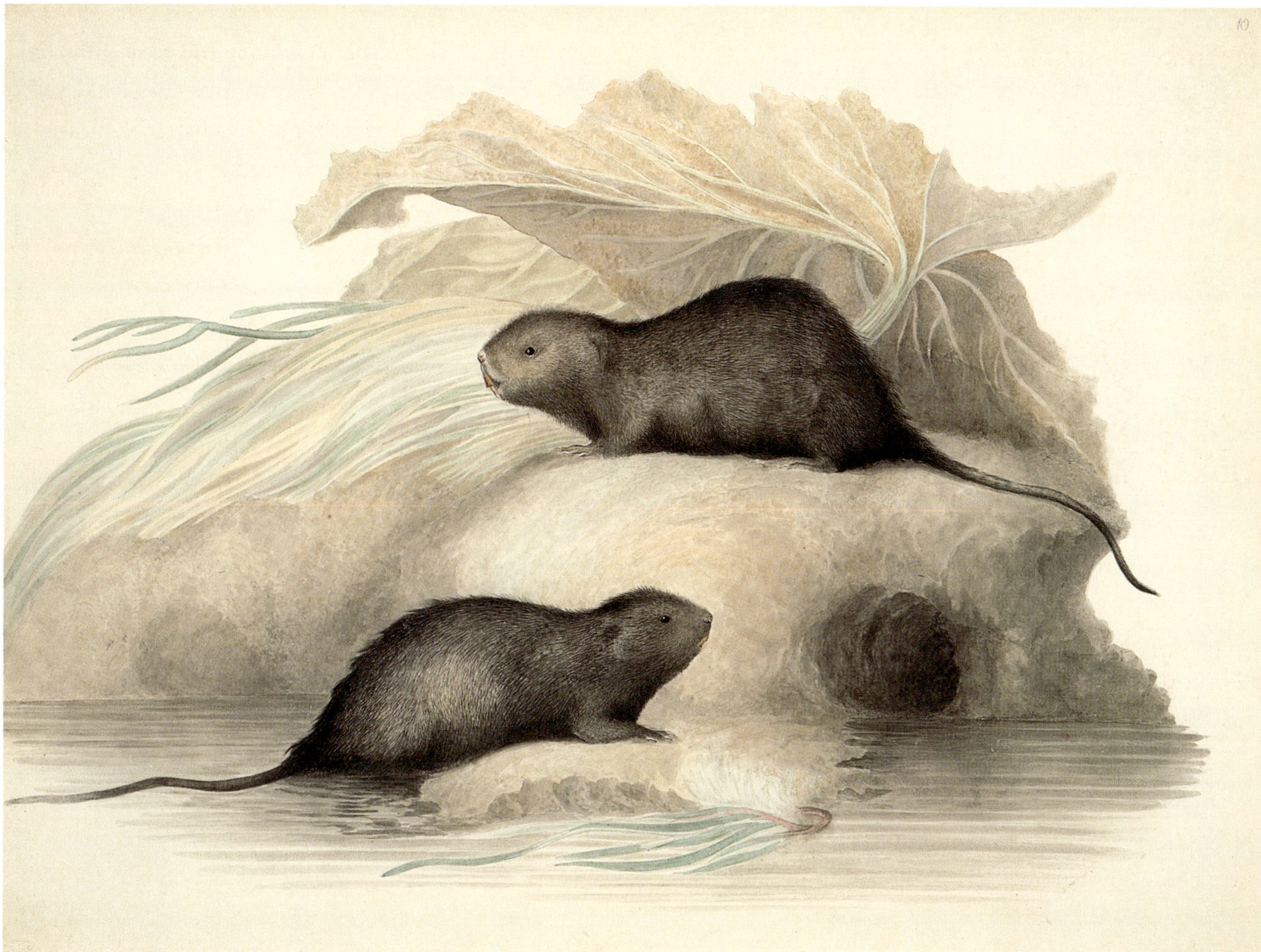

PLATE 55 Water vole *Arvicola terrestris* melanic (i.e. black) form or variety [Black water rat. *Arvicola ater.*] *From individuals sent from Aberdeenshire, one of them by the Rev. McCowie of Cairnie. Edinburgh 1832.*

supporters, not acknowledged in his letter to Harley, was probably Robert Grant FRS, the Professor of Comparative Anatomy and Zoology at the University of London. He had worked in Edinburgh in the early 1820s and he and MacGillivray had become close friends. MacGillivray moved to Aberdeen on 1 May 1841 and threw himself into his new post with his customary energy, beginning his first botany class just two days later. In another letter to Harley he described his new situation:

"It appears that I have at length found a temporary refuge from the storm. Yet the anchorage seems unsafe, for the blasts of adversity still shake the frail bark, and the sunshine of peace comes in fugitive glimpses. However, here I am, as the Professor of Natural History in the University of Aberdeen, and Providence has assigned me the station for good to me and others. There are two towns here, the new and old, the former large and populous, the latter a village rather than a town. In each is a college, and Marischal College is a university, with power to grant degrees in Arts, Medicine, Law, and Divinity. The two universities are not only separate and distinct, but rivals and enemies. Marischal College and University is situated in the New Town, at the distance of a mile from King's College, of which I am an alumnus, although now a Professor in the rival and more modern institution. Being fond of rural shades and solitary rambles, and having always in mind the health of my family, I have chosen for my habitation a house in the midst of a large garden, a mile and a half distant from Marischal College, and half a mile beyond King's College. The professors of the two universities are not on friendly terms, and those of my own are probably not well pleased at my having settled in the midst of the enemy. Strange to say, those of King's College have been more friendly than those of my own. Yet I am not sure of their having any great dislike of me, although no doubt they would have preferred another. Be this as it may, I find my situation in many respects most pleasant. I have been lecturing on Botany since I came here to a class of twenty-five most attentive and respectful pupils. The district is in a great measure unexplored, and must yield many interesting objects. In the last six weeks I have walked more than in the whole previous year, and have slept less than at almost any time of my life; so that, although in excellent health, I am getting so thin that my clothes are quite loose about me. Just opposite my house in a fine old granite cathedral [St Machar's Cathedral], with two tall spires, on one side of which is a clock, the sight and sound of which is most pleasing to me. I love to sit in the old church and listen to the reading of the Scriptures, and the exposition of their doctrines. Many times I have been struck by passages that bore reference to my own case. I have never been very regular in my church goings, but here I find difficulty in staying away. The Ministers are not eloquent, vigorous, or in anyway impressive, but they really preach sound doctrine, and although both moderate, are in my judgement quite evangelised.

As there are heaths, pastures, fields, woods, pools, rills, and rivers, as well as marshes, sands, and the ocean, the country furnishes ample materials for study. There are few naturalists here, but a very friendly and agreeable person, who is remarkably fond of Zoology, resides beside me, and is my daily companion in my short rambles."[3]

MacGillivray's teaching took on a set pattern, with classes in zoology and geology in the winter, and botany in the summer. He had taught botany at King's more than two decades before but since then had had little formal contact with students. He clearly took a great delight in teaching and his lectures were always very popular. One of his students wrote of him:

"I had a very great regard for him not only as an ornithologist but as a man. He was exceedingly loveable and undoubtedly the first ornithologist in Europe, and we were all proud of his fame. One thing always made a great impression on me; he treated his class as men and gentlemen, and we reciprocated his action. It was far from otherwise with some of the professors.

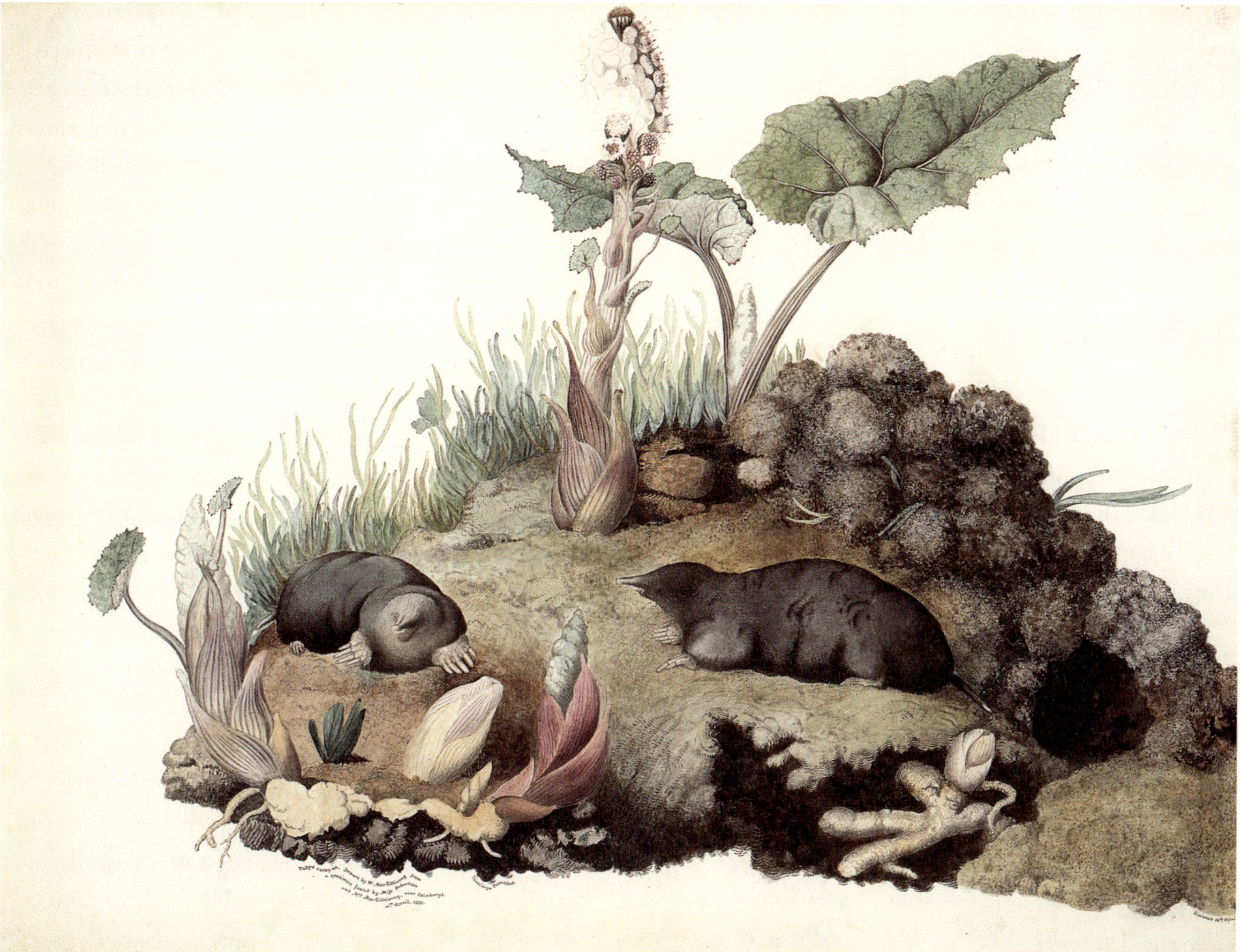

PLATE 56 Mole *Talpa europaea*

[Common Mole. *Talpa Europaea.*] *From a specimen found by Miss Robertson and Mrs. MacGillivray.* Fussilago petasites [now *Petasites hybridus* – butterbur]. *Edinburgh, 10th April, 1831. W.Mc.G.*

His interest in the habits of his students was remarkable. If he saw a good student careless he would remonstrate with him privately, whilst earnest attention gained his favour. With his rapid power of observation he could detect even a temporary lapse from diligence. As an examiner he was patient, tender and gentle, unwilling to say an angry word. He would rather help out the hesitating student, but it was easy to see that carelessness was an abomination to him."[4]

When MacGillivray arrived in Aberdeen, the natural history courses were simply lecture courses, there were no laboratory classes or field work, so students never examined specimens. MacGillivray changed all this. He insisted on taking his students on excursions into the field where according to one of them "he could walk the most active of us into limp helplessness". Given his museum background, first with Jameson and then with the Royal College of Surgeons, he felt the need for a museum, and during his time at Aberdeen established one, largely at his own expense. The Zoology Department at Aberdeen still has a major undergraduate teaching museum, but very few specimens in it can be ascribed to MacGillivray's collection, other than the bird specimens that Audubon gave him. Not all of his time was devoted to teaching. Just two years after arriving in Aberdeen he published *A History of the Molluscous Animals of the Counties of Aberdeen, Kincardine and Banff*,[5] the first book to be produced by a Professor of Natural History at Aberdeen. It is an account, with detailed taxonomic descriptions, of nearly 300 species of terrestrial, freshwater and marine molluscs, two-thirds of which were collected by MacGillivray himself, the others by members of his family and by students. This was a dramatic change of subject for MacGillivray, who had spent most of his life working on birds, but his plan was to produce a book that could be used by his students; at any time of the year, they could get out into the field collecting molluscs, from streams and ponds, from the beach or from the lines and creels of the local fishermen. The book cost MacGillivray a great deal of time and effort; there was much fieldwork to be done as he was working in an area of natural history previously unknown to him, and the library available to him was inadequate, but the work may have been a welcome diversion from the poor prospects of completing his life's major work, with the last two volumes of *A History of British Birds*.

The next few years were as busy as ever for MacGillivray, with publications coming thick and fast; in 1846 he published a new edition of his *A Manual of British Ornithology*.[6] He also produced an eight-part work on domestic cattle and a revised edition of Thomas Brown's *The Conchologist's Textbook*.[7] There were many articles for the *Scottish Farmer and Gardeners' Journal* on subjects as diverse as 'The Alpaca' and 'Remarks on the improvement of the links of Aberdeen, and on the securing of maritime sands' and, in 1847, he became editor of the journal as well as continuing to contribute articles. In spite of the rivalry between the two Aberdeen universities, he was awarded an LL D degree by King's College, a measure of the esteem and respect that he had gained.

In the autumn of 1850, he embarked on a project to describe the natural history and geology of Deeside and Braemar. It was more than thirty years since he first explored the area, on his journeys to and from Harris, and on his walk to London. It was probably his favourite area and, certainly, Lochnagar was his favourite mountain. MacGillivray spent nearly six weeks at Ballater and Braemar, accompanied initially by his son Paul and then by one of his daughters. He was out almost every day, surveying the area, making observations on the geology and on the distribution of the many species of plants.

Many of the days were long and strenuous. One spent exploring Ben Macdui, at 4296 feet the highest mountain in the Cairngorms, began at five o'clock one morn-

PLATE 57 Field vole *Microtus agrestis*
[Common Meadow Mouse *Arvicola agrestis.*] *Male. From a specimen caught near Roslyn by John MacGillivray. 13th May 1837. Edinburgh 16th May 1837.* Arum maculatum [Cuckoo pint], Caltha palustris [Marsh marigold].

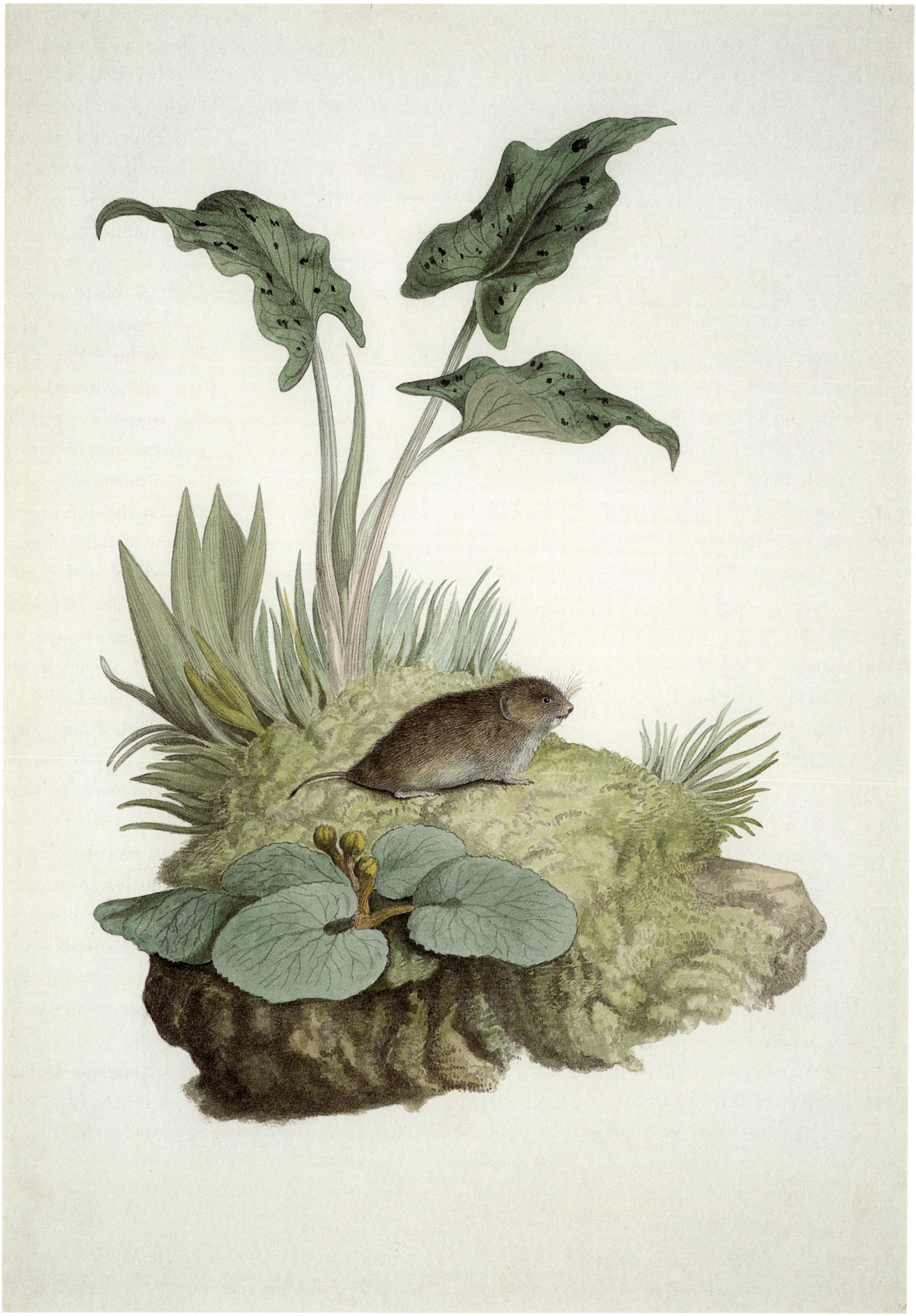

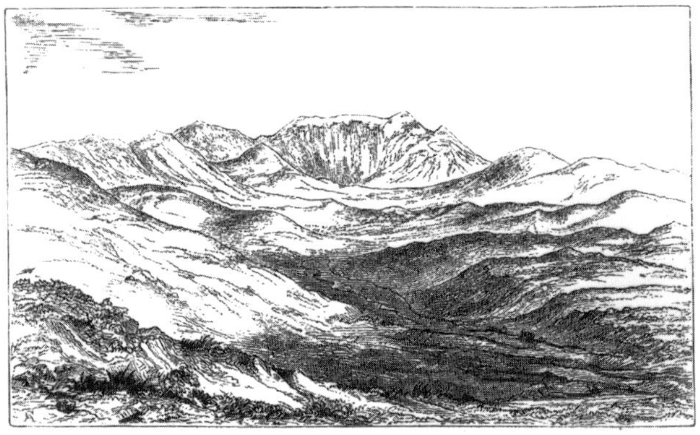

35 Lochnagar – MacGillivray's favourite mountain
from *The Natural History of Dee Side and Braemar*, p. 231, 1855

ing to end at three o'clock the next. On other occasions he set off with frost on the ground, was drenched with perspiration climbing in the heat of the day, only to return late at night as chilling frost set in again. Days were often spent soaked to the skin by rain. At the end of the trip he claimed to have been relaxed and invigorated by the fieldwork, but he was fifty-four and the years and the miles were catching up on him. A few months later he fell ill and was unable to take his classes.

His old friend and companion Audubon died in America on 27 January 1851. It is not clear if the news of this ever reached MacGillivray; if it had it could only have added to his gradual decline. Despite his ill health he was actively working on four major books: *The Natural History of Dee Side and Braemar*,[8] a work on the whole of the north-east of Scotland, and, surprisingly, the completion of his life's main work, the last two volumes of *A History of British Birds*, although he must have been depressed at the prospect that none of them might be completed. The planned book on the natural history of the north-east of Scotland was never published and any notes or parts of a manuscript that MacGillivray might have written have been lost. Presumably it was for this proposed work that he began painting British fishes, both freshwater and marine, with some of these paintings being among his best. By the autumn of 1851 he was so ill that his doctor insisted that he should avoid the coming Aberdeen winter, and, accompanied by one of his daughters, he left for Torquay. For a while things seemed to improve. There were daily walks along the shore, and fish and rockpool animals to draw. From there he managed to publish volume 4 of *A History of British Birds*.[9] The opening lines of the Preface give an indication of his state of mind:

"As the wounded bird seeks some quiet retreat where, freed from the persecutions of the pitiless fowler, it may pass the time of its anguish in forgetfulness of the outer world, so have I, assailed by disease, betaken myself to a sheltered nook, where, unannoyed by the piercing blasts of the North Sea, I had been led to hope that my life might be protracted beyond the most dangerous season of the year. It is thus that I issue from Devonshire, the present volume which, however contains no observations of mine made there, the scenes of my labours being in distant parts of the country."

MacGillivray was unable to be completely forgetful of the outer world. In February he received news of his wife's sudden death, at home in Aberdeen. She was just forty-seven, they had been married for thirty years and she had borne him thirteen children, four of whom had died in infancy. It is not difficult to imagine the hardships that Marion, the tall, genteel, simple and unsuspecting girl from North-town, endured in their marriage. In the first years of their marriage during the 1820s when MacGillivray had no settled employment, she had at one time five children under the age of seven to feed and clothe. Money must always have been a problem; even in the most settled period of their lives back in Aberdeen the family moved five times in ten years, each time to a smaller house.

Shortly after receiving the news of Marion's death MacGillivray became ill again and his doctor in Torquay, perhaps sensing that he had not long to live, urged him to return to Aberdeen. This he did and the final, fifth volume of *A History of British Birds*[10] was published at the end of July. The preface is especially poignant:

"I have finished one of the many difficult and laborious tasks which I had imposed upon myself. Twelve years have elapsed since the first three volumes of this work were issued to the public, and I had scarcely hoped to see its completion, when I was most unexpectedly encouraged to revise the manuscript of the two remaining volumes, containing the Wading and Swimming Birds, of which the History, as far as I am acquainted with it, is now given on the same plan as that adopted for the Land Birds."

There is nothing in anything MacGillivray wrote to show why he should have returned to the last two volumes of *A History of British Birds*. The first three volumes, published twelve years earlier, had been almost destroyed by the critical reviews that caused MacGillivray so much heartache and distress, and had failed financially. The last two volumes were both dedicated to Queen Victoria. The Queen and Prince Albert had begun visiting Deeside in the 1840s, leasing Balmoral House in 1848, before buying it in 1852 and beginning the building of Balmoral Castle. She was no stranger to the mountains climbing Lochnagar, Beinn a' Bhuird, Ben Macdui and many others. There is no record of her or the Prince ever meeting MacGillivray, but the dedication of the last two volumes to Her Majesty may reflect "the unexpected encouragement" he received. The preface to the final volume continues:

"Commenced in hope, and carried on with zeal, though ended with sorrow and sickness, I can look upon my work without much regard to the opinions which contemporary writers may form of it, assured that what is useful within it will not be forgotten, and knowing that already it has had a beneficial effect on many of the present, and will more powerfully influence the next generation of our home ornithologists. I had been led to think that I had occasionally been somewhat rude, or at least blunt, in my criticisms; but I do not perceive wherein I have much erred in that respect, and I feel no inclination to apologise. I have been honest and sincere in my endeavours to promote the truth. With death, apparently not distant before my eyes, I am pleased to think that I have not countenanced error, through fear of favour. Though I might have accomplished more, I am thankful for having been permitted to add very considerably to the knowledge previously obtained of a very pleasant subject. If I have not very frequently indulged in reflections of the power, wisdom, and goodness of God, as suggested by even my imperfect understanding of his wonderful works, it is not because I have not ever been sensible of the relation between the Creator and his creatures, nor because my chief enjoyment when wandering among the hills and valleys, exploring the rugged shores of the ocean, or searching the cultivated fields, has not been in a sense of His presence. "To Him who alone doeth great wonders" be all glory and praise. Reader, farewell."

Death was indeed not far distant; William MacGillivray died at his home in Crown Street in Aberdeen on 8 September 1852 aged fifty-six.

NOTES

1 James Harley was a prosperous wool merchant in Leicester. He began corresponding with MacGillivray when he wrote to him about the distribution of the Dartford warbler in Leicestershire. There is no evidence that the two men ever met but they became very regular correspondents and MacGillivray clearly regarded Harley as a friend and confidant. Harley's diaries and correspondence are in the Record Office for Leicestershire, Leicester and Rutland (Accession number 13D56).

2 Letter to James Harley, 2 April 1841 – Leicester RO.

3 Letter to James Harley, 10 June 1841 – Leicester RO

4 MacGillivray (1901), p. 44. In 1900 a number of MacGillivray's former students collected funds to raise a memorial to him. A brief biography was published, written by another, unrelated, William MacGillivray.

5 MacGillivray (1843).

6 MacGillivray (1846).

7 MacGillivray (1845).

8 MacGillivray carried out the fieldwork for *The Natural History of Dee Side and Braemar* but died before he could get it published. The manuscript was bought by Queen Victoria and the book was eventually printed, for private circulation, in 1855.

9 MacGillivray (1852).

10 MacGillivray (1852).

Postscript

MacGillivray was buried in the New Calton cemetery in Edinburgh where Marion and two children who had died in infancy were buried. For nearly fifty years his grave was left unmarked, until at the turn of the century, a group of his former students and surviving relatives, by then themselves elderly, put matters to right. They collected enough money for a splendid granite monument to mark his grave, and for a fine bronze memorial tablet, which today hangs on the wall of the Aberdeen University Zoology Department Museum, the museum founded, of course, by MacGillivray. The inscription on his gravestone reads:

In memory of William MacGillivray M.A., LL.D. born 1796 died 1852. Author of British Birds and other standard works in natural science. Professor of natural history and lecturer on botany in Marischal College and University of Aberdeen from 1841 to 1852. Erected in 1900 together with a memorial brass in Marischal College Aberdeen by his relatives and surviving students who affectionately cherish his memory, and by others desiring of doing honour to his character as a man and to his eminence as a naturalist.

When MacGillivray died he left several unpublished and unfinished manuscripts, the most important being the text of *The Natural History of Dee Side and Braemar*. This was taken up by Queen Victoria, who with Prince Albert, had just bought the Balmoral estate on Deeside. With her growing interest in all things Highland, she bought the manuscript and the book was published by royal command in 1855. The publishing details on the title page simply say "London – Printed for Private Circulation". Copies seem to have been distributed individually, each with a printed presentation bookplate from Prince Albert. There is no record of how many copies were printed and to whom they were sent but in the copy that was sent to Selby, someone, perhaps Selby himself, has written "Only 100 copies printed". It is widely regarded as MacGillivray's finest work, in its style the most accessible to the general reader.

MacGillivray spent much of his life as a museum-based zoologist but he was always insistent on observing birds in the field and believed that the only way to understand nature was by observing it directly:

NIGHT HERON. NIGHT RAVEN.

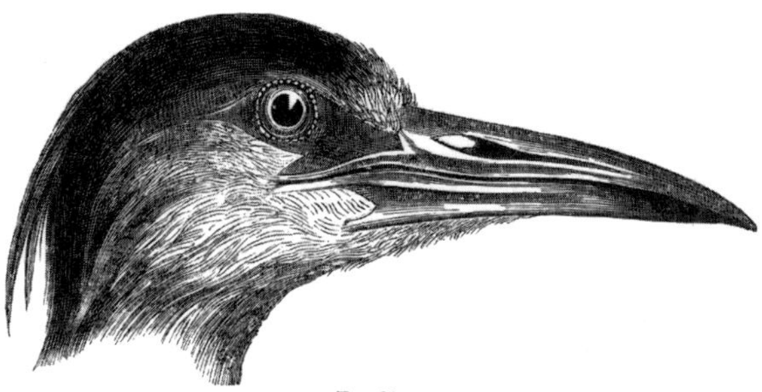

FIG. 36.

36 Night heron *Nycticorax nycticorax*; 'grey night heron', *Nycticorax gardeni* from *A History of British Birds*, vol. 4 (1852), p. 433

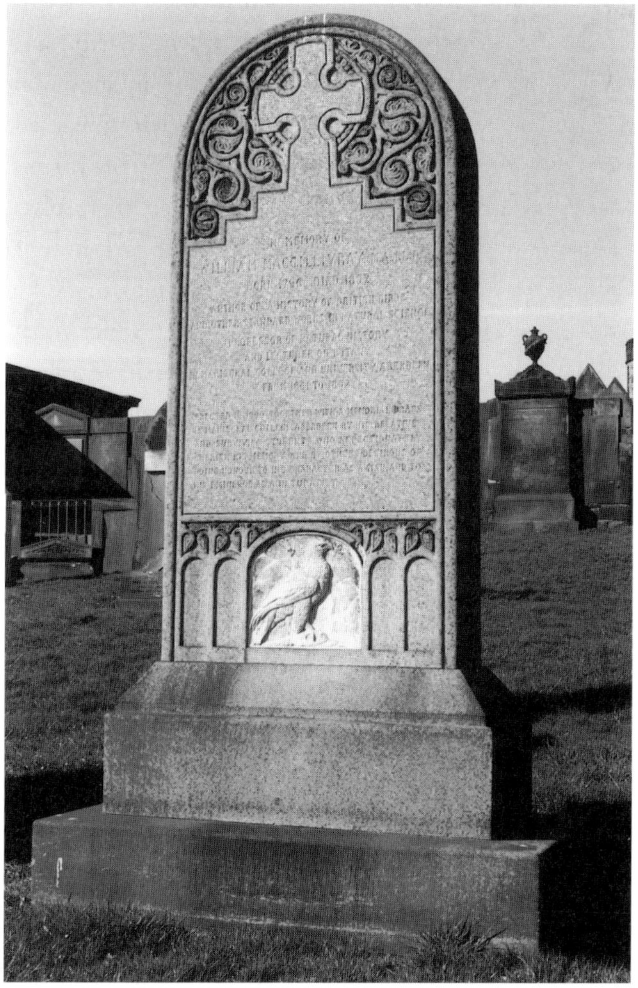

37 MacGillivray's grave in New Calton Cemetery, Edinburgh. The tombstone was erected in 1900 at the same time as the bronze memorial plaque was presented to Aberdeen University. The inscription on the stone is the same as on the plaque.

"Is there a man so dead to Nature that, regardless of the leafy woods, the green fields, the gliding brooks, and the wave-washed shores, among which one can only study birds to advantage, he gathers around him the spoils of every land, arranges them in circles and groups which he imagines to be concentric, parallel or diagonal, measures their bills and counts their feathers, and having thus performed his task, chuckles over it with the consciousness of being a philosopher? Let him alone; you cannot kindle his heart with a spark of ethereal fire; but come along, and let us study wherever we find her glories displayed."[1]

In many ways it was probably this insistence on field observations that made him so many enemies among the cabinet-naturalists. MacGillivray worked at a time when ornithology had three clearly distinct groups of people working in it. The first were the anatomists and morphologists, spending their time in dissecting rooms; the second group were the cabinet-naturalists, who examined skins of birds in museums, arguing over varieties and taxonomy and endlessly devising methods of classification. The third group, of which MacGillivray was the master in his day, were the naturalists in the field. If there was just one thing on which the cabinet-naturalists were agreed, it was that they had a common and united hatred of the field naturalists. It is not clear why this should have come about. Most of the cabinet-naturalists would have been men of independent means, able to afford the expense of accumulating their own collections and libraries, socially at ease at scientific societies, and confident in expressing their own opinions. Perhaps they regarded the field workers as intellectually and socially inferior. Whatever the reason, in MacGillivray's case, there was no love lost between him and them. Elliott Coues, the American ornithologist summed up the complexities of MacGillivray's character and his relationship with his contemporaries:

"Opinions differ greatly respecting the merit of MacGillivray's work, and it is not easy to decide in a case where one's estimate must depend so much upon whether one likes the author or not. For instance MacGillivray is to me personally so agreeable a companion, that I doubt not my warm appreciation of his ability and acquirements is open to a charge of favoritism. His writings attract me strongly; and possess for me the nameless fascination that thousands have felt in perusing the pages of Gilbert White or Alexander Wilson. MacGillivray appears to have been of an irritable, highly sensitized temperament, fired with enthusiasm and ambition, yet contending, for some time at least, with poverty, ill-health, and a perhaps not well founded though not therefore none the less acutely-felt sense of neglect; thus ceaselessly nerved to accomplish, yet as continually haunted with the dread of failure. The author was undoubtedly unwise in his frankness; but diplomacy is a stranger to characters ... and MacGillivray's way of handling people whom he disliked or despised often savoured of arrogance. If he never hesitated to differ sharply with anyone, or to express his own views pointedly – if he scarcely disguised his contempt for triflers, blockheads, pedants, compilers, and theorisers – if he was also fallible, even as the rest of us – he was nevertheless a lover of nature, an original thinker, a hard student, and finally, an ornithologist of large practical experience, who wrote down what he knew or believed to be true ..."[2]

Without his unstinting, though largely unrecognized assistance to Audubon and the *Ornithological Biography*, American ornithology might not have had such a secure foundation. Sadly, his own major work *A History of British Birds* languished in obscurity, but even today there is much of value in his work, and anyone with an interest in a particular British bird could do worse than to see what MacGillivray has to say about it. If he had been able to publish his paintings, life-sized, in the same style as *The Birds of America*, surely their merit, and the merit of his written work would have been recognized in his day, and been enough for him to "merit the name of ornithologist".

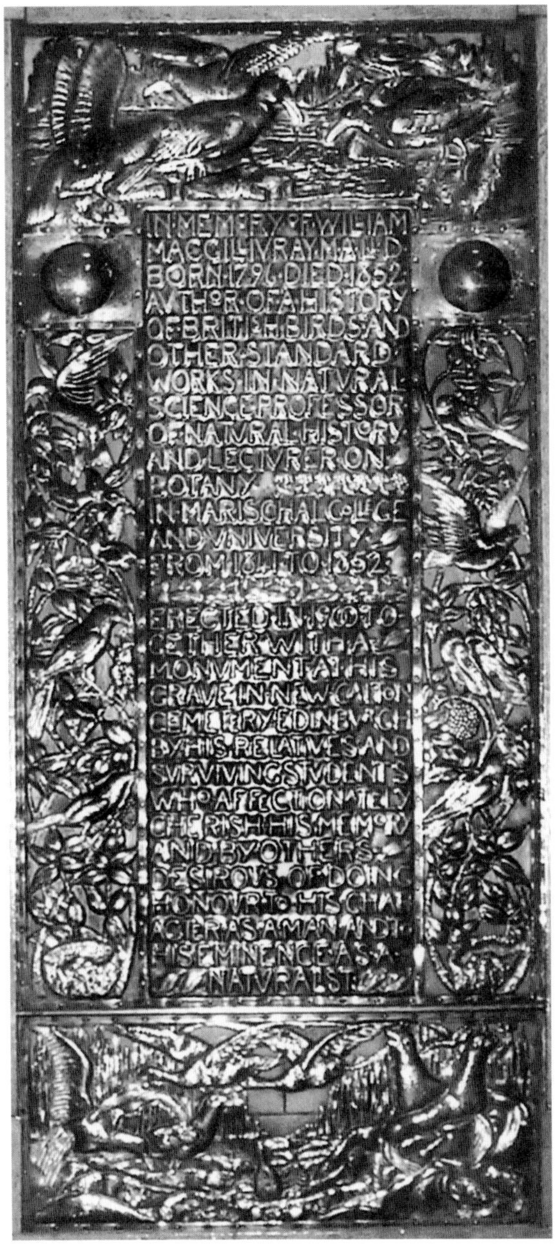

38 The bronze plaque to MacGillivray's memory presented to Aberdeen University in November 1900. The inscription reads: *In memory of William MacGillivray M.A., LL.D. born 1796 died 1852. Author of British Birds and other standard works in natural science. Professor of natural history and lecturer on botany in Marischal College and University of Aberdeen from 1841 to 1852. Erected in 1900 together with a monument at his grave in New Calton Cemetery, Edinburgh by his relatives and surviving students who affectionately cherish his memory, and by others desiring of doing honour to his character as a man and to his eminence as a naturalist*

NOTES

1 MacGillivray (1839).

2 Coues (1880), p. 395.

Bibliography

AUDUBON, J.J., 'Account of the Habits of the Turkey Buzzard (*Vultura aura*) particularly with the view of exploding the opinion generally entertained of its extraordinary power of Smelling', *Edinburgh New Philosophical Journal*, 2, 1826, pp. 172–84

AUDUBON, J.J., 'Prospectus – The Birds of America', issued by Audubon, Edinburgh 17 March 1827

AUDUBON, J.J., 'Notes on the Rattlesnake (*Crotalus horridus*)', *Edinburgh New Philosophical Journal*, 3, 1827, pp. 21–30

AUDUBON, J.J., *The Birds of America from original drawings by John James Audubon*, 4 vols., published by the author, London 1827-38

AUDUBON, J.J., *Ornithological Biography*, 5 vols., Edinburgh 1831–39

AUDUBON, M.R., *Audubon and his Journals*, 2 vols., New York 1897

BARLOW, N. (ed.), *The Autobiography of Charles Darwin 1809–1882*, London 1958

COUES, E., 'Behind the Veil', *Bulletin of the Nuttall Ornithological Club*, 5, 1880, pp. 193–204

COUES, E., 'Ornithological Bibliography', *Proceedings of the United States National Museum*, 2, 1880, p. 359

DARWIN, C., *The Descent of Man*, London 1871

DEANE, R., 'Unpublished letters of William MacGillivray to John James Audubon', *Auk*, 18, 1901, pp. 239–249

HARMONSON, J.S.W., *Life of the American Woodsman*, New Orleans 1937

HERRICK, F.H., *Audubon the Naturalist*, New York 1938

JARDINE, SIR W., and SELBY, P.J., *Illustrations of Ornithology*, 4 vols., Edinburgh 1826–43

MACGILLIVRAY, W., 'Occurrence of the sea-horse (walrus or morse, *Trichecus rosmarus*, Lin.) in the Hebrides', *Edinburgh Philosophical Journal*, 2, 1820, pp. 381–90

MACGILLIVRAY, W., 'Notice relative to two varieties of *Nuphar lutea* found in a lake in Aberdeenshire', *Memoirs of the Wernerian Natural History Society*, 4, 1822, pp. 186–89

MACGILLIVRAY, W., 'Remarks on the specific character of birds', *Memoirs of the Wernerian Natural History Society*, 4, 1823, pp. 517–40

MACGILLIVRAY, W., 'Descriptions, characters, and synonyms of the different species of the genus *Larus*, with critical and explanatory remarks', *Memoirs of the Wernerian Natural History Society*, 5, 1824, pp. 247–76

MACGILLIVRAY, W., 'Description of a new species of *Ornithorhynchus*', *Memoirs of the Wernerian Natural History Society*, 6, 1826, pp. 127–32

MACGILLIVRAY, W., 'Description of *Anatina villosiuscula*, a new species, and of *Venerupis nucleus*, a species new to the British fauna', *Edinburgh New Philosophical Journal*, 2, 1827, pp. 370–71

MACGILLIVRAY, W., 'Description of a species of *Arvicola* common in Aberdeenshire', *Memoirs of the Wernerian Natural History Society*, 6, 1830, pp. 425–29

MACGILLIVRAY, W., 'Account of the series of islands usually denominated as the Outer Hebrides (Climate, Soil and Vegetation)', *Edinburgh Journal of Natural and Geographical Science*, 2, 1830, pp. 87–95

MACGILLIVRAY, W., *A Systematic Arrangement of British Plants*, London 1830

MACGILLIVRAY, W., *Lives of Eminent Zoologists from Aristotle to Linnaeus*, Edinburgh 1830

MACGILLIVRAY, W., *Elements of Botany and Vegetable Physiology*, Edinburgh 1831

MACGILLIVRAY, W., *The Travels and Researches of Alexander von Humboldt*, Edinburgh 1832

MACGILLIVRAY, W., *Descriptions of the Rapacious Birds of Great Britain*, Edinburgh 1836

MACGILLIVRAY, W., *A History of British Birds*, vol. 1, London 1837

MACGILLIVRAY, W., *A History of British Quadrupeds*, vol. 7 in *The Naturalist's Library conducted by Sir William Jardine*, Edinburgh 1838

MACGILLIVRAY, W., *A History of British Birds*, vol. 2, London 1839

MACGILLIVRAY, W., *A History of British Birds*, vol. 3, London 1840

MACGILLIVRAY, W., *A Manual of Botany*, London 1840

MACGILLIVRAY, W., *A Manual of Geology*, London 1840

MACGILLIVRAY, W., *A Manual of British Ornithology; Part I, The Land Birds*, London 1842

MACGILLIVRAY, W., *A Manual of British Ornithology; Part II, The Water Birds*, London 1842

MACGILLIVRAY, W., *A History of the Molluscous Animals of the Counties of Aberdeen, Kincardine and Banff*, London 1843

MACGILLIVRAY, W., *The Conchologist's Textbook*, Edinburgh 1845

MACGILLIVRAY, W., *Portraits of Domestic Cattle of the Principal Breeds Reared in Great Britain and Ireland*, Edinburgh 1845

MACGILLIVRAY, W., *British Ornithology: Manual of British Birds*, London 1846

MACGILLIVRAY, W., *A History of British Birds*, vol. 4, London 1852

MACGILLIVRAY, W., *A History of British Birds*, vol. 5, London 1852

MACGILLIVRAY, W., *The Natural History of Dee Side and Braemar* (edited by Edwin Lankester, printed for private circulation by Queen Victoria), London 1855

MULLENS, W.H., 'Some early British ornithologists and their works, IX. William MacGillivray (1796–1852) and William Yarrell (1784–1853)', *British Birds*, 2, 1909, pp. 389–99

RALPH, R. (ed.), *William MacGillivray – A Hebridean Naturalist's Journal*, Stornoway 1996

RALPH, R. (ed.), *William MacGillivray – A Walk to London*, Stornoway 1998

RICHARDSON, J., and SWAINSON, W., *Fauna Boreali-Americana*, 2 vols., London 1831

SELBY, P. J., *Illustrations of British Ornithology*, 2 vols., Edinburgh 1821–33

WITHAM, H., *Observations on Fossil Vegetables*, Edinburgh 1831

WITHERING, W., *A Systematic Arrangement of British Plants*. 4 vols., London 1776

YARRELL, W., *A History of British Birds*, 4 vols., London 1837–43

Works about William MacGillivray

MACGILLIVRAY, W., *A Memorial Tribute to William MacGillivray*, Edinburgh 1901

MACGILLIVRAY, W., and THOMSON, J.A., *Life of William MacGillivray*, London 1910

RALPH, R., *William MacGillivray*, London 1993

WYNNE-EDWARDS, V.C., 'The centenary of William MacGillivray 1796-1852', *The Scottish Naturalist*, 64, 1952, pp. 65–69

Index